IN
OUR
PRIME

———

ALSO BY SUSAN J. DOUGLAS

Celebrity: A History of Fame (with Andrea McDonnell)

The Rise of Enlightened Sexism: How Pop Culture Took Us from Girl Power to Girls Gone Wild

The Mommy Myth: The Idealization of Motherhood and How It Has Undermined Women (with Meredith Michaels)

Listening In: Radio and the American Imagination

Where the Girls Are: Growing Up Female with the Mass Media

Inventing American Broadcasting, 1899–1922

IN
OUR
PRIME

How Older Women
Are Reinventing
the Road Ahead

SUSAN J. DOUGLAS

W. W. NORTON & COMPANY

Independent Publishers Since 1923

For information about permission to reproduce selections from this book, write to
Permissions, W. W. Norton & Company, Inc., 500 Fifth Avenue, New York, NY 10110

For information about special discounts for bulk purchases, please contact
W. W. Norton Special Sales at specialsales@wwnorton.com or 800-233-4830

Manufacturing by LSC Communications, Harrisonburg
Book design by Buckley Design
Production manager: Lauren Abbate

ISBN 978-0-393-65255-0

W. W. Norton & Company, Inc., 500 Fifth Avenue, New York, N.Y. 10110
www.wwnorton.com

W. W. Norton & Company Ltd., 15 Carlisle Street, London W1D 3BS

1 2 3 4 5 6 7 8 9 0

For Lynette Anderson, Margaret Bartiromo, and Jeffrey Golden
BFFs since childhood, and, yes, forever

One of the really important things, I think,
is that women have found their voices.

—GLENDA JACKSON, 2018

This is one time when older women and younger
people are going to make a difference.

—CHER, 2018

Revolution is not a one-time event.

—AUDRE LORDE, 1984

I got fury in my soul,
fury's gonna take me to the glory goal . . .
Save the people, save the children,
save the country now.

—LAURA NYRO, 1969

CONTENTS

IN

OUR

PRIME

———

Women Coming of Age

I AM A BABY BOOMER, and thus a woman, as we would say politely, of a certain age. And as I blink my eyes and wonder (as so many of us do these days) "How did I get here?" I am feeling once-settled tectonic plates rumbling beneath our feet, changing what it means to be an older woman in America. They are especially shifting about what older women want and how we see ourselves. While not yet widely noticed—given everything else on our nation's over-crowded and hyperventilating screens—it is an impending, and major, upheaval in our cultural terrain.

On the one hand, our culture seems intent on trying to rope women of my vintage off into a honey-hued, quiet, quilted pre-serve, where we are as relevant (and as stimulating) as pet rocks. All too many drug ads on television, for example, suggest that we are supposed to go plant peonies and play peekaboo with our grand-children (unless you're as beautiful and famous as Helen Mirren or Susan Sarandon and can be commissioned to be "the face" of a skin cream company). We're also supposed to keep quiet about and ignore the muscular efforts by the mostly white-haired men our age—or older—to reverse so many of the gains women of our generation achieved.

On the other hand, the ropes are giving way, because the numbers are adding up: there are more women over the age of fifty than ever before in our country. And millions of us are not pottering in the garden or inclined to say "OK, whatever" to the trashing of our legacy, the mowing down of women's rights, the marginalizing of our generation, what we have accomplished, and who we are. So I see this as a major turnstile moment in our culture, and our history.

Look around: women over fifty and well beyond are everywhere—working, shopping, traveling, going to concerts, yoga studios, restaurants and bars, and, importantly, working to get more women elected to public office as well as serving in public office themselves. Many feel they are in their prime. In the 2018 New York City marathon, eighty-eight people over the age of seventy-five competed, including seventy women in their seventies and eighties.[1] Millions of us are more confident, more financially independent, more socially engaged, and more outspoken than our mothers were at this age (or than even some of us were in our twenties); we are dramatically changing how these years are lived and experienced.[2] The number of older women today doing jobs that in 1970 were reserved primarily—or only—for men is unprecedented, and our accomplishments have given many of us self-assurance, even power, and, for some, money. Some are working beyond the traditional age of retirement because we want to, others because we have to. Yet, still, all too many businesses, political leaders, and certainly the media have put their blinders on when it comes to us. They do so because older women are supposed to be, for the most part—and even more so than younger women—quiet, docile, and invisible.

Even feminism, which would not have happened in the 1970s

without so many of us and which is enjoying a much-needed, at times even fiery resurgence, is cast in the media primarily as a young woman's game, with its high-profile embrace by Beyoncé, Lena Dunham, Emma Watson, and other celebrities, and with the explosion of the #MeToo movement across our nation in 2017. The battle over Brett Kavanaugh's 2018 Supreme Court nomination provoked women's open-wounded fury over so many male Republicans' dismissive attitudes toward sexual assault, in particular, and women in general. Like a sensational discovery of intact Mastodon bones, many girls and women of all ages are seeing, starkly, how sexism and patriarchy still structure our society, our politics, and our culture at their very core—and this nearly fifty years after the women's movement. Feminist writers like Rebecca Traister and Brittney Cooper have written and spoken passionately about the current, pressing need for women's rage. And in the 2018 midterms, a record 117 women were elected to Congress—the vast majority of them in opposition to the throwback politics of misogyny.[3]

Women like me are standing up and cheering about this renewed feminist tsunami. ("Feminism, back by popular demand" was a recurring sign at the 2017 Women's March.) According to a 2016 *Washington Post* poll, 68 percent of women aged fifty to sixty-four and 58 percent of women over sixty-five identify as feminists or "strong feminists" with majorities (64 percent and 56 percent, respectively) finding feminism "empowering." Yet the voices, concerns, and interests of older women have gotten minimal attention as part of this new, revitalized feminist movement.[4] We have been sidelined—at least in media imagery and political discourse. Even worse, we have at times been cast by some as outdated, clueless antagonists to younger women, fuddy-duddy "second-wave" feminists stuck in the past (with "second wave" even becoming an insult), stereotyped as "hidebound relics who are too timid to push for the real revolution." As entertainment writer Laura Hudson lectured in a tweet, it was time for older feminists "to listen, to learn, to step aside" because "age tends to correlate with not being on board with progress."[5] But here we still are, hugging young women's concerns close to our hearts, and hugging our own as well.

There is something quite incongruous here, then, between our flesh-and-blood visibility in everyday life, the vitality of our past and present, our ongoing feminist concerns and energy, and our invisibility, or dismissal, in too many sectors of our country's cultural imagination. According to one survey, the majority of older women believe that if the media were reflective of the population, a person would likely suppose women over fifty do not exist. This same survey found that 93 percent of women aged fifty to sixty-four felt there were major misconceptions about older women, including that they are not productive in society (71 percent), do not care about their appearance (70 percent), do not have a full social life (69 percent), and do not enjoy sex (72 percent). Not surprisingly, 91 percent believed it is about time for society to change the way it looks at aging, especially for women.[6] This near-total eclipse is even more obscuring for older women of color, who are virtually absent from the screens of America.

The question before us then is this: are we going to accept this manufactured invisibility, or rip off the invisibility cloak? Many increasingly impatient women are saying, let's choose option B. To do so, we need to confront our media's, our culture's, and our own dismissive attitudes about aging—especially for women— and how they seek to marginalize and silence us culturally, economically, and politically. And we need to do so with humor, irreverence, and, yes, anger.

This is a major piece of the unfinished business of the women's movement and it matters now more than ever. Because, while many of us are, in fact, doing better than ever, others of us are not—not at all—because of poverty, racism, or bigotry. This remains a totally unaddressed, hidden, and pressing feminist issue. No agenda can be feminist if it doesn't bring all women forward. Older women are 80 percent more likely to be poor than older men, with 17 percent of women over sixty-five living in poverty, nearly twice as many as men. And the number is even higher for women of color and those who never married.[7] Is this not a feminist issue?

So I'd like to propose that it is now time for a "lifespan feminism," which sees the issues facing older women as part of a continuum of concern, attention, and activism that begins with the well-being of girls and young women and sees feminism as a mainstay and resource throughout the entire arc of a woman's life. Just because a woman may no longer be the target of sexual harassment, or may no longer need paid maternity leave or decent day care, or may no longer be under threat of having her reproductive health hijacked by a bunch of intrusive, grizzled white guys, doesn't mean that sexism—now, for her, further polluted by ageism—doesn't still structure her life also.

Lifespan feminism is tied to something else we very much need right now: a bridge feminism among girls and women of different generations that links us together in a common cause to confront the unfinished business of the women's movement. Too many forces—and, indeed, some of our own blind spots and mistakes—can pit us against each other, but for women especially, we should not allow gendered ageism, let alone media-stoked dramas about "generational warfare," to be one of those dividers. If more of us see that the concerns of older women should be folded into the ongoing project of feminism, then an appreciation of lifespan feminism can lead to the bridges we need. And, ironically, Trumpism—and not only Trump, but the movement he has come to represent, including all his allies and the misogynistic forces they have breathed life into and unleashed—is making that bridge more essential than ever.

Today, women of a certain age find ourselves once again at a major juncture: pulled between the colliding crosscurrents of what we've accomplished, what we're still doing, and how we feel, versus utterly ossified notions of what it means to be an older woman. We are at the vanguard of reinventing what this stage of life means for women, including how we ourselves experience and think about it. Yet we are in a cultural and media environment that is, for the most part, either clueless about this transformation or does not wish to recognize it.

This matters because there are now and will continue to be more older women in our country than at any time in our history.[8] Thus the next phase of our collective history has begun. The first baby boomers—those born between 1946 and 1964—turned sixty-five on January 1, 2011, and for the next nineteen years after that, according to the Pew Research Center, about 10,000 more people will turn sixty-five every day.[9] As of 2017, one third of the population is fifty or over.[10] Women make up a significant majority of the older population, and our share increases with age because women live longer than men.[11] Studies show that many of us typically feel ten to fifteen years younger than our chronological age, with millions of us still active in the world.

So, while we certainly don't think of ourselves as young (nor do many of us miss our youth), we don't think of ourselves as "old" either, given what "old" has come to mean in our culture. We are healthier, living longer, and even working longer: almost 30 percent of women sixty-five to sixty-nine are still working. When we include those who are working at an even older age, we have the largest number of older women workers ever.[12] And millions not working after sixty-five are energetic forces in their families and communities. Today, what constitutes "being old" continues to shift and be redefined. While some have snidely mocked baby boomers as being so narcissistic and delusional that we refuse to see ourselves as old, many of us find it much more productive to unmoor ourselves from rigid, chronologically anchored notions of aging, and instead foreground the importance of how we feel and what we can and still want to do.

Of course, my friends and I bemoan the annoying and, yes, melancholy aspects of aging, but it is these that dominate our cultural landscape. Yes, we joke about never being able to find our glasses, even though we've purchased nine pairs of those really fashion-forward ones from Walgreens at $14.95 a pop. We compare notes about how, at least five times a day, we walk into a room and then ask ourselves why the hell we needed to go in there and have to retrace our steps to remember. And every day we curse our new worst enemy: gravity. We've noted sardonically that aging is like puberty in reverse: your body does strange, alien things you don't want it to, betraying and embarrassing you at every turn—except that at the end of puberty you're still only in your teens. Certainly, losing dear friends and family members is utterly wrenching. Some women lose their jobs, or are sidelined or silenced at work, or struggle to make ends meet because of their age. Getting older and being seen as irrelevant (or not) is experienced differently by millions of women. So I'm hardly going to go to the other extreme and claim that aging is a total hoot, or plan to emulate former President George H. W. Bush, who went skydiving for his ninetieth birthday.

At the same time, here's how millions of women actually experience this stage of life, which for the most part remains unheralded. We are often happier as we get older, with various studies documenting that older women are happier than women in their twenties.[13] We typically have more time to become recommitted to friends and family in profoundly satisfying ways. We know a lot more than we did thirty years ago and are sought out for advice and mentoring. We often care a lot less what people think about us, and instead focus on what is important to us. Many of us have all sorts of personal and professional accomplishments that have made a difference to ourselves and others, that have given us a strong sense of self, and that have meant, in some situations, that people do not mess with us. And finally to be able to walk down the street and not be barraged by catcalls from cave men? Such liberation.

This, then, is a major demographic revolution—an underappreciated, under-covered revolution—and one that is and will be defined especially by women. These are women—all kinds of women—who initially came of age during the height of the women's movement, women who have defied the numerous, corseted stays that have sought to confine us. Our whole lives have been an experiment, doing things our mothers rarely did or simply couldn't do. There was a go-for-broke sensibility that filled the air. Millions of us were able to say no to the double standard, no to job discrimination, no to male-only quotas at medical or business schools, and yes to working outside the home while raising small children, and much more. We are women who changed history, women who are still changing history, women who now need to change the future, politically, economically, and culturally, and not just for us, but for those who will come after us.

As a result, we continue to experiment and to defy hand-me-down recipes about what we can and cannot do—not just because we want to but also because we have to. The world we grew up in is gone, with tumultuous and massive transformations in technology, institutions, politics, cultural values, and the economy upending previous expectations about the stages of life: when one would get married, buy a house, have kids, change jobs, retire. Back in 1975 (of course, this affected mostly white men), 85 percent of those working in the private sector had a guaranteed pension based on their salary, how long they had worked, and similar critieria; by 2013, only 18 percent could count on such a benefit.[14]

Uncertainty surrounds public-sector pensions as well. Social Security, Medicare, and Medicaid have all been under relentless right-wing attack. Scholars are noting how "people of all ages are faced with new levels and kinds of uncertainties" in the twenty-first century, leading to unprecedented shake-ups and prompting the need to restructure how we imagine and live the course of our lives.[15] What sustained many of our parents financially, but also fenced them in culturally, is being dismantled. Thus many of us are confronting this stage of life by boycotting circumscribed notions about what it means to be an older woman while also looking over our shoulders, warily, at what historical surprises may be sneaking up from behind us.

Now, it's true that, as a baby boomer, I assumed aging was optional; didn't most of us? After all, we were the first generation to be given a name (and with "baby" in it, no less) and, more importantly, to become the biggest youth market—76 million strong—our country had ever seen. With that goiter in the population known as the boomers, the writer Susan Sontag noted that there was a "reevaluation of the life cycle in favor of the young."[16] We were the generation that drove youth marketing—teenage culture was truly developed because of us. Branded as young and hip, the glowing irons of that marketing left an indelible imprint on our psyches as well. From the 1950s through the 1980s at least (when we allegedly became "yuppies"), the producers of Hula Hoops, *Beach Blanket Bingo*, Motown records, Stridex medicated pads, television shows like *Shindig!*, designers of power suits with padded shoulders, and then the purveyors of balsamic vinegar coveted us. Everyone wanted a piece of us, and to sell to us they hailed us as *Mod Squad* rebel types, way cooler and different from our parents. And at least three things happened: we became convinced of our importance as a generation, as well as the superiority of youth, and the media obsession with youth became as permanent as Stonehenge.

Baked into this, of course, was the understanding that getting older was not only remote—and that it just wouldn't happen to us—but also that it meant being washed up, irrelevant, uncool, and, especially for women, unattractive—or, worse, grotesque. In the 1960s, you were more likely to see a talking horse or a Munster than a woman over thirty-five on television. When you did, you saw the potion-stirring Grandmama on the *Addams Family*, whose shock of white hair looked like she had just stuck a fork in an electrical outlet. In Disney movies, older women were sadistic stepmothers with too much turquoise eye shadow who made princesses scrub the floor with their hair, or envy-engorged witches proffering poison-infused apples to unsuspecting young things they hated. (Disney even gave us his cartoon version of a white-and-black-haired cigarette-smoking ogress who kidnapped little puppies so she could sell them for their fur.) Older women with mouths on them, like the cartoon and then television character Hazel, were pushy, nosey, asexual battle-axes.

A whole raft of traits was supposed to shrivel up when you got old: optimism, rebellion, energy, sexuality, being hip.[17] All of this was part of our mediated, generational DNA—older women were repellant and antithetical to who we saw ourselves to be. Instead, back in the day, in our bellbottoms and India print tops, we all smiled knowingly (and smugly) at the Beatles' "When I'm Sixty-Four" ("Yours sincerely, wasting away") because we just never thought Paul McCartney—or we—would ever be that age.

Well, here we are.

So now we face a dilemma. What do we do with this identity we were schooled to shun and seduced into thinking we would never inhabit? In other words, we need to fully grasp that we were urged, in our youth, to internalize a set of values that now work against us psychologically, politically, and economically. We must come to terms with the legacy of those media images, and the assumptions that go with them. After all, the negative, even phobic, attitudes about aging, especially for women, that stippled our psyches when we were young are still with us and are part of the problem we must now purge. Will we acquiesce to the disparaging attitudes about older women that we grew up with— think the shotgun-toting Granny on *The Beverly Hillbillies*—that burrowed into us, and now still grip so much of our culture? Or will we rebel against them, given how ridiculous (and insulting) they were and how positive many of us feel now about who we are and what we are doing?

As baby boom women, we've shot through such contradictory rapids before. In the 1950s and '60s, in one ear we (well, middle-class white women) heard that our only destiny was to be housewives and mothers, that our mission was to master the art of making Jell-O molds, and that we were too emotional, hormonally driven, and irrational to have credit cards in our own names, balance our checkbooks, or sell washing machines, instead of lipstick, at Sears. The very last arena we were supposed to dare enter was the rope-guarded ring of politics. In the other ear, though, spurred by Sputnik-driven calls to go to college, what-you-can-do-for-your-country appeals to join the Peace Corps, and grass-roots summons to participate in the civil rights and antiwar movements, we were encouraged to become political, to change the world. Told we were subordinate, yet told we were equal, told we were passive, yet hailed as active, told to whisper, yet driven to shout, we could not sustain the mixed messages, the contradictions, and we opted for equality and activism; hence the women's liberation movement.[18] Millions of us didn't acquiesce; we rebelled. Down came the ropes—well, at least, many of them.

Today, another jailbreak is afoot, and gaining more traction every day. It is propelled by our history, and what feminism—and we—made possible. This book is about that jailbreak and the two

revolutions—one demographic, the other in consciousness—
that are mobilizing it. It is especially about the role of the media
in mostly reinforcing, but also at times challenging, how older
women are seen and thought about—because older female stars,
politicians, and public figures are also rebelling, and staking their
claim to remain in the spotlight with, for some, infuriating, and
for others, inspiring results. For many of us, it was enraging to see
how the coiling together of ageism and misogyny served as a powerful weapon against Hillary Clinton in 2016 ("an angry, crotchety old hag" as one Trump rally attendee put it to the *Washington
Post*).[19] I mean, Donald Trump, at the age of seventy in 2016, had
the chutzpah to suggest that Hillary Clinton, at sixty-nine, was too
old and didn't "have the stamina" to become president. "She goes
home, goes to sleep." Of course, we wished he did that much more
often. Next, Nancy Pelosi, initially urged by some to step aside as
Speaker of the House, in part because of her age, rose up phoenix-
like to demonstrate that she was *the* force that could take on and
chasten a rogue president. And she's been accompanied by the
equally fearless Maxine Waters.

So, just like in the 1960s and 1970s, we are pulled between the
anchors of the past and the propelling sails of a more liberated, fulfilling future. Hailed, on the one hand, by those LifeCall and Life
Alert ads in which women (like one "Mrs. Fletcher") are seen lying
prostrate next to their equally horizontal walkers ("I've fawllen and
I can't get up!") and on the other by the ever-luminous Helen Mirren who is still opening movies and is a spokesmodel for L'Oreal,
we are threatened with supine decrepitude or lured by gutsy glamour. As I'm not really interested in the former and can't possibly
achieve the latter, I think it's time for everyday women to chart a
new, different way. It involves being seen, being heard, and insisting
that we are in our prime. Millions of us are already doing this. So it
is a movement that is already afoot.

Yet we are enacting this revolution in a culture in which the word "aging" (unless it has the word "anti" hyphenated in front of it) is to women what kryptonite was to Superman. Indeed, our culture is positively phobic about getting older (and, especially for women, looking it!), an obsession that pumps collagen-infused billions into what can best be called our anti-aging industrial complex, an industry that has become morbidly obese over the last twenty years. Ageism—a bias and discrimination against older people, simply because they are old—is so ingrained, so woven into the weft and warp of our culture that it goes unnoticed as a bias and indeed is pretty much taken for granted. As a growing cadre of anti-ageism authors and activists—nearly all of them women—have made clear, unlike public awareness of sexism or racism or homophobia and their consequences, most people, especially those under, say, fifty, remain clueless about ageism; they lack an understanding or even an awareness of it as a ubiquitous form of bias, both among individuals and in institutions. As the inimitable Cher put it, "At sixty-five, you have to retire and go eat dog food or whatever. It's a shame to be discarded because of something that happens to everybody. Old is like an enemy you have to make peace with before you get there." Amen, sister.

Every day, women are bombarded by media imperatives to "Reverse Aging" and "Look Younger!" "Welcome to the Age-Free Life!" heralds O, The Oprah Magazine. "Stop Aging Now," commands New Beauty. A battalion of industries seeks to fuel, exploit, and, most importantly, earn massive profits from the fear of aging.[20] Look at any of these ads—for skin creams, of course, omega-3 supplements, kale—and one word stands astride them all like the Colossus of Rhodes—DEFY. (Yes, men are targeted with ads for Grecian Formula and the ceaseless ones promising to energize a certain flaccid, inoperative male appendage, but these are nothing compared to the fusillade directed at us.) There is an endless inventory of things that are supposed to make women feel bad about ourselves for the last third of our lives—eye bags, "brown spots," "puppet lines," gray hair, the whole neck situation—that advertisers suggest are somehow our fault and require termination with extreme prejudice. And studies show that the more that young women internalize these standards of thinness, beauty, and youth, the greater their negative attitudes are toward older people.[21] Thus it's hardly surprising that after a successful day at work, or a deeply affirming get-together with friends or family, we still wince at our reflections as we catch them in a mirror or storefront window.

Can we stand back from this for just a minute and note how strange it is (although hugely profitable for so many businesses) for seasoned women like us to be repeatedly ordered to defy an ineluctable biological process and to feel badly when we can't? We are supposed to feel ashamed of how we look and to see this as our own lonely dilemma. Worse, we're supposed to continue to compete with each other, compare ourselves to each other: well, at least I don't have as many wrinkles as *she* does! So let's appreciate how we are all in this together, that this shame is how we're all supposed to feel, because it is actually designed to keep us quiet and in our places. And then let's exorcise it. We want and need to be accepted and respected for who we are, not how we look.

Despite the defiance mantra, and despite our numbers (about 36 million baby boom women alone!), the media mostly ignore us or pin our wings to ageist tropes. The media matter crucially because they are the major storytellers of our time; as some of the most powerful institutions in our country, separately and together they shape what we see as success and failure, who is worthy of admiration and who is not, what is just and what is unjust, who deserves the spotlight and who should stay in the shadows. And in our youth as now, with a few exceptions, its imagery has skewed very white and mostly middle to upper-middle class (or rich). As the first television generation, who gorged ourselves on a smorgasbord of pop culture pastries—rock, R&B, and folk music, movies, *Seventeen*, and *Glamour*, and the relentless ads seeking to grab us by the lapels—our entire lives have been mediated by these funhouse mirrors shaping our sense of ourselves and our relationships to each other and to society.

Today they are more embedded in our lives than ever and, like it or not, they play a role in our lifelong identity construction and reconstruction. Between traditional media like television and magazines, and social media like Facebook, Twitter, YouTube, and Instagram, Americans in the first three months of 2016 spent, on average, over 10½ hours a day—a day!—consuming media, up a full hour from 2015.[22] And because of our smart phones and tablets, the media can be and are with us all the time, buzzing, beeping, flashing, insisting, "Open me up! Look at me! Listen to me! Let *me* be your guide!"

In this ever-beaming, luminescent ecosystem, visibility has become the coin of the realm. Media visibility means you are important, you matter; it's a resource you can convert into other kinds of power. Just because so many media outlets give us the side eye does not mean that the media do not matter in how we negotiate our coming into this phase of our lives. Back in the 1960s, our Etch-a-Sketch media drew us front and center on their screens; today, those powdered images have been shaken away to the bottom of the frame. When our collective biographies have been so thoroughly mediated, such retractions matter. So it is in fact essential to explore the role that all these pulsating screens are playing as we confront aging and ageism in such a world.[23]

It is hardly surprising that there has been a gaping lack of imagination when it comes to telling stories, fictional or not, about older women. Since most images of older women are not made by older women themselves, we are represented in the media through the eyes of others. And those others are typically younger and male. On television in 2013, for example, fewer than two percent of prime-time characters were sixty-five or older, and twice as many of them were men.[24] In a 2014 study of the few people over the age of fifty in television commercials, researchers found that 73 percent were men and only 27 percent were women.[25] And aside from Tyler Perry's often-reviled (yet, yes, also often beloved), overweight, loudmouthed Madea character, how many older black women have we seen? With a few exceptions—Cicely Tyson in *How to Get Away with Murder*, Rita Moreno in the reboot of *One Day at a Time*, for example—older women of color are indeed hidden figures. And where are older Asian American or Native American women?

In addition, existing research shows that negative portrayals still outweigh positive ones.[26] Study after study has shown that older people (when they appear at all) are depicted in the media "through a lens of decline and diminished value."[27] They are often cast as less intelligent, less competent, less responsible, more forgetful, and more childlike than younger adults.[28] They are also frequently cast as grumpy, conservative, clueless about new technology, and resistant to social change.

This remains a sedimented layer in the media, deposited over the years, that equates getting older with deterioration, disease, and dependency. As recently as 2014, Esurance aired an ad featuring a seventy-something "Beatrice," who brags to her comparably aged female friends that instead of mailing everyone her vacation photos, she's "saving a ton of time by posting them to my wall." Cut to an actual wall in her house with her photos taped to it. Yep, older women are dumber than box turtles when it comes to social media, even though more than a third of people over sixty-five are on Facebook and, indeed, know how to use it. (In a comment that should add to Mark Zuckerberg's woes, an eighteen-year-old said to me in 2018, "Facebook is for old people.")

Having endured so many double-standard indignities throughout our lives, which we indeed sought to defy, we now confront the double standard around aging. Because all women are still judged, first and foremost, by our appearance, and because our worth is so tied to how we look, our value is supposed to decline much more sharply as we age than it does for men. While it has become a recurrent cliché to observe that men get to be regarded as "dignified" when their temples gray but women don't (and that sixty-year-old male actors are routinely paired with thirty-year-old love interests), less acknowledged is the simple erasure and silencing of older women.[29] What is not visible and not heard is harder to notice.

Hollywood, of course, has been at the forefront in hitting the delete button when it comes to us. In its 2016 study of roles featuring those over forty in the media, the Annenberg School at the University of California found that nearly 79 percent of the older characters in film, 73 percent of the older characters on broadcast television, and 70 percent of the older characters on cable were male.[30] A 2015 study by *Time* magazine found that while male actors' careers peaked at forty-six (and many continue to get roles well beyond that: think Harrison Ford, Clint Eastwood, Robert De Niro, Morgan Freeman), female actors' careers peaked at thirty, with the number of roles offered them declining sharply after that. Even worse, "Women today who are under the age of sixty are seeing the number of roles they are cast in decline faster than their older peers once did."[31] Helen Mirren, one of the few exceptions to this statistic, noted simply that ageism against women in Hollywood is "fucking outrageous! It's ridiculous, honestly. . . . We all sat there watching . . . as James Bond got more geriatric as his girlfriends got younger and younger. It's so annoying."[32]

It has also become a cliché, and a rallying cry in Hollywood, that men vastly outnumber women as directors: only a puny 11 percent of the directors of the top 250 films in 2017 were female.[33] But worse, when they're older, they and their audiences are scorned as shriveled up and pathetic. (Remember, in most media outlets men constitute about 70 percent of movie reviewers.)[34] Let's take Nancy Meyers (*Something's Gotta Give, It's Complicated, The Intern*). Dismissed as a "mom-com director," Meyers is actually the most commercially successful woman director of all time, her films having grossed, collectively, over $1 billion! Her movies together have sold more tickets than those of Quentin Tarantino, for example, yet because they're dusted off reviewers' shoulders as "chick flicks," she doesn't get nearly the same respect. *Something's Gotta Give* (for which Diane Keaton was nominated for an Oscar) was, according to male reviewers, nothing more than a "menopausal screwball," a "fantasy exercise" for "gal pals taking a movie break after returning Christmas presents." *It's Complicated*? "[A]n older woman's emasculating revenge fantasy." Meyers herself? "[T]he world's foremost purveyor of crack-cocaine-strength gastro-lifestyle fantasy porn to the menopausal classes."[35] So here's an industry that worships at the feet of adolescent boys fantasizing about being a superhero in tights who can sucker punch Godzilla, but scoffs at older women's desire to see themselves at the multiplex as active, passionate, funloving, attractive, and, okay, having a kitchen not unlike one you might find at Versailles.

In the news media, older men like Bill Plante (eighty-one), David Martin (seventy-five), and Bob Schieffer (eighty-one) at CBS remain on the air while women in their fifties and sixties, with a few exceptions, get moved to radio or have to leave the business entirely and are replaced by model-ready women in their twenties and thirties with their de rigueur sleeveless dresses. (When I see some of the few older, seasoned women reporters like Barbara Starr on CNN or Elizabeth Palmer on CBS, they immediately stand out because of all the contrasting men and young women.) On the Sunday morning talk shows, where men constituted 74 percent of the guests in 2014, there were plenty with gray hair (or none at all), wrinkles, eye bags, paunches, and jowls.[36] Their presence—and our absence—simply affirms, without saying a word, that older women don't really have a place as experts or authorities about public affairs, most of which do or will impact our lives and those of our family and friends, including those much younger.

While *Glamour, Allure, Marie Claire, Elle,* and *Cosmo* battle for the millennial market (who mostly don't read magazines except on Snapchat), we have only one magazine geared to us now that *More* has bit the dust: the *AARP* magazine. Although we may account for up to one quarter of the readership of fashion magazines, women over forty are rarely portrayed.[37] In the 250-page, February 2017 edition of the *New York Times Style Magazine,* only one older woman, Lauren Hutton, appeared as a model amid the hundreds of mostly white teenage waifs. When we see older women in celebrity gossip and all the proliferating "red carpet" events, many have obviously taken great pains (literally) to eradicate the visible signs of age and to make sure any telltale lines are photoshopped out of their pictures, further validating that aging for women is disastrous.[38] It did not escape our attention that the first sixty-five-year-old woman to grace the cover of *Vanity Fair* was Caitlyn Jenner, dolled up like a contestant on *Toddlers & Tiaras.* Such media imagery matters, because being sidelined or marginalized in the media interlocks with being sidelined or marginalized in work, government policies, and everyday life.

Our youth-obsessed media have barely caught up with us or just simply keep missing the mark. They are driven and consumed by the media-driven dictates of demographics, with the eighteen-to-forty-nine age range (and, for women, eighteen-to-thirty-four) being the most highly prized. Back in 2007, television shows whose viewers were in the thirty-four-to-forty-nine range could charge 30 percent more per ad minute than those whose viewers were fifty-five and older, and twelve years later, this hasn't changed much.[39] This even though older people watch more television: by 2014, the median age of CBS's audience was fifty-seven, for ABC it was fifty-three, and for NBC, fifty.[40] Since advertisers know they're going to get these viewers anyway, they don't feel the need to target or even feature them in ads, except for Big Pharma bent on medicalizing everything, even "shaky legs."[41] Indeed, as the trade journal *Broadcasting & Cable* noted in 2013, because the viewing practices of the over-forty-nine demographic weren't even tracked, "just like that, more than 80 million viewers—with an estimated spending power of more than $3 trillion—will no longer be considered relevant."[42] This outdated logic governing advertising on television, where we have the numbers yet they don't matter, is the result and impact of ageism in the media. It's also foolish, because various researchers have found that "subjective age"—how old we feel—is a better predictor of what we'll watch and buy than chronological age, which actually "predicts little."[43]

Meanwhile, celebrity culture has come to dominate so much of the media that it has become a central site where the struggles over what it means to be an older woman, and battles over our "common sense" about aging, are being fought out. At the same time that "aging does not sit well with celebrity culture," to put it mildly, and the faces and bodies of older female stars are dissected, often viciously, against the standards of youthfulness, an increasing number of female stars are insisting that being older should not be an obstacle to ongoing visibility, status, and success.[44] Older female celebrities have never been more visible, and often defiantly so, and they enact our resistance to gendered ageism (for which we cheer). Their example lifts us up. At the same time, we also need to weigh how their rebellions redefine yet also up the ante for the expectations we, and others, may have of ourselves, especially how we should look.

Thus at the very same moment that millions of women, famous and not, are resisting out-of-date notions about what older women can and should do, we are confronting that double helix of ageism and sexism that still, despite everything, courses through our culture and warps how others see us, and even, at times (and more than we'd like to admit), how we see ourselves.

Given our numbers, our experiences, and where we are now, the time is long overdue for older women to talk back to this. It's time not for a personal makeover, but for a cultural one. We now need to take on a culture that primarily worships and rewards youthful femininity.[45] Because as we learn as the decades pass, while youthful femininity doesn't last forever, strong womanhood does.

The time is ripe for us to flip the dominant narratives surrounding us, individually and collectively. Rather than seeing ourselves as aging (which of course we are), we need to see ourselves, and have others see us, as in our prime, and coming of age, yet again, as a generation, which is quite different. Aging is seen in our culture as negative and as passive; it happens to you. Coming of age is positive and active; you grab the reins as you jump over the fence. Seeing ourselves this way, and not through someone else's occluded lens, is an important feminist project.

"Coming of age" typically refers to the passage from youth to adulthood, as if that is the only transition people experience in their lives as they move from one phase of being to another. But coming of age is an ongoing, fluid process we experience throughout the life span, often marked by life-defining events like having children, assuming leadership positions or taking on more responsibility at work, losing parents, and retiring, as well as by (as the greeting card industry reminds us) hitting certain ages: thirty, forty, fifty, sixty-five. Coming of age includes an awareness of entering a new stage of life, one with different challenges and opportunities. It is seen as producing new insights, new strengths, new awareness, and new responsibilities—as well as new losses—and this does not only happen when we turn eighteen or twenty-one. And it involves finding a new, more aware, more empowered voice.

In addition, coming of age, especially for young men, is often cast as an individual experience. But for baby boom women, our initial coming of age in the late 1960s and 1970s involved connecting with each other as we went to college, protested, aspired for careers; it was very much a collective and a feminist experience. Our biographies changed dramatically from those of our mothers. We were part of a revolutionary and arm-in-arm social movement. When the first issue of *Ms.* was published in January 1972 (which ABC newsman Harry Reasoner dismissed as "an irrelevant shock magazine" and predicted would last no more than three issues), 250,000 copies flew off the newsstands in eight days, as its contents gave full-throated voice to what millions of us were feeling.[46] We shared a sense of a daring and new trajectory for our lives that millions of us internalized and drew strength from.

We need to resuscitate this sense of common cause and harness it again as a force. It has been heavily battered over the years by the politics of neoconservatism, market fundamentalism, individual responsibility, the gated-communities approach to ever more exclusionary market segmentation, and the consumerist mantra of inward-looking self-actualization. A female-driven common cause is being revived by social forces like the #MeToo movement and in response to antifeminist political initiatives and laws, and increasingly hostile discourses and violence against women, which seek to undo much of what we have fought for, sought to improve, and, indeed, changed throughout our lives. To cite just one infamous paleo-chest-beating moment, in May of 2017, we saw thirteen lone white men drafting a Senate health care bill that included decisions on which aspects of women's reproductive health would be covered.

With the number of women over fifty growing every day, we confront a new coming-of-age experience, a process that involves internal and external liberation.[47] It is one that millions of women are going through personally and individually all around the country as we seek both to defy and to ignore outmoded and insulting attitudes about women of our vintage. As a result, once again, the personal is becoming political. Yet, with the exception of comparing notes with a few friends, especially about the gap between the images of us (or lack thereof) and reality, we don't yet appreciate that it is a national phenomenon. Certainly there is barely a glimmer in the eyes of Madison Avenue or Hollywood that such a change in consciousness is afoot.

Most important, and what I seek to emphasize, is that this new collective female experience—coming of age—is an incipient social movement. It is a change in sensibility still hovering under our country's radar, but there are increasing numbers of blips starting to echo ever more loudly on our nation's screens. Few have connected the dots, in part because of the invisibility, especially in the mainstream media, that hides us from view and mutes our voices. Back in the 1970s, when women saw themselves in the media both as a coveted market and as masses of demonstrators in the streets, their collective identity and rebellion were hypervisible, documenting that they constituted a movement that had to be taken seriously. Today we don't see older women on the screens of America as a group (and barely as individuals); if we did, we would realize how much we matter and how much power we have.

So let's pull back the shades and wake up to what so many older women are thinking about and doing in common. Let's see how what might seem like lone, individual, everyday rebellions can instead be seen as a percolating social movement on the verge of erupting. In addition to remaining visible in the workforce, out of choice or necessity, or becoming more politically active, increasing numbers of older women are finding each other online and pushing back against geriatric images and assumptions about who they are and what they can do. Niche websites like *Fashion Over Fifty*, *Boomer Café*, *LivingBetter50*, *Midlife Boulevard*, *Sixty and Me*, and *CoveyClub*, to name a few, feature the voices of older women talking back to ageist stereotypes as well as sharing common experiences. When Jessica Bennett's *New York Times* article "I Am (an Older) Woman. Hear Me Roar" appeared in January 2019, it garnered 314 comments and was one of the most emailed stories of the week. I was quoted in that article and saw my inbox explode.

This movement has strong similarities to what we went through in the early 1970s, when the women's movement transformed our country, as so many of us realized our experiences were not isolated or just our own. They were collective, and thus mattered on a much larger scale. So many women went through internal conversions in how they saw themselves and what they felt themselves capable of doing, and that's happening again. These awakenings drove and resonated with the external changes women fought for, in our laws, business practices, media imagery, and overall attitudes about women's roles. That can and needs to happen again now.

It is time to connect the dots, to open our eyes and see that we are doing and feeling this simultaneously, en masse—together—and to own it. It is time to marshal this demographically driven social movement and make it vocal and visible. We are at a crossroads where consciousness-raising is essential again, this time about the role and image of older women in our culture and media, our economy, and our political realm. It is time to make this an empowered generational identity, an emerging resistance that gives us strength and clout, that can chart out a new mission for women culturally, politically, and economically. And we need to see it as essential to the latest feminist turn.

We also need to insist on the value and importance of our voices, and raising them. Older women have been expected to be soft-spoken, nurturing, and retiring grandma types and to silence themselves, and, if they don't, they are stepping out of character and thus out of line. To quote Rebecca Traister's perfectly timed *Good and Mad: The Revolutionary Power of Women's Anger*, the refusal to hold in female anger has "often ignited movements for social change and progress" and has indeed been "crucial in determining [women's] political power and social standing."[48]

While a rising chorus of voices, from activist Ashton Applewhite to sixty-something Bill Maher to Cher, are talking back to fossilized notions of aging, not enough has been done to hitch this issue to feminism.[49] Feminism has, since the 1970s, focused primarily on issues of crucial importance to younger women, from reproductive rights to equal access to education and employment to campaigns against sexual harassment and violence. These issues of course have been and remain pivotal, especially today.

It's just that issues affecting older women—how they're treated at work, their economic prospects, how government policies hurt or help them, whether doctors take them seriously, the negative attitudes and discrimination they may face, how all of this is shaped by race and class—and how the media promote, undermine, or simply ignore their needs and rights, have not been central to feminist agendas. Worse, from television shows to political commentary over the years, "second-wave" feminists (and their issues) have been cast as now irrelevant, grim, dowdy, beside the point. Some have even asked whether "ageism is entrenched within feminism itself."[50] Framed as "outdated antagonists" to younger women, this is a stereotype that can also legitimate our invisibility.[51] It too is one we must combat, as baby boomers and millennials—in fact, all women who believe in equality—need each other more than ever.

The media especially love pitting older women against younger ones, as when Gloria Steinem, appearing on Bill Maher's *Real Time*, having emphatically praised young women as being "way more feminist" and more activist than her generation, blurted out that some younger women might be supporting Bernie Sanders because "that's where the boys are." Despite the fact that the comment was uncharacteristically dumb and flippant, Steinem noted, correctly, that it was taken out of context; she had to issue an apology, despite her paean to millennial women. Alan Rappeport in the *New York Times* lost no time in hyping this "generational clash" in his story "Gloria Steinem and Madeleine Albright Scold Young Women Backing Bernie Sanders," which neither woman did.[52] After backlash from readers who saw the word "scold" as a sexist stereotype of nagging older women, the paper changed it to "rebuke."[53] That Gloria Steinem, who has said, written, and done so much for women over five decades, could be so trashed because of a gaffe is testimony to how gendered ageism can seek to fell even the most consequential of female icons.

These media-stoked wars that crudely stereotype entire generations mask our now quite pressing common interests as women. What unites us across generations is feminism; starting in the 2010s (and especially after the 2016 election), many have discarded the "I'm-not-a-feminist-but . . ." deflector shield. In addition to the majority of older women's embrace of feminism, 63 percent of those eighteen to thirty-four say they are feminists or strong feminists, with 83 percent of them seeing it as empowering.[54] They—and we—need to see ourselves as part of this renewed feminist rally that must prevent our troglodyte politicians from taking us back to 1958. And we also need to appreciate how the anti-aging industrial complex, and its defiance mantra, is profoundly depoliticizing. It urges us to use a microscope to focus inward, when we need telescopes, to focus outward, as we did in the 1960s and beyond, to work, still, to make the world for girls and women a better place.

Claiming and raising our voices matters. It is time for us to be mouthy once again and to enjoy and take pride in doing so. As Traister urges, "You're right to be mad . . . being mad can be joyful and productive and connective."[55] Our mission involves calling out the intertwining of ageism and sexism when we see it and hear it, talking back to a youth-obsessed media that either sidelines us or insists that aging is inherently bad, and opposing public policies that hurt all women and especially older women, particularly older women of color. It also involves forging a cross-generational bridge feminism with younger women who will someday be where we are and need to see how ageism—and the policies that go with it—will affect them too unless we all tackle it now. Because of what we did in the 1970s, 1980s, and beyond, we opened up enormous possibilities for subsequent generations; it's time to do that again, and in partnership with them.

Women of a certain age do not want to be marginalized or constrained by obsolete and dismissive attitudes about older women. Millions of us are embracing a more positive and socially active role. When Katie Couric (sixty-two), one of our many role models over the years, was at an event recently and overheard someone say, "Wow, she really looks old," she thought to herself, "Well, I am older, and that's okay." She insists we should celebrate age and make older people more prominent, adding "the more we can present ourselves the way we are and be okay with it, the better off we'll be."[56] Indeed. We need to make our emerging, inchoate movement visible, strong, and influential. To do this, it is important to review what we've achieved, what mistakes we may have made, and which tactics from our past are best suited to the pres-

ent moment—even as we embrace newer strategies to dismantle gendered ageism. It's time to talk back to the media, past and
present, to review how they helped get us here, and to point out
how they may be advancing yet thwarting our needs and desires.
And those of us who are more privileged need to work together
for institutional changes with those women who are not. Lifespan
feminism affirms the ongoing struggles of young women while
also foregrounding what is necessary for older women in this new
stage of our lives.

There is no manual for throwing off the cloak of invisibility,
just as there was no manual back in the 1970s, 1980s, and 1990s for
reinventing what it meant to be an American woman. Let's write
one together and dethrone outmoded and derisive attitudes and
change the road ahead, for ourselves and for others. Let's make
this moment count. We once changed the world. Let's do it again.

CHAPTER 2

Why the Seventies Mattered

"THE 1970S WERE WILD TIMES," begins "The CNN Quiz Show, Seventies Edition." "From Watergate to Disco . . . The Vietnam War to *Star Wars* . . . Test your 1970s knowledge and see if you're Dyn-o-mite!" The questions grill you about the television show *Good Times*, who made the Concorde supersonic jet, the miniseries *Roots*, which horse won the Triple Crown, and whether pet rocks were really a thing. Its "Who were you in the '70s?" wonders whether you were a bell-bottomed, shaggy-haired, and/ or polyester-wearing type. Not exhumed in this have-a-nice-day, smiley-face time capsule are more frowny-face topics like Watergate, Vietnam (although they are mentioned in the quiz teaser), long gas lines, and plane hijackings, not to mention "Escape (The Piña Colada Song)" or, worse, "Muskrat Love."

Not surprisingly, especially erased in this disco-ball refraction of history is the rise and impact of probably the most far-ranging and consequential social movement of the 1970s, the women's liberation movement, which, despite an ongoing list of pressing, unfinished business, changed everything from the workplace to the family to educational institutions and more. In the popular imagination, women's history, and especially the history of feminism, has been pretty much silted over; it has become the obsolete, irrelevant history of a bygone, maxi-skirted movement whose work has allegedly been done. There is an amnesia about what it took— by feminist leaders, by everyday women, and, yes, by Congress— to tackle women's deeply entrenched second-class status.

This movement, which included liberal and radical feminism, was hardly perfect: some leaders and activists were homophobic, racist, and class-bound, making many lesbians, women of color, and women from the working class feel excluded and marginalized. Nonetheless, its impact, however flawed and partial, was meteoric. And despite the stereotype that all white feminists of this era were exclusionary, or that women of color were not foundational to the second wave, that is false. When the New York Radical Women in 1968 organized their deliberately incendiary, history-making demonstration against the Miss America Pageant ("the degrading Mindless-Boob-Girlie Symbol"), they also protested the pageant's rank racism.[1] White and black activists— including feminist Robin Morgan and civil rights lawyer Florynce "Flo" Kennedy—picketed together, and Kennedy, who had chained herself to a giant Miss America puppet, proclaimed the demonstration "the best fun I can imagine anyone wanting to have."[2] Other such pioneers included African American activist Pauli Murray, who told Betty Friedan in 1965 that the country needed "an NAACP for women." A year later, Murray helped found the National Organization for Women (NOW) with Friedan and others.[3] Aileen Hernandez, another African American activist, also a founding member of NOW, became its second president in 1970; Hispanic activist Inez Casiano was on NOW's first national board. Murray and Hernandez were especially outraged that the Equal Employment Opportunity Commission, formed in

1965 to enforce antidiscrimination provisions of the Civil Rights Act, refused to prohibit sex-segregated job ads.[4]

Very few of these women of color enjoyed the media coverage (and thus credit for their pathbreaking work) that white feminists, and especially Gloria Steinem, got. Two exceptions were Shirley Chisolm, the first black woman elected to Congress in 1968, and Flo Kennedy; her trademark cowboy hat and quips like "There are very few jobs that actually require a penis or vagina. All other jobs should be open to everybody," helped. (I loved Kennedy; when a male heckler taunted her, asking, "Are you a lesbian?" she shot right back, "Are you my alternative?") Kennedy was, along with Chisolm and African American feminist activists Dorothy Height, Eleanor Holmes Norton, the Native American rights leader LaDonna Harris, and Steinem, one of the founders of the National Women's Political Caucus in 1971.[5] Kennedy also founded the National Feminist Party in 1971, which proceeded to nominate Shirley Chisolm for president in 1972.[6]

Gloria Steinem—who was always committed to inclusion and diversity in the movement—posed side by side, clenched fists raised, with activist Dorothy Pitman Hughes, and in 1974 hired poet and novelist Alice Walker as an editor at *Ms.*[7] The media gave minimal attention to the role of women of color in the movement, further whitewashing it. Also erased from this history—despite the setbacks, insults, and humiliation heaped on so many feminist women—is how fun it was to burst the barricades, to talk back to white male authority, and, well, to win!

As we gather ourselves to stake our claim to continue to be seen and heard, we need to remind ourselves that it took being visible, being vocal, being political—and unruly—enduring ridicule, and, yes, being irreverent and sarcastic, to crack major chinks in the wall of patriarchy. And we need to remind ourselves, and others too, of this past, as this is a place, baby boom women can assure you, we definitely do not want to go back to. As we confront what it might take to dismantle the ageism-sexism dyad, we can build up some muscle mass by remembering, celebrating, and drawing lessons and sustenance from what our generation, and those surrounding ours, older and younger, have done since 1970.

Former NBC news anchorman Tom Brokaw famously labeled those who came of age during the Great Depression, and saved us and the world from fascism, as "the Greatest Generation," and there is much to be said for this tribute. But I would argue that women who proved themselves pioneers by entering jobs and professional schools previously reserved only for men—where they were often greeted with considerable animosity, resentment, and degrading comments; who had to go back to work when their babies were only six weeks old because that was all the unpaid maternity leave they got (if they even got that); who then worked full-time jobs while raising small children in the face of crappy, overpriced, or nonexistent childcare; who had to learn how to be managers and supervisors with no mentors, role models, guidelines, or support; who only had themselves to rely on financially; who held their families together financially and emotionally after their husbands divorced them for younger women (often after their wives had helped put the men through college or professional school); who taught their daughters how to stand up for themselves and their sons to respect women; who insisted that making coffee for all the male coworkers in the room wasn't their job; who spoke up about and resisted sexual harassment, or who just had to put up with it to keep their jobs; who insisted their husbands also do the dishes and know the name of their kids' pediatrician; who had the guts to file often stressful and expensive lawsuits against gender-based discrimination; who came out as lesbians when it could mean losing their job, their friends, and the love of their family; who pioneered in exposing domestic violence as widespread and criminal; who had the enormous courage to testify against rapists in thoroughly hostile courtrooms; who endured the double whammy of racism and sexism, or homophobia and sexism, or the triple whammy of all three in doing any or all of this; in other words, a generation of women who, through what Gloria Steinem famously called "outrageous acts and everyday rebellions," helped transform the nation's educational system, the workplace, marriage, family structure, our laws and policies—that this is the Greatest Generation of Women.

And we are not done yet. Plus, what is exciting about where we are now is that an invigorated cohort of younger women, pushing further for progressive change, may be poised to assume that mantle.

So what did we do then that helps us see what we might do now?

As part of this history refresher, we will be deploying an age-old tool that women have used for years, publicly and privately: the bullshit detector. It is important to identify and itemize all the bullshit said about women, as well as the bullshit warnings about what terrible things would happen—to our economy, our culture, and our families (not to mention the bathrooms of America)—should women be granted equality.

Let's start with a particularly noxious geological stratum of our history: the 1950s, an era some white men see as a golden age and seem to be pining for. What attitudes did our country's media gatekeepers have toward us and how did they depict us? The 1958 guidebook *What Makes Women Buy* opined that "at least half of all women are turned into 'witches' of varying degrees once a month," that they "like to see pictures of food," that they are "not inclined to be interested in automobiles," and that their "verbal aptitude accounts for the fact that they like to gossip *and* have the last word."[8] We were technophobes who supposedly couldn't drive or play a hi-fi (but had somehow mastered the vacuum cleaner and washing machine), and weaklings who shouldn't lift anything over thirty pounds (the average weight of a three-year-old). Television commercials featured housewives who sang "Mr. Clean, I love you" while scrubbing their bathtubs, at the same time that print ads showed men holding their wives facedown over their knees and spanking them—really—for making "flat, stale coffee" or, weirdly, because they just got a new, seemingly testosterone-infused Van Heusen shirt. We were suited only to clean house and produce babies, had a built-in maternal instinct, were by nature passive and inherently domestic, and lived to be deferential to men. (Women of color, by contrast, who were mostly invisible in the media, could work outside the home—as maids, bathroom attendants, or tending to white people's children, for example.) Such put-downs had a persistent grip on Madison Avenue's mindset; in 1970, the year the women's movement burst onto the scene, *Ad Age* opined, "She likes to watch television and she does not enjoy reading a great deal . . . she finds her satisfaction within a rather small world . . . she has little interest or skill to explore . . . mental activity is arduous for her."[9]

And then there were the infamous quotations: "Women are usually more patient in working at unexciting, repetitive tasks" and "when women are encouraged to be competitive too many of them become disagreeable" (pediatrician and best-selling author Dr. Spock, 1970); "It would be preposterously naïve to suggest that a B.A. can be made as attractive to girls as a marriage license" (Grayson Kirk, president of Columbia University, 1968); and especially notorious, "The only position for women in SNCC [Student Nonviolent Coordinating Committee] is prone" (Stokely Carmichael, 1964).[10]

In the early 1960s there were more women, married and single, in the workplace than ever before, but they earned just over half of what men made, often for doing the exact same job, such as being a teacher or working in retail. Activist women, some galvanized by his New Frontier vision, pushed President John Kennedy to take on gender-based discrimination. He established the

Presidential Commission on the Status of Women, headed by former first lady Eleanor Roosevelt. Its 1963 report, *American Women*, documented that women were second-class citizens, who endured gender-based job discrimination, unequal pay, and inequality in their marriages, and deserved paid maternity leave and affordable childcare.[11] Meanwhile, Esther Peterson, head of the Women's Bureau in the Department of Labor, drafted a bill for Kennedy that would become the Equal Pay Act of 1963, which Congress passed despite opposition from the U.S. Chamber of Commerce and the National Retail Merchants Association.

The Equal Pay Act prohibited differential pay for men and women employed in equivalent jobs requiring the same "skill, effort, and responsibility." However, it excluded domestic and agricultural workers (millions of whom were women of color) and left employers free to not hire women for certain positions.[12] Of course there were loopholes, where "merit," seniority, and quality or quantity of work produced could allow for differential pay. While women, on average, still earn about 82 cents to a man's dollar (and that depends on what state we're in—in New York it's 89 cents, in Louisiana it's 70 cents—with race making a difference too), that's an improvement from 1963.[13]

What lies were women (and the country) told? A spokesman for the U.S. Chamber of Commerce, a perennially conservative voice, warned that "working girls" would be "fired wholesale if equal pay ever becomes law" and that with equal pay required, businesses "will always hire the man except in the most unusual circumstances"; and it predicted that the law would eliminate "thousands, even hundreds of thousands of job opportunities for women."[14] But what really happened? Women's participation in the workforce increased from 38 percent in 1960 to 43 percent in 1970 and to 52 percent by 1980.[15]

In 1964, Lyndon Johnson, in part to honor President Kennedy's legacy—and much more to cement his own—pushed for passage of a Civil Rights Act initially introduced by Kennedy in 1963. Because it would outlaw segregated facilities and job discrimination based on race, color, or national origin (Title VII), and would provide greater protection for black voters, Southern congressmen vehemently opposed the bill, emphasizing, as Russell Long from Georgia did, that they would resist "to the bitter end" any bill that would allow for the "intermingling and amalgamation of the races" in the South.[16]

In an effort to deep-six the legislation, Howard W. Smith (D-VA), chairman of the House Ways and Means Committee, decided to add "sex" to the list of categories one could not discriminate against, because women, and their rights, remained a joke among most male politicians. When he introduced his amendment, reportedly the chamber erupted into jeers and laughter. Representative Emanuel Celler of New York, regarding the amendment as ludicrous and unnecessary, noted that women "are not the minority in my house . . . I usually have the last two words and those words are 'yes, dear.' "[17] Representative Martha Griffiths (D-MI), who helped get the votes needed to pass the bill, noted that "if there had been any necessity to point out that women were a second-class sex, the laughter would have proved it."[18]

To combat this me-Tarzan you-Jane mindset, which permeated pretty much every nook and cranny of American society—its laws, its politics, its economic system, its detergent commercials—feminist organizations like NOW and their leaders, using Title VII as well as the Equal Pay Act of 1963, started suing companies and institutions for sex discrimination. NOW also took on knuckle-dragging media imagery in the early 1970s with their annual Barefoot and Pregnant Award for the most sexist, Neanderthal ads and helped expose these stereotypes as preposterous. Equality hinged crucially on reconceiving how women were depicted in popular culture, because derogatory and objectifying imagery of women was rampant and it justified discriminatory laws and practices.

Just as important, the women's movement invented one of the most powerful and effective forces for social change: consciousness-raising. Women began getting together in groups to crack open their feelings about often previously unspoken experiences in their relationships at work and in their everyday lives. For many, these were revelations. What women had seen as their own lonely struggles, frustrations, and indignities now emerged as a jigsaw puzzle taking form into a picture of collective oppression, alienation, and, increasingly, collective outrage. Consciousness-raising helped transform women's feelings into a propulsive social movement, stoking the rallying cry "the personal is political." While most of the participants in CR groups were white and middle to upper-middle class, and thus privileged in their experiences and concerns, the resulting activism sought to further broadcast their cumulative realization: that all women were oppressed by sexism.

To remind ourselves of the strength, and chutzpah, all these efforts fueled, let's start with August 26, 1970. (Although the 1968 demonstration at the Miss America contest—"Atlantic City is a town with class; they raise your morals and they judge your ass"—remains a personal favorite.) It was the fiftieth anniversary of women getting the right to vote nationally. To mark it, and that rising seismic shift coming to be labeled the women's liberation movement ("women's lib" for short in the news media), Betty Friedan and other feminists announced a "Women's Strike for Equality" to be held that day. The idea was simple yet incredibly defiant for the times—women should stop cleaning, cooking, waitressing, taking dictation, or doing any kind of a job "for which a man would be paid more"—and participate in a mass walkout to show how the country would come to a screeching halt if women's underpaid— and unpaid—work was not done. There was concern among the movement, especially among some in the National Organization for Women, that the strike would be a flop because most women would not risk losing their jobs, no less refuse to, say, change their babies' diapers, just to make a point.

But it was a sensation. It's true that most women did not strike at their workplaces, but a diverse group of women came together nationally and rallied in cities all over the country, including Chicago, Seattle, Los Angeles, Indianapolis, and Washington, DC: it was at that point the largest demonstration for women's rights in the history of the country. Five thousand women gathered in Boston Common; women in Detroit staged a sit-in in a men's room protesting against unequal facilities; two thousand demonstrated in San Francisco's Union Square; and in New York City, where one lane of Fifth Avenue had been set aside for marchers, tens of thousands surged onto the street, shutting it down completely. Signs ranged from "Sisterhood is Powerful" and "Don't Iron While the Strike is Hot" to "Don't Cook Dinner—Starve a Rat Today." Women chanted at men who heckled them: "Go do the dishes! Go do the dishes!" For Friedan, the nationwide turnout exceeded her "wildest dreams."[19]

The rallies brought together the "leading edge" of baby boom women who were between fifteen and twenty-four with women of prior generations. Millions more women watched on television. The women's movement was one of the biggest stories of 1970, and this event in particular garnered massive coverage. However, not surprisingly, given that the news media was a nearly total white boys' club, much of the coverage was snide and condescending, with all three major television networks quoting West Virginia senator Jennings Randolph's characterization of the movement as "a small band of bra-less bubbleheads." News anchor Howard K. Smith on ABC insisted that women were already more than equal and had more money than men because they inherited it from "worn-out husbands." Frank Reynolds, also on ABC, chuckled that having women serve in the military would end the country's role as "world policemen" because female troops "could simply never be ready on time." Eric Sevareid, editorializing on CBS, suggested that women wore the pants in most marriages and that "most American men are startled by the idea that American women in general are oppressed."[20]

So were women actually "oppressed"? Here is what a woman faced prior to the 1970s. She could be fired from her job if she was pregnant. In many states a woman's property and income were legally under the control of her husband. Until the Equal Credit Opportunity Act of 1974, a bank could deny a woman a credit card if she was single; if married, her husband typically had to cosign for her to get one. If she worked, she made 59 cents to a man's dollar. She could be a schoolteacher but not a college professor, a nurse but not a doctor, a secretary but not a manager (although a few women did soldier their way through to these upper echelons). And if she was a schoolteacher, she was paid less than her male counterpart for doing the same job because supposedly she didn't have to support a family and instead only worked for what was quaintly called "pin money." Until a 1973 Supreme Court decision outlawing the practice, newspapers could post job ads by sex (Help Wanted–Men, Help Wanted–Women), and you know where the better jobs were versus the crappy ones. If you were a "steward-ess" (what we call a flight attendant) you had to be white, between 5 feet 2 inches and 5 feet 9 inches in height, 105–135 pounds in weight "in proportion to your height," not need glasses, maintain "soft hands," quit if you got married, and retire by age thirty-two—and of course put up with drunk male passengers grabbing your ass and propositioning you.[21]

Restrictive quotas kept female students at law schools to a minimum: between three and five percent. Women reported that they were rarely called on in class, and if they answered incorrectly, they were told to "go back to the kitchen." Some classes had "Ladies Day" in which the few women were grilled to the amusement of the male professor and students.[22] Women fared little better when they applied for jobs after graduating. Those whose applications were rejected by major law firms in the 1950s and 1960s include Sandra Day O'Connor, Ruth Bader Ginsburg, Janet Reno, and Elizabeth Dole. Female applicants in the early 1970s were told, "We don't like to hire women," "We just hired a woman and couldn't hire another," and "We don't expect the same kind of work from women as we do from men."[23]

It was the same for medical and other professional schools; women were barred altogether or admitted in extremely limited numbers. Many states excluded women from jury duty or allowed them to automatically opt out because they were deemed too emotional to objectively assess evidence and might simply swoon when confronted with violent criminal cases. The ACLU filed various suits against this practice, and Supreme Court cases in 1975 and 1979 deemed the practice unconstitutional (the latter case being argued successfully by Ruth Bader Ginsburg).

By 1971, female law students at Columbia and New York University were fed up. Citing violations of Title VII of the 1964 Civil Rights Act, they filed a complaint with the NYC Commission on Human Rights against ten New York City law firms. The litigation grew into a class-action suit, and after massive resistance by the law firms, in 1977 they agreed to guidelines ensuring the hiring of female associates. Similar suits around the country also succeeded. Result? The percentage of women in the legal profession jumped from 4 percent in 1970 to 12.5 percent in 1980; by 2017, women constituted 45 percent of associates (but only 22.7 percent of partners) in major law firms.[24]

Pushed further by women activists and the groundswell of the women's movement, Congress in 1972 passed Title IX of the Education Amendments, which barred sex-based discrimination in any federally funded education program or activity.[25] Thus medical schools, business schools, and other graduate programs could no longer use quotas to keep women out. This led to a huge increase in the number of women in many professions. In 1950, only 6 percent of working physicians were women (and I remember them being regarded as weird); by 1990, the figure was 17 percent; by 2015, 36 percent.[26] The number of female civil engineers increased by 977 percent between 1970 and 2010; pharmacists by 434 percent; lawyers and judges by 681 percent.[27]

Title IX also applied to athletic programs and required equal opportunity for women to participate in sports. Representatives of the NCAA warned that the law would "signal the end of intercollegiate athletic programs" and that money would be channeled into "non-money-making sports,"[28] which I guess is why each of the five major college football conferences in 2014 was "projected to see its base revenue increase to about $50 million,"[29] with the Ohio State Buckeyes valued at $1.5 billion in 2017.[30]

At magazines like *Newsweek* in 1970, college-educated women could be "researchers," which included "sorting mail, collecting newspaper clippings and delivering coffee."[31] They could not be writers and only rarely reporters. They were told, "Women don't write at *Newsweek*. If you want to be a writer, go someplace else." The women who left as a result? Nora Ephron, Ellen Goodman, Jane Bryant Quinn, and Susan Brownmiller.[32] So here was a truly in-your-face move: on the very same day—March 23, 1970—that *Newsweek*'s cover featured the silhouette of a naked women breaking through the symbol for the female sex under the all-caps headline "WOMEN IN REVOLT," forty-six women on the magazine's staff held a press conference announcing they were suing the publication for gender discrimination. The women were represented by civil rights attorney Eleanor Holmes Norton—white and black women working together. In August—and on the same day as the Women's Strike for Equality—*Newsweek* signed an agreement with its female employees laying out specific steps to provide equal employment opportunities for women.[33] (The 2016 Amazon series *Good Girls Revolt*, based on journalist Lynn Povich's memoir of the lawsuit, was not renewed by studio head Roy Price for a second season; Price subsequently resigned amid allegations that he had sexually harassed another show's executive producer.)[34]

Dolores Huerta, an activist for the rights of the mostly Mexican farm workers in the 1960s and '70s, met Gloria Steinem, and the two fused workers' rights and feminism. During the national boycott of California table grapes, designed to secure a minimum wage for those who picked them, the well-connected Steinem got Huntington Hartford, the heir to the A&P supermarket fortune, to actually picket A&P headquarters.[35] This was inspired theater; it is also another example of how women united across racial and ethnic divides from fifty years ago.

Reviewing the dizzying level of activism, ferment, writings, lawsuits, and court cases in the 1970s reminds us of how many women, all over the country, and their allies, famous and not, were mobilized to press for change. By 1974, the Fair Housing Act was amended to prohibit discrimination based on sex. In 1977 the Chicago-based group Women Employed, which clearly had a sense of humor as well as of justice, took up the cause of legal secretary Iris Rivera, who was fired for refusing to make coffee for the men in the office. The group brought fifty women to her office who staged a "how to make coffee" lesson complete with instructions like "turn the switch to on. This is the most difficult step, but, with practice, even an attorney can master it."[36] Rivera got her job back. Women Employed also solicited women to tell them the most menial rules and chores they had to do in their offices and then publicized them: having to sign in and out to go to the bathroom, balancing the boss's checkbook, dusting the office plants. These chores for women also began to disappear.[37] In other words, irreverence and humor mattered too.

Women had minimal control over their reproductive processes, and abortion was illegal, extremely dangerous, and sometimes deadly. This was very personal to many of us. One of the first stories I heard when I got to college was about a student who had died in a local motel from a botched illegal abortion. Women who had survived the procedure spoke out, loudly and publicly, burying their earlier shame and pushing for the right to control their own bodies and to make abortion legal. In 1969, Flo Kennedy organized a group of feminist lawyers to challenge the constitutionality of New York State's restrictive abortion law. A year later, the state legislature legalized abortion.[38] Such "speak outs" spread around the country, and in 1973 the Supreme Court struck down many of the restrictions on abortion.

Even when having babies, women had minimal control over their bodies. In the 1950s, many women were subjected to what was called "twilight sleep" during delivery, when they were partially knocked out (including with scopolamine, an amnesia-causing drug that erased all memory of giving birth). They were expected to take orders from the male doctors, and were strapped down so they wouldn't thrash around too much during labor, which resulted in the bruising and even scarring of some women's wrists. Some babies, having imbibed the drugs as well, were born limp and in need of resuscitation. Another delivery-room method involved numbing women from the waist down with what was called a "spinal," so they couldn't feel enough to push, sometimes requiring doctors to use forceps to pull the baby out, which could scar the babies' head and tear the woman's vagina.[39] Fathers were barred from the delivery rooms.

A feminist health movement, spurred by the sharing of collective horror stories and, later, by the publication of *Our Bodies, Ourselves*—that earthquake of a book that educated women about knowing and taking control of their own bodies—launched the natural childbirth movement. Men helped too, some husbands handcuffing themselves to their wives' gurneys so they could participate in the delivery.

Meanwhile, women around the country began revolting against the standard rules that then governed marriage and child rearing, leading some to embrace a phenomenon called "the marriage contract." Pioneered by the feminist writer Alix Kates Shulman and her husband, they wrote up an agreement affirming their equality in their marriage and that all domestic chores—waking up the kids, making their lunches, finding babysitters, and the like—would be split fifty-fifty between them. Their contract got considerable media coverage—a six-page cover story in *Life* and a feature in *Time*. *Redbook* published it under the editors' title "A Challenge to Every Marriage" and got over two thousand letters in response. By 1975, *Time* reported that there were at least 1500 different versions of marriage contracts being used.[40] At the same time, many marriages collapsed as women with less egalitarian husbands decided to go it alone. The divorce rate soared in the 1970s, doubling between 1969 and 1979.[41]

In part because of the women's movement, the 1973–75 recession during which some families needed two incomes, and the rising divorce rate, an unprecedented number of white middle-class mothers with small children entered the workforce, transforming the workplace and family life. The number of working mothers with infants under one year of age doubled between 1970 and 1985. By 1984, working mothers had reached a record number, with six out of ten women with children under eighteen working outside the home.[42] They were repeatedly warned by various "experts" and "family values" disciples that their children would, as a result, become maladjusted, more aggressive, and insecure if they went to day care, or worse, they might be molested by pedophiles who allegedly were the primary employees at these childcare centers. (Most of the various day-care child molestation scandals, wildly sensationalized by the media, turned out to be bogus.)[43] As *Parents* warned in 1982, day-care kids were "more easily frustrated, less cooperative with adults . . . more destructive and less task-oriented."

Various studies later showed that these accusations, trumped up as facts, were false. Actually, they have found that children of working mothers enjoy a variety of benefits—economic, educational, and social. Daughters completed more education and earned more money than the daughters of stay-at-home mothers, and adult sons spent more time on childcare and housework.[44] Despite all the dire warnings—as well as the overwhelming lack of decent, affordable day care—millions of mothers had to work. They had to figure out childcare on their own, juggling work and family, with much less pay than men. And they simply did it.

This is only a partial history of what women in the 1970s and early 1980s were up against and the status quo they challenged. Women were told they should be quiet. They weren't. Women were told it was unladylike to protest, to mouth off, to defy norms. Many didn't care. Women talked to each other to share and validate their experiences; they organized and pushed for legal protection against discrimination. Congress actually responded because women were in the streets and in the courts, protesting and fighting. They challenged the retrograde images of women in the media, and more women were hired to be television reporters and anchors. Having a political agenda mattered, marching and protesting mattered, talking back to outdated, retrograde attitudes about women mattered. It still matters. A lot.

Because despite all these victories, there was still much unfinished business, thwarted by a brawny backlash that gained enormous power in the 1980s and beyond.

— • • • —

Meanwhile, another rebellion was afoot, and there is a stunning amnesia about this as well, given how nationally prominent it was at the time and the revolutionary changes it sought, with some being achieved. It is here that we see the antecedents of where we are today, of taking a defiant stance on behalf of older women.

On Johnny Carson's *Tonight Show* on February 18, 1977, a gray-haired, seventy-two-year-old white woman wearing a Mao jacket with her hair in a bun strode out as one of Carson's guests. In his opening monologue, he mistakenly introduced her as Maggie Kuhn of "the Black Panthers" and then, cracking up as he realized his not-inconsiderable mistake, corrected himself while emphasizing that she was the founder of the Gray Panthers, *not* the Black Panthers, and that she was a champion for "old people's power." When the time for her segment came, Carson emphasized that her organization was "a national liberation group aimed at eradicating ageism."

When Carson welcomed her, Kuhn in turn assured him it was OK to mix up the name in the monologue because she said the Black Panthers and the Gray Panthers were collaborating on "some very good things," like a health center in Oakland, California, devoted to preventive care. Kuhn may have been less threatening to mainstream America than gun-toting black men in leather jackets and berets, but she was no less radical in what she took on.

That a woman who happily described herself as an "old woman" and a "wrinkled radical" would get on a late-night talk show is testament both to Kuhn as a force of nature and to the format of *The Tonight Show* in the 1970s, which did not confine its guest roster only to those celebrities who had their latest projects to promote. Plus, her segment lasted seven minutes, a solid chunk of time on a late-night talk show.

In one of his recurring skits, Carson donned a long dark-gray dress, a lacy ruffled collar, a gray wig, and a cane. His sidekick Ed McMahon welcomed him as "dear, sweet, lovable, *old* Aunt Blabby." The jokes typically relied on double entendres, casting Aunt Blabby as sexless yet sex-starved, and about her being hard of hearing and generally infirm, with her repeatedly reminding the audience, "I'm *old*." For example, in one joke, McMahon asks her if she likes vegetables and she says she loves them, "some of my best friends are vegetables." In another bit she comes out swinging a tennis racket and McMahon asks her how she scores. She replies, "Badly; I don't score anymore." Such jokes, and they were numerous, cast her sexual desires as absolutely preposterous, inappropriate, and a source of ridicule.

In her February appearance, Maggie Kuhn says, "I have a special request to make of you, Johnny." "Certainly," he responds. "And I hope you will be open to this," she adds. "When we were talking together some time ago, I talked about Aunt Blabby," she continues. "I think Aunt Blabby, at least the way you portray her, is antediluvian." Remember, this took considerable chutzpah: here Kuhn is, on national television, taking on one of the most powerful and popular men in show business. "Really?" he asks. "Yes, and I think you ought to bring her into the twentieth century . . . you ought to liberate her," Kuhn responds along with some laughs from the audience. "I'm quite serious about this, for older women," she goes on. She gives him a present to help radicalize Aunt Blabby. The audience laughs and claps as he holds up a Gray Panthers T-shirt. Carson promises to wear it, adding, "The next time I do Aunt Blabby, guaranteed, and I will try to bring her up to date."

Mostly forgotten today, Kuhn's spirited advocacy on behalf of older Americans, and especially older women, constitutes the origins of the quest for visibility for those over fifty. If you think that some of the images of older women in the media have changed for the better since Granny on *The Beverly Hillbillies* (1962–71) dimwittedly mistook a TV set for a washing machine, you have Maggie Kuhn to thank.

By the mid-1970s, Kuhn had become a nationally and even internationally recognized political leader. In addition to appearing on *The Tonight Show* four times,[45] she was all over the media: on *The Phil Donohue Show*, *The Today Show*, and *Good Morning America*. And she was chosen as the very first guest on the new *Larry King Live* show in 1985 on CNN.[46] Media monikers for Kuhn included "Ball of Fire," "Feisty," "Dynamo," "Fiery," and "Pied Piper for the Aged."[47] In a time when Clairol relentlessly admonished women to "hate that gray, wash it away," the columnist Ellen Goodman observed that Kuhn "carries her white hair like a bumper sticker."[48] Kuhn had speaking engagements all over the country, and by 1977 was reportedly traveling 100,000 miles annually, giving at least 200 talks a year. In March of 1980 alone she spoke 22 times in 11 states. Her speeches blasted various myths about old age: that it's "mindless," a time "when you stop learning and growing"; that it's "a disease nobody wants to admit they have" ("we'd rather have syphilis," she quipped, "at least you know you can cure syphilis"[49]). In 1978 the *World Almanac* named her one of the 25 most influential women in the United States.[50] Shortly before she died in 1995, ABC News profiled her as their "Person of the Week." Maggie Kuhn mattered, big time.

Kuhn had worked for the United Presbyterian Church in New York for twenty-five years until 1970, when she hit what was then the mandatory age for retirement: sixty-five. Kuhn, still full of energy and a longtime social activist, especially on behalf of women, found this outrageous and discriminatory. As she wrote, she felt "suddenly shocked and wounded, then angry, at having to be sent out to pasture. Then I figured there must be thousands of old people like me, so I decided it was time to fight back."[51] She drew inspiration from the antiwar, civil rights, and women's liberation movements. Their calls to end discrimination were everywhere, but discrimination against older people was left out. And she now had a new term, coined by Dr. Robert Butler in 1969, "ageism": the "systematic stereotyping and discrimination against people because they are old."[52]

Kuhn's response to her forced retirement was to found the Gray Panthers along with several friends. In addition to advocating for the end of mandatory retirement and for fully subsidized health care by the government—what we would call single payer—her main goal was to change how people looked at, thought about, and treated older people. She also sought to forge an intergenerational alliance between the young and the old. She had already been arrested alongside twenty-somethings demonstrating against the Vietnam War, and she saw "a contrived effort to set the old against the young, to persuade the young people that old people are getting too much . . . which is not true."[53] Young people joined the organization, and Kuhn called them "Panther Cubs."[54] The Panthers' motto was "age and youth in action." Throughout her older years she shared her two homes in the Germantown section of Philadelphia with a variety of young people because she felt that intergenerational alliances enriched everyone involved.

Given the vibrancy and visibility today of so many people over sixty-five—celebrities and everyday people alike—it's hard to believe that back in 1970 the accepted wisdom among gerontologists about aging was governed by "disengagement theory"[55]— meaning it was best for society, as Kuhn put it, to stay "out of the way" and go play "bingo and shuffleboard." She called this "wrinkled babyhood," and she cast age-segregated housing for older people as "glorified playpens."[56] There was virtually nothing at this time in the popular press or elsewhere in the media about women over the age of sixty-five having fun or full, meaningful lives.[57]

Kuhn set out to shatter every stereotype she could about older people. Here she seemed to delight in shocking people, as when she insisted repeatedly that sexual desire did not shrivel up at age sixty-five and proved it by having an affair with a man in his twenties when she was in her seventies.[58] Kuhn was a badass; for example, in 1973, she threatened to have the Gray Panthers, including those with wheelchairs and canes, stand on the tracks to stop the trolleys in Philadelphia, until its transit authority cut fares for senior citizens to ten cents during non-rush-hour times. They did.[59] Kuhn successfully lobbied against the mandatory retirement age, which Congress raised to seventy in 1978 and eliminated altogether in 1986.

Kuhn also saw the impact of media activism by feminists and African Americans, who protested demeaning imagery. She too looked at the media, especially television, and did not like what she saw. She was not alone: a 1976 poll of people between the ages of fifty-five and eighty found that nearly half of those surveyed responded negatively to the representation of older people in ads. Another study of television commercials found that people in their sixties and seventies were represented as having ten times the number of health problems as those in their thirties and forties, a gross exaggeration.[60] "Old age has been so negatively stereotyped that it has become something to dread and feel threatened by," the Panthers asserted.[61] Through the Gray Panthers, which grew to 100,000 members (most of them women) in over thirty states,[62] Kuhn launched the Media Watch Task Force of volunteers around the country, headed in 1977 by seventy-four-year-old Lydia Bragger, who monitored how older people were depicted—if they appeared at all—on the three networks.

Kuhn scrutinized everything and didn't miss a trick when

watching television, including noting that in one yogurt ad, the younger actors were eating the strawberry flavor while the camera zoomed in to older people eating prune yogurt. "In commercials, we're buffoons. In programming we don't exist," the Panthers charged.[63] In 1975, Bragger and Kuhn sent a letter of protest to Arthur Taylor, president of CBS, criticizing their "pervasive put-downs of the old." Their protest led to a meeting with the National Association of Broadcasters, where they asked that age be added to the topics—race, sex, creed, color—that the NAB's code said should be "treated with sensitivity." The NAB agreed.[64] By 1977 the Gray Panthers had partnered with the National Council on Aging and their Media Resource Center—a two-woman office in Hollywood "whose sole purpose [was] to lobby television's creative community to do a little better by the old."[65]

This was Maggie Kuhn. In the fall of 1977, she was testifying before Congress (which she had done before) in hearings before the Select Committee on Aging (which the Gray Panthers' activism had helped establish) presided over by Representative Claude Pepper (D-FL), who was seventy-seven. Pepper's hearings and Kuhn's testimony sought to build on the momentum of the August report by the U.S. Commission on Civil Rights titled *Window Dressing on the Set: Women and Minorities on Television*. The report was a damning indictment of television for continuing to underrepresent and stereotype women and minorities (especially minority women). However, it had not considered examining ageism in television at all. By this time Kuhn had already been raising hell with the networks, using Lydia Bragger's work, writing to their presidents to attack offensive stereotypes. Pepper hauled in network executives to answer for their portrayals—or lack thereof—of older Americans.

It is important to review what these hearings found, as they remind us how far we have—and have not—come. The hearings were accompanied and informed by a study supervised by Kathleen Hall Jamieson, who later became the dean of the Annenberg School for Communication, of the images of older people in television. Her study found that older women constituted less than one percent of major characters in prime-time television and that when they did appear they were often the victims of fatal crimes—so, not much screen time. The dean of the Annenberg School at the time, George Gerbner, found it was even worse for African American women: "Old black women are 'only cast to be killed. They rarely have any other role.'" (In reality, people over sixty-five had the lowest rate of criminal victimization.)[66]

"Are the elderly the lepers of television?" Pepper demanded of the executives in the hearing, noting that older television characters were "toothless, sexless, humorless, witless and constipated." Pepper and other members of Congress at the hearings listed a host of negative stereotypes of older people: "rigid, decayed in intelligence, unproductive and uninformed, doddering, senile, deaf, and useless." One representative noted that older people were often depicted as residing in nursing homes when, actually, only five percent did.[67] "We have instilled the notion that aging is an affliction," Pepper proclaimed and added, "It is my hope that these hearings [will lead the networks to] completely eliminate age stereotyping, even if it is inadvertent." Age stereotyping matters so much "because we all age."[68] It also matters because older people, especially those who were retired, tended to watch more television than younger people, so their self-image was at stake.

Then, in January of 1978, the committee held hearings on the images of older people in advertising. Pepper again asserted that "age stereotyping is a pandemic in this country" and Edward R. Roybal (D-CA), the presiding chair, said the media cast aging as something that should be battled as if it were "a communicable disease." The Gray Panthers added, "You see these TV grandmothers in 1890s clothing and silly hats all agog over a sink cleaner. It makes you sick."[69] Older women, Pepper continued, were exhorted to "wash out the gray," to drench their skin in skin creams. Soon enough, "constipation becomes a whispered preoccupation, their teeth fall out, their digestive systems revolt and they are overtaken by aberrant behavior." Pepper urged the industry to "spurn" ageism in ads and "to declare defiantly that gray is beautiful."[70]

In the study of older people in advertising that accompanied these hearings, again supervised by Jamieson, the researchers found that older people were comparatively healthier than their portrayal in commercials where they needed a bleacher-sized rack of medications. Also, in real life, older women outnumbered older men, but in television ads, older men outnumbered older women and were more likely to appear as authority figures.

Simply put, ads, especially those for cosmetics or hair dye, held women more personally accountable for physically aging than men—when, of course, neither could control the process. As women aged, the likelihood that they would sell a beauty product plummeted (no sixty-nine-year-old movie star as "the face" of anything back then). It was younger women who pitched anti-aging products. And of course, just like today, ads for beauty creams used "old" as a pejorative term, especially for women. In a typical ad of the time, a young woman expressed outrage over her first wrinkle as she slathered on Oil of Olay, declaring simply, "This is war!"

By the 1980s, in part because of the Gray Panthers and Pepper's activism, the networks debuted a variety of shows featuring older actors, including older women—*Murder, She Wrote* and *The Golden Girls* (on the air for seven years and still in continuing syndication for twenty-four years). This was groundbreaking work. Kuhn's crusade provides crucial lessons in consciousness-raising, self-pride and empowerment, and media activism that it is time to resurrect and revitalize. It is time to pick up where she left off.

Thus, while most feminists were focused on young women's issues—education, jobs, reproductive freedom, sexual equity, and childcare, Kuhn led a revolt against ageism and, especially, against the invisibility of older women. In many ways these were parallel and, indeed, often unconnected movements, although Kuhn saw them as of a piece in changing women's lives. It is time to remember and celebrate both revolutions, to remind ourselves of what we need to preserve, what we must build on, and what we can no longer let be undone.

So don't waste your time with CNN-style quizzes about who played Starsky and who played Hutch. The 1970s was nothing less than a major, national upheaval in gender relations that profoundly shaped the fortunes and fate of millions of young and middle-aged women (and men too), and it continues to do so today. Maggie Kuhn was paying it forward to us. She promoted a visibility revolt that had real consequences. Let's have a drink in her honor, and then let's pick up her torch.

CHAPTER 3

The Rise of Aspirational Aging

DURING THE 2017 SUPER BOWL, in between the usual ads for Budweiser, Snickers, and the NFL itself, and one in which an allegedly adult woman has sexual fantasies about a silver-haired, totally ripped, booty-shaking, animated Mr. Clean, viewers got something a little different. A pewter-bearded biker in a dive bar sees Steppenwolf's classic "Born to Be Wild" on the jukebox and hits Play. As the music pounds, we see a poster for the 1969 film *Easy Rider* and then various aging male bikers headbanging each other. Into the bar storms one very angry compatriot announcing, "Blocked in!" The music screeches to a halt. "Blocked in?!?" they all yell and rush out to discipline the offender, and now a lone, leather-faced female also appears as part of the group. But the culprit is Peter Fonda himself, wearing the same American flag–emblazoned leather jacket from his most iconic movie, who drives off in the go-to vehicle for anarchists, a Mercedes convertible. Cue the music and the tag line "Born to Be Wild, Built to Be Wild" as Fonda, tearing up the road, flashes the peace sign.

This is one example of how some in the media construct us

in their mind's eye, think about how to hail us as consumers, and reflect some version of us back to ourselves. So when some marketers not selling denture cream or diuretics think, however fleetingly—and reluctantly—of baby boomers, one default generational touchstone seems to be the *Easy Rider* rebels.

Ads targeting older viewers, using male avatars of the counterculture, started over a decade ago. In November 2006, writing his "Ad Review" column for *Advertising Age*, the journalist Bob Garfield, now the cohost of *On the Media*, deliciously noted that Dennis Hopper, a "drug smuggler in *Easy Rider*," a "brutal pervert in *Blue Velvet*," and a "sociopathic bomber in *Speed*," whose "off-screen life hasn't been especially orderly," was now "fronting for freakin' Wall Street." (Garfield wondered whether Squeaky Fromme, would-be assassin of Gerald Ford in 1975, was unavailable.) The ad in question (still viewable on YouTube should you be so inclined) was for Ameriprise, the financial planning firm. One ad in this campaign blared Iggy Pop's bom-bom-bom, bom-bom-da-bom "Lust for Life," while we saw retirees—men—windsurfing. Another had Hopper on a tropical beach, reading a dictionary. "To go away. To disappear. That's how the dictionary defines retirement." He then hurled the tome on the sand in disgust. Cue the phallic backbeat guitar hook from "Gimme Some Lovin'" by the Spencer Davis Group. "Your generation's definitely not headed for bingo night! . . . There's no age limit on dreams . . . 'cause I just don't see you playing shuffleboard, ya know what I mean?" Cut to a man building his own catamaran and sailing it on an azure sea. Wow, that's one self-actualized, enterprising retiree!

While Garfield was taken aback by the choice of spokesperson, he admitted to being "thrilled by the ad" because it was so different from the usual "brain-dead, condescending" ones by companies like Colonial Penn Insurance and Craftmatic adjustable beds that presumed older people were "doddering old fools . . . badly dressed and a little slow on the uptake." As if channeling Maggie Kuhn, he added, "It's as if a switch goes off in your 60s. One day you're a vibrant worker with responsibility, income and possibly even a sex life and—wham—the next you're a fearful dullard, being insultingly spoken down to by the very people who want your business." Could advertisers, he wondered, be tiptoeing toward addressing this growing population of older people with dignity?[1]

The Ameriprise-Hopper gambit was one of the early salvos of what can best be called aspirational aging, one media response to our demographic revolution that envisions getting older as a life stage of throbbing empowerment and privilege. Aspirational aging is a media-crafted, marketing-created zeitgeist whose central tenets are self-actualization, the ongoing importance of personal, proactive transformation, and developing another new potential self to ward off (and pretend we aren't) aging. It draws from over a decade of market research—some of it silly and some of it on the mark—about how baby boomers see themselves as very different from the retirees of yore and the stereotypes that encased them. Aspirational aging recognizes that many older people are active in the world, feel younger than their age, and hate ageist stereotypes, and then seeks to exploit this positive sensibility in ways that can commodify, and distort, what we need and how we are supposed to see ourselves.

The Ameriprise ads contained two of aspirational aging's initial, defining characteristics: the focus on men through male boomer icons, and its address to those privileged enough to be able to afford a financial adviser. As various marketers and advertising analysts in the early twenty-first century began turning their attention to what they were realizing was a rather enormous sector of the population that they were either ignoring or talking down to—reportedly only 10 percent of ads were directed to people over fifty[2]—they struggled to develop some conventional wisdom about baby boomers that would help inform sales pitches.

And gradually, some advertisers—or, more to the point, those advising them—began to discover that what had been considered "elderly" in, say, the 1980s—people in their fifties!—was now middle age. What was thought of as "old" had become a moving target, and the age many baby boomers felt themselves to be—their subjective age—was often years younger than their chronological age. People in their sixties and seventies who were healthy, active, and financially comfortable were especially offended by geriatric images in the media.[3] One notorious example was a line of stews introduced by Heinz called "Senior Foods," which were designed to be as pureed as what Beech-Nut produced for babies. Failing to recognize that older people might not want to be reminded that their teeth weren't what they used to be or that they would want to be seen in the checkout line buying something labeled "Senior," this product bombed miserably.[4]

In addition to the obvious reason why aspirational aging became such a rising marketing trend—a huge and growing customer base of older Americans who didn't want to see themselves as old—there is a broader explanation as well that has shaped so much marketing, not to mention public policy. That is the triumph of market fundamentalism, whose onward trudge began in the 1980s and now powerfully shapes the experiences of and attitudes toward aging. It was a tectonic shift in political attitudes, and the media gave it a very large megaphone. Academics call this doctrine neoliberalism, but for me that's actually a misnomer, as liberalism has nothing to do with it—neoconservatism does. Stay with me for a moment, because this new creed is a central building block of aspirational aging, and it is especially toxic for women.

Market fundamentalism seeks to take a wrecking ball to a general agreement that emerged during the suffering of the Great

Depression and was cemented in the post–World War II period and up through the 1970s: the government has a responsibility to mitigate inequality and to provide the public, especially those in need, with basic services like unemployment benefits, Medicare and Medicaid, and Social Security. Advanced aggressively by the Reagan administration, and holding sway with a percentage of Americans since then, market fundamentalism calls for limiting the role of government, a belief in "trickle-down" economics (the discredited notion that tax cuts for McMansion owners would float money down to help people in trailer parks), the irrelevance of social solidarity, and the absolute centrality of individual responsibility to personal success. Market fundamentalism holds complete faith that the market (as all-knowing and just as Yahweh), not the government, is the best arbiter of wealth distribution.

Thus the government should get out of providing services, especially for the needy, the poor, or retired people, because the state is allegedly less efficient, and more corrupt than, say, Goldman Sachs or Wells Fargo. To justify this shrinkage of government services, the gospel of market fundamentalism glorifies individualism and individual responsibility as if they were sacraments. We and we alone create our own circumstances by the choices we make; individual enterprise makes up for the gap and the economic pitfalls left by deregulation.[5] In this gilded world, there are no structural, institutional obstacles that might thwart such choices for some or, conversely, offer opportunities and advantages that make them possible for others. As the scholar David Harvey succinctly put it, "All forms of social solidarity were to be dissolved in favor of individualism, private property, personal responsibility and family values."[6] So the notion of "we're all in this together" was to give way to a vision of society as a collection of self-governing and especially self-serving atoms.

Not emphasized nearly enough is how market fundamentalism

was linked to and embodied by a tough-talking, six-gun-toting version of government as personified by Ronald Reagan in his cowboy boots and hat. Drawing from World War II movies, Westerns, football, and the Clint Eastwood "Dirty Harry" movie *Sudden Impact* ("Go ahead, make my day," Reagan warned Congress, about his eagerness to veto a tax increase), he effectively cast himself as a man's man and a hero. This was, in part, in direct contradistinction to President Jimmy Carter, whom one writer in the *Wall Street Journal* dismissed as "a 'woman' president [who] lost no time revealing his true feminine spirit." With his pugnacious, militaristic foreign-policy stance, and his persona as a tough, aggressive, supremely self-confident man, Reagan made clear that social programs designed to help those less fortunate were a marker of governmental and national weakness.[7] So market fundamentalism became intertwined with a cold-hearted hyper-masculinity that cast the need for social welfare programs as signs not just of individual laziness and indifference (or corruption, as Reagan emphasized with his repeated made-up stories about Cadillac-driving "welfare queens") but also of national vulnerability.

How, then, are we meant to internalize the market fundamentalism mantra? What persona must we assume when the mesh of the safety net has been gnawed away? The mantra insists on and promotes the need for idealized, productive citizens who must learn how to govern themselves. They must be enterprising and achieve self-mastery. If they can, they will control their own destiny, becoming autonomous and fulfilled. Our very selves become an ongoing project; we must work on, transform, and improve ourselves, no matter what our age, so we can survive and even prosper in this self-determining environment.[8] Feminist writers have emphasized, persuasively, how young women especially have been called on by the media to constantly make and remake themselves physically, to objectify themselves as a sign of their "empowerment." They are asked to be feisty girl-power types who are simultaneously "hot" and able to reinvent themselves for any new economic, political, or cultural paradigm to succeed.[9] As ads, magazines, reality television, and makeover shows have made clear, such individual self-actualization comes through buying the right stuff: being a persistent and shrewd consumer. Market fundamentalism relies crucially on consumerism, and vice versa.

At the same time, almost no attention has been paid to how this new gospel of wealth affects older women. Market fundamentalism has led to decades-long, serial bashing of Social Security and Medicare by the conservative news media and politicians, so the idea of a larger public and collective responsibility—a social contract—that would also support older Americans is under constant threat.[10] To survive in this society, marked by insecurity and a bench-pressing competitive individualism, we too are urged to succumb to the siren call of never-ending self-improvement and transformation. Do you want to be successful at aging via windsurfing and learning to salsa dance? Or do you want to end up in a refrigerator box under the overpass? Aspirational aging insists on the importance of continuing to be a self-actualizing, self-constructing, autonomous individual, no matter how old you are.

Market fundamentalism has also powerfully shaped public attitudes about our society's relationship to older people. A 2015 study about attitudes toward aging found that those interviewed held older people "responsible for the quality of their financial lives" as well as for their income security and health. "People need to assert control over their financial life, make smart decisions, and plan ahead for their older years," respondents insisted.[11]

So, yes, aspirational aging is a positive media response to our refusal to be associated primarily with prune juice and adult diapers, and to address us as just a tad more enlivened. And, yes, it contradicts hoary stereotypes. But it also stems from, and under-girds, the ruthlessness of market fundamentalism. Aspirational aging, then, in its commercialized form, and inadvertently or not, is the handmaiden of market fundamentalism, beguiling us to see ourselves primarily as cool consumers instead of, God forbid, polit-icized and thus tiresome citizens.

Hence the rise and promotion of aspirational aging. Since the early twenty-first century, *Advertising Age* and others have been repeatedly warning Madison Avenue that the baby boom gener-ation is, once again, one of the most important entities you can become in the United States: a market. When you're a market in America, you matter. Marketers break this group into two, distin-guishing between "leading-edge" boomers (born between 1946 and the late 1950s) and "trailing" boomers (born between the late 1950s and 1964). Marketers see each group having its own dis-tinct, petrified traits, yet they also see all boomers as obsessed with "self-actualization."[12] Remember that generations—how they are named, constructed, thought about, and talked about—are almost entirely defined by market research; marketers are the dominant arbiters of generational identity and significance. They can elevate a generation on a national pedestal as the ones to venerate and flat-ter, and then kick it to the curb as obsolete, to be replaced by a new, differently named, shinier, cellophane-wrapped cohort.

So, as we get kicked to the curb, we face a conundrum. Millions of us hate ads, or at least most ads. (And for women, who were told his "ring around the collar" was somehow our fault, or by Hard-ee's that "We all know a woman's place is in the home, cooking a man a delicious meal," many ads were especially loathsome.) If we are able to, we fast-forward through them on the shows we've recorded (although often the technology doesn't allow us to); we use AdBlock on our computers, try to block them on Facebook, and scroll through them as fast as we can on Instagram; we pay extra for Spotify Premium to not hear them; we hit "skip ad" on YouTube. We revile "sponsored stories" and clickbait (want to eliminate belly fat, anyone?) on websites.

Why should older women complain that they're not featured in the avalanche of sales pitches that dominate American life? Because advertising supports virtually every media outlet and platform and is a major site for visibility and legitimacy in our culture. Such visibility often equals validation and can convey recognition of a group's relevance. More to the point, when people are not seen as consumers, except for bunion pads or hearing aids, they are not seen as productive members of society or as contributing to the economy or culture. Quite the opposite: they're a "burden." Older women are rarely seen consuming the same products that most adults, including them, use: clothing, cars, iPads, wine. And there may be some ads they *do* want to see and not have to learn about cool new products or services from their twenty-something children and friends. So while we all may hate being advertised to, we may hate even more being exiled from this media landscape as irrelevant, uncool, and (despite what L'Oreal assures us) not worth it.

In the 1990s and early 2000s, after being dropped faster than a leper colony in favor of millennials, baby boomers were hailed as an abandoned gold mine ripe for renewed excavation. "New Old Won't Go Quietly," *Ad Age* proclaimed in 2006 (with a hint of resentment?), noting that boomers envision an older age "characterized by youthful vigor, prosperity and personal fulfillment" and asked, "Is 55 the new 40?" In particular, the article warned advertisers, "We'll be seeing more economically independent women over the age of 50."[13] A year later, in an article subtitled "'Crazy Aunts and Uncles' Spend $1.7 Trillion," the magazine cautioned yet again how "woefully out of touch" most marketers were with baby-boomer buying power.[14]

Six years later, Nielsen issued a major report titled "Introducing

Boomers: Marketing's Most Valuable Generation." According to
Nielsen, in 2012 boomers represented 44 percent of the population (a seemingly inflated figure) and controlled 70 percent of the
country's disposable income, making us "marketing's tidal wave"
for advertisers.[15] In 2012, boomers racked up nearly $230 billion
in spending on consumer-packaged goods. Advertisers, marketers,
and media producers, Nielsen warned, ignore this demographic
revolution at their peril. A Google search "Marketing to Baby
Boomers" now produces over five million results. (One piece of
advice? "This is a generation that's stuck in the psychedelic '60s and
'70s," one marketer noted. "I recommend clients use psychedelic
colors and music."[16])

All sorts of gambits have been trotted out, some retrograde,
some indeed progressive. Just as boomers were the first truly massive youth market, and corporate America had to figure out how
best to reach us (which involved some serious miscalculations, like
"feminine hygiene spray"), now they have to figure out how to
market to older people, many of whom do not feel particularly old
except for the usual physical giveaways. Should you use sixties and
seventies rock music or not in your ads? Does nostalgia sell or does
it remind boomers they aren't young anymore? Should you feature
people in their fifties, sixties, and seventies so boomers see people of their own age and have the importance of their age group
affirmed? Or do you use actors in their forties, or even younger,
because "boomers see themselves as a decade younger than their
chronological age," so "don't use language which implies they're
'old' in any way."[17] "Avoid posed pictures like the plague. Motion
conveys vitality. Posed pictures convey lifelessness," admonished
another article.[18] So in marketing to older people, the conventional
wisdom goes, you have to acknowledge their age while simultaneously denying it, thus often reaffirming ageism.

To say that the generational stereotypes—covering over 76 mil-

lion people of different genders, races, religions, geographical loca-
tions, sexual orientations, political persuasions, educational levels,
and income—were preposterous would, of course, be an under-
statement. Baby boomers may be the most negatively stereotyped
generation ever (although the much-maligned millennials are giving us a run for our money). All too many pundits have depicted
the baby boom, from the start, as a monolith, characterized by
extreme narcissism, self-indulgence, and a totally engorged sense of
entitlement. A typical headline from 2010 read: "Boomers Hit New
Self-Absorption Milestone: Age 65."[19] Even the late George Carlin,
a favorite comic among boomers, called us "whiny, narcissistic, self-
indulgent people with a simple philosophy: Gimme, it's mine!"

Boomers could allegedly grab whatever they wanted because
they were repeatedly cast as the group with "the most disposable
income, the generation in better shape than any previous generation, the ones who buy convertibles, run corporations, buy second homes, influence legislation, take adventure vacations [and]
consume more durable goods than anybody else."[20] The difference
between "leading-edge" and "trailing" boomers, as one column
in *Advertising Age* opined, is that older boomers might go for the
"designer name" in clothes and the Jaguar while younger boomers
prefer the "cashmere sweater from Costco" and the Prius.[21] Failing to "monetize" boomers was thick-headed because "boomers
are a wealthy cohort," as if the reported $2.3 trillion in disposable
income was somehow evenly distributed along race, class, and gender lines.[22] "They tend to be big spenders . . . they've bought and
sold as many as five to six homes to constantly upgrade their lifestyle."[23] Wow, I so missed this trend!

Despite the conventional marketing assumptions such articles
sought to overturn—older people are set in their ways, not willing to try new things (especially brands), don't have much if any
money, and in incessant need of laxatives—the ad industry itself

favored young people, especially as digital media began to explode
as a potent form of advertising, particularly for individualized, targeted ads. In one marketing firm headed by a fifty-one-year-old
woman, half of the 150 employees as early as 2007 were under the
age of thirty.[24] By 2012, 40.3 percent of those working in advertising
were between twenty and thirty-four, even though they were just
31 percent of the workforce overall; those over fifty-five were only
15.8 percent of the industry.[25] Some critics saw a direct relationship
between the youth of those in the business and the ongoing failure to address what they saw as the lucrative baby boom market.
When Unilever in 2007 began researching the shopping patterns
of baby boomers—those typically considered demographically
irrelevant—the company's younger employees sent emails asking,
"Who cares about these people?" For many marketers, this report
noted grimly, "the average boomer was already zipped up in those
body bags the AARP puts in its ads."[26] Or as a column in *Adweek*
put it, "Sick of hearing about baby boomers? Be patient, they'll die
off soon enough."[27]

One unwavering marketing assumption that left boomers
ignored—or, as *Ad Age* put it more starkly, "left for dead"[28]—was
the straitjacket of advertising demographics: that "human life
begins at 18 and ends at 49."[29] This mismatch was especially true
for broadcast television, where by 2018 the median age of viewers
for top-rated shows ranged between forty-eight and fifty-eight.[30]
While financial services, insurance companies, and drug companies
pitched their products to boomers, few in the travel, clothing, or
electronics industries were doing so because of ageist stereotypes.

Many boomers—45 percent according to one survey—felt over-
looked by marketers.[31] And older women were especially given the
cold shoulder as marketers concentrated on women eighteen to
thirty-four.[32] As one woman put it, she was "useless and washed
up at age 35," no longer a market for "premium liquor and Lexus;

from here on, all my dedicated marketing would be for arthritis medicine and hearing aids."[33] Despite ten years of the trade journals harping on the importance of boomers as a market, in 2014 *Broadcasting & Cable* wondered again, "Age-Old Question remains: Why Not Target Boomers?" The answer? "It's not fashionable" to market to older people; they are just "not desirable enough a demographic."[34]

Not much has changed. "Baby Boomer Women Remain Invisible to Marketers," reported the American Marketing Association in 2016. Boomers remain "the forgotten generation," Robert Passikoff, president of Brand Keys Inc., told the *New York Times* in 2017, because "marketers have gotten so hot for the millennial generation." *MediaPost* asked, the same year, why baby boom women were virtually neglected during the holiday shopping season when they buy, among other things, food and wine for all the meals they cook and collectively spend billions on presents for family and friends and especially grandchildren ($35 billion a year).[35]

Some preserves in our niche-driven media landscape, especially cable channels like Decades showing Johnny Carson and Ed Sullivan reruns, do have ads geared to older viewers, but they are still stuck in the 1970s and continue to bombard their audiences with images of failed and risk-filled aging—ads for reverse mortgages, medical-alert buttons, and security systems. They seem to see their viewers as rigidly and primarily defined by the infirmities of aging. Others, seeming to heed the Nielsen and *Advertising Age* admonitions, have embraced aspirational aging, depicting successful aging, but often in ways that are filled with exasperating contradictions.

This leads us to the one industry that has not ignored the over-forty-nine demographic: Big Pharma. Big Pharma has played a complicated role in the construction of aspirational aging in the media, addressing and even representing older people living their lives in fulfilling, self-actualizing ways, but also as sick and needing medications—and able to afford them! I haven't exactly counted this up, but aside from those peddling assisted-living centers and pitches to sell back your life insurance policy, Big Pharma seems to be the main industry portraying older people in the media. If you watch, say, CBS News, 72 percent of the commercial breaks have at least one Big Pharma ad.[36] So, on the one hand, Big Pharma offers more positive images of older people in ads than appeared on television thirty years ago. On the other hand, being older is central to these people's roles in the commercials (unlike, if older women were, say, pitching cars or clothes), because their age itself is a condition that needs treatment.[37]

Today, especially if you watch any television that "skews older"—the network news programs, CNN, or the Weather Channel, for example—you completely take for granted the onslaught of pharmaceutical ads, often for ailments you never heard of like pseudobulbar affect and for products with phony pseudo-scientific names designed to roll off your lips. (It seems important for these drugs' names to end in an A—Latuda, Lyrica, Humira, Viagra of course—or have an X in them—Chantix, Xeljanz, Celebrex, Xarelto.) These ads also provide innocuous, even cool abbreviations seemingly designed to camouflage the ailments they treat— ED (erectile dysfunction; don't have to say impotent), IBS (irritable bowel syndrome; don't have to say diarrhea, constipation, or gas), COPD (chronic obstructive pulmonary disease; don't have to say emphysema). The advertising barrage has led to a truly wonderful term: "disease mongering."

It's easy to forget that Big Pharma couldn't really do direct-to-consumer ads until the late 1990s; we are the only country besides New Zealand that permits them. Starting in 1985, the Food and Drug Administration relaxed its rules and allowed drug makers to publish and air ads, but they had to follow very strict rules about disclosing all possible side effects and a complete list of risks, which made doing so on television prohibitive. Then, under industry pressure, the FDA relaxed its rules in 1997, allowing drug companies to make specific claims about treatment of specific ailments, to mention only "major risks," and then to refer viewers to the more detailed print ads and websites where microscopic print itemized all the other possible side effects.[38] And, of course, the ads pushed you to "ask your doctor" about the drug in question.

We pay more for drugs and medical devices than any other country on the planet.[39] While Americans spend, on average, about $1000 per person a year on prescription drugs, those in France and Britain pay about half that and the Swedes pay only $351. (And it's not that we take more prescription drugs; we're just gouged more for them.)[40] For some top-selling drugs, Americans pay seven times what the British pay. The annual price of one drug to treat lung and pancreatic cancer is nearly $80,000 in the United States and just under $24,000 in Canada.[41] Why? Other countries with state-run health systems drive hard bargains with Big Pharma, setting price caps and demanding to see proof of the drug's effectiveness; by contrast, Medicare (as of this writing) is not allowed to negotiate pricing. To seek to keep their swollen profits high—earning over double the net profits compared to other companies in the S&P 1500[42]—Big Pharma's main trade organization spent a record $27.5 million on lobbying in 2018 alone.[43] And while Big Pharma claims the high prices in the United States are necessary to fund ongoing research, the exorbitant fees here underwrite something else: the juggernaut of marketing muscling its way through television, magazines, and doctors' offices.[44]

The industry's expenditures on advertising put the lie to their claim that they need, and use, all their lucre for research. The industry as a whole spent about $360 million on all direct-to-consumer ads in 1995; by 2006, ad outlays had surged to $5 billion, most of that going to television commercials.[45] Three of the top four Big

Pharma companies spent up to twice as much money on marketing in 2015 as they did on researching and developing new drugs.
For example, in 2013, Pfizer spent $11.4 billion on advertising and
marketing and $6.6 billion on R&D; Johnson & Johnson, $17.5 billion on marketing and $8.2 billion on R&D; Novartis, $14.6 billion
versus $9.9 billion.[46] While the majority of this was spent on mar-
keting to health care professionals, between 2012 and 2017, spending on television commercials increased 62 percent.[47] And who
helps pay for this saturation bombing of ads? Why, we do. American taxpayers subsidize Big Pharma ads to the tune of about $6
billion a year! The federal government allows companies to deduct
some of their advertising costs as an expense, lowering their tax
bill, which only helps sustain the blitz.[48]

So how do pharmaceutical companies construct and represent
who older women are and what they are doing? Here the ads show
some upscale, happy older people doing active things, although
the silver-haired men are driving tractors, fighting fires, kayaking, coaching basketball, or playing guitar in a rock band, while
the women are gardening, shopping in a farmer's market, or, most
frequently, playing with their grandkids. Older women's identi-
ties tend to center on their roles as grandmas, not as independent
women, let alone working women.[49] Such gendered images aside
(and the upper-middle-class ones as well), the onslaught of these
direct-to-consumer prescription drug ads suggest that a metastasizing epidemic of psoriasis, diabetes, restless leg syndrome, dry
eye, and irritable bowel syndrome is ravaging the country. (Psoriasis, for example, affects about 2 percent of the population; restless
leg syndrome, which my husband, and thus I, have lived with for
decades, affects somewhere between 5 and 8.8 percent of adults,
although data are sketchy.)[50] Alleged treatments for all of these ailments are targeted to older viewers; you do not see these ads, for
example, on *The Daily Show* or *Saturday Night Live* (except in paro-

dies mocking them), or sponsoring media events meant for a mass audience like the Academy Awards.

So, despite the images of smiling kayakers and women beaming over a head of radicchio, there is the ongoing, relentless equation between getting older and disease. Then there were the what-were-they-thinking 2013 commercials for MiraLAX targeting older women ("It may seem strange," the voiceover croons, "that people love their laxative"—uh, yeah, it does) that urged us to run out and buy bracelets, throw pillows, and a smart-phone case all emblazoned with a jumbo, bubblegum-pink heart proclaiming "I ❤ My Lax," as if we were trinket-obsessed children desperate to broadcast our lavatory experiences to the world. Or the ones for Viberzi with the intentionally annoying thirty-something actress Ilana Becker in a flesh-colored jumpsuit with intestines and a colon drawn on it so she could personify irritable bowel syndrome with diarrhea, in case you weren't in enough agony.

Women are especially targeted for irritable bowel syndrome, depression, and osteoporosis. Some commercials use female actors in their thirties or forties, presumably to give us flattering reflections of ourselves as still young, but also to rope in as large a group of potential sufferers as possible. Others actually feature older women. And here we enter a soft-focus, honey-hued world where a celebrity known to boomers like Blythe Danner (seventy-six at the time), on a walk with her friends through a redwood forest, accompanied by sotto voce guitar chords, asks, "When it comes to strong bones, are you on the right path?" While she and her friends stroke a redwood, pet a horse, and hug each other, the male voice-over warns about possible side effects like "trouble breathing, throat tightness, face, lip or tongue swelling . . . severe jawbone problems . . . serious infections which could require hospitalization . . . or severe joint or muscle pain." But then back to Blythe. "Why wait?" she asks cheerfully. "Ask your doctor about Prolia." Um, I think not.

Several elements of these ads have become especially laugh-able as well as condescending. Some advertisers seem to imagine people in their sixties or older to have the mental age of a toddler. One ploy is transforming either a product or an ailment into an animated character. This approach is especially used to sell to kids: animated M&Ms, Lucky Charms cereal as a leprechaun, Frosted Flakes as Tony the Tiger. This infantilizing strategy of using car-toons is now being turned on us. Big Pharma ads for drugs like Lunesta, Zoloft, and others have trotted out various forms of animation—black-and-white drawings that move, rotoscopes (drawing over live-action scenes and turning them into animation so they look more realistic), and cartoon images of nonhuman mascots—all to get our allegedly addled attention.

With the risk of fungal nail infection increasing with age, Novartis gave us "Digger the dermatophyte," a creepy, purple-spotted, horned and tailed goblin personifying the fungus that burrows under toenails who needs to be mowed down by Lamisil. (*Slate* called the ad "stomach-turning.")[51] Or the Mucinex globby green mascot that grown adults actually talk to before taking the cough medicine. Abilify, an antidepressant targeted to women, was depicted in a cartoon as an animated letter A with a smile and happy eyes, there as a friend to the cartoon female in distress, but you do need to "call your doctor" if you get suicidal thoughts. While con-gestion and depression affect people of all ages, it is on programs like the news (as opposed to *The Tonight Show* with Jimmy Fallon) where we get the endless parade of such drug plugs. The FDA in 2016 became concerned that the use of such animation, designed to "grab attention, increase ad memorability, and enhance persua-sion" and that produced higher recall of the ads for some viewers, might inflate perceptions of a drug's effectiveness and minimize its risks. Against industry objections, it launched a study of their per-suasiveness, which is still in progress.[52]

In addition to using mascots and cartoons, other Big Pharma approaches include soothing music, preferably piano or acoustic guitar; idealized older couples lovingly holding hands, snuggling, and caressing each other; and, most important, ecstatic images of happy, empowered women enjoying time with family and friends (pets work here too), to arrest our eyes and tug at our heartstrings so our ears won't pay attention to the sometimes terrifying list of potential side effects. Some ads use different voices: an upbeat, happy one to pitch the drug, another, flatter-toned, reduced-volume one to drone on rapidly about the side effects.

While the ads have to warn viewers about side effects (you know, like death), they use buoyant, joyful images of a closed-world intimacy to visually overwhelm the verbal alerts about everything from rashes to liver failure. But they also seek to wheedle you into believing that it is the drug itself that enables the enhanced physical and psychic experiences we see these women enjoying. The scenarios are totally aspirational. Verzenio, a breast cancer medication, deploys dulcet piano music, as we see softly lit, slim, attractive women in their late forties or early fifties tending to and blowing bubbles with their grandchildren, snuggling with their husbands as if they were newlyweds, and hugging friends they are meeting for coffee. One woman ecstatically bakes a latticed-top pie with her daughter in their country-style kitchen; the one African American woman in the ad nuzzles her husband as he plays a baby grand piano in their Pottery Barn–style living room. No women who might need Medicare or Medicaid here. No lesbian couples, either.

The women's faces beam with smiles at these emotionally enriching moments as the voice-over warns us that "diarrhea is common, may be severe." As a younger woman (we presume to be the daughter) shows the older women an ultrasound image of the baby she is carrying—new life!—the voice-over advises that Verzenio "may also cause low blood count which may cause serious infection that may lead to death"; at the very moment we hear the word "death," the two women's faces become incandescent with joy. When the older woman shares hot chocolate with a child we assume is her granddaughter, and then snuggles her in her arms in front of a crackling fireplace, we hear that "blood clots that can lead to death have also occurred." You get the idea. In another ad for the same product, we do see one working woman, a school-teacher, cuddling a child in her arms. So women dealing with met-astatic, or stage IV, breast cancer are still supposed to devote their time and energy on nurturing and tending to others.

And it's not just Hollywood that pairs fifty-five-year-old men with thirty-five-year-old women, reinforcing the double standard around aging. Cialis ads for ED, although targeted primarily to men, with their ever-perplexing images of a man and a woman in separate and obviously impenetrable bathtubs, repeatedly feature a man with salt-and-pepper-flecked hair coming on to his wife who is twenty years younger. We do see some African American cou-ples here (and also, especially, in ads for diabetes medicines), but at least in my media market, there have been no Asian American or Latinx actors to be found in any of these Big Pharma pitches.

What these ads do, of course, is target primarily older con-sumers leading, because of ballooning marketing budgets and the quest for more drugs to pitch, to more ads featuring older people. The inclusion of older women is a change for the better, but it also suggests that their lives are defined by all kinds of ailments, which they are not. Intermixed with images of aspirational aging where you take control ("ask your doctor") is the message that this psychically energized life is primarily enabled through overpriced medications. And the dominant image of older women here is that of women who are nurturing caretakers, loving wives, and sooth-ing friends—compliant, upscale, unthreatening women who know their place.

Of course, this barrage of direct-to-consumer commercials has been controversial (as well as incredibly annoying). Critics argue that such ads urge people to self-diagnose, to ask for, even demand, medicines they don't need, and that they convert pretty normal if somewhat unfortunate things—hair loss, shyness, a tendency to shake your legs while sitting, unattractive toenails—into diseases that need cures. Many of these drugs are quite expensive in the United States (60 capsules of Lyrica cost about $400 in 2017) and urge people to ask their doctors for medications that may be only marginally effective or even inappropriate.[53] A *Consumer Reports* study found that about three-fourths of doctors said that patients have asked them for drugs they have seen advertised, yet many of them are unaware of the negative side effects.

Indeed, what is masked by these cascading images of women finding personal transcendence and harmony through Big Pharma is the billions the industry has spent on criminal and civil settlements resulting from fraudulent advertising.[54] One notorious example was Vioxx, promoted by skater Dorothy Hamill, an Olympic champion in 1976, seen in their ads skating with children as "It's a Beautiful Morning," the 1968 hit by the Rascals, sought to pull at boomer women's heartstrings. Pitched as curing osteoarthritis, it had to be yanked from the market after it was linked to increased risk of heart attack or stroke.[55] The makers of Xarelto, a blood thinner, have agreed to pay $775 million to settle approximately 25,000 lawsuits alleging that the companies failed to warn patients that the drug could cause excessive bleeding, and even death.[56] In 2015, the American Medical Association, in what is most certainly a futile bid, citing "the negative impact of commercially-driven promotions," asked for a ban on these ads given that these drugs inflate the cost of health care and that there are less-expensive options.[57]

In addition to the Big Pharma flotilla of ads, aspirational aging struts its stuff almost exclusively in age-segregated outlets that very few people under fifty ever see. It thrives in the precincts of *O, The Oprah Magazine* and *AARP* magazine, and showcases windsurfing, yoga-stretching agesters and, especially, extremely well-preserved celebrities. Unlike the *National Enquirer* and other celebrity tabloids that consistently feature stories about stars who are "tragic," "broke," and "alone" now that they're older, AARP reminds us that aging is a democratic process affecting even the rich and famous who are, not surprisingly, doing just fine. While showcasing mostly white celebrities, AARP has also profiled Rita Moreno, Alfre Woodard, and Viola Davis. In its magazine, whose cover motto used to be "Feel Great. Save Money. Have Fun" and now is the more future-looking aspirational "Real Possibilities," sample headlines have been "Diane Keaton: How She Stays Forever Young," "24 Hours to a Longer Life," "Energize Your Body, Brain—and Sex Life," "Sally Field—Her New Life," and the like.

It is celebrity profiles that insist we are always transformable and that we can, even must, continue to work on who we are and how we look. In these profiles, aging is, at the same time, something to be celebrated yet also something to be fought.[58] Aspirational aging in these publications, with its counter-stereotypical imagery and its celebration of older people, has considerable pleasures and significant benefits because it acknowledges our coming-of-age sensibilities and affirms that we are still in our prime. It also promotes eating well, exercising, and remaining socially active and connected.

To be fair to *AARP* magazine, it does also address the struggles around aging, including scams targeting older people and the wages of ageism and inequality. In the fall of 2018, it profiled seven people with very different income levels: two of them African American, whose annual incomes were $18,000 or $20,000, and a Native American man who somehow lives on $13,800 a year. Nonetheless, of the seven profiled, five were men, two of whom were millionaires, and only the minorities were presented as poor. Except for the lone African American woman, sixty-four, suffering from Crohn's disease and trying to live on $18,000 a year, older women and their disproportionate financial hardships were underrepresented here, as they are in most issues. This is hardly surprising given the you-can-do-it, cheerleading ethos that dominates its pages.

But it is the ongoing celebrity-generated exhortations, or how they are presented as media-constructed role models, that can be a bit daunting, as the goading to still be a self-actualizing, self-igniting ball of fire can feel like an extension of the media brow-beating that women have gotten their whole lives. Let me give you a few examples. The magazine puts cool agesters like Smokey Robinson or Sharon Stone on the cover and offers stories on how neat it is to be Bruce Springsteen and the benefits of flower arrang-ing. And AARP has been moving down the age chain, seeking to recruit people in their late forties and early fifties. Thus it featured Brad Pitt who, at forty-fucking-nine years old, had the temerity to say, "Personally, I like aging." (Come back to me in thirty years, buster. And as a woman. With no health insurance.) Another issue featured Jamie Lee Curtis (age fifty-two at the time), Kristen Bell (thirty), and Betty White (eighty-eight) in a cover story about how to stay "hot." (I think it's safe to say that no one in my life, includ-ing myself, is interested in my concentrating my energies on being "hot" at this stage of the game.)

Month in and month out, this glossy features well-preserved, wealthy, successful, broadly smiling celebrities on its cover who suggest that aging can be defied, and also that it's just a hoot. "With projects galore," it noted about William Shatner, eighty-seven, in 2018, "his focus is on go, go, going!" In its features like "New Adventures, New Risks, New You!" it urges readers to "escape your comfort zone." "Whatever scares you, do it. Now!" ordered one headline.[59] Like bungee jumping? Snake handling? Trying on a bathing suit? Other comparable magazines, like *O, The Oprah Magazine*, geared to middle-aged women, blare "How to Get Better with Age," which showcases Dr. Oz, who offers "4 Easy Ways to Reverse the Effects of Time." While many older people are enjoying life, and welcome seeing celebrities doing the same, such entreaties push for aggressive self-transformation, and for "defying" aging just when we need to get comfortable exactly where we are. There is something highly regulatory, narrowly prescriptive, and even punitive in all this overheated advice. I *have* a comfort zone; I've earned it. I don't want to be more scared than I already am, of stink bugs, of flying on United Airlines (or worse, Spirit), and now, of course, of falling on my ass. One of the good things about aging is that you can tell people trying to shove you *out* of your comfort zone to go screw themselves.

In "Life's a Kick When You're Diane Keaton" (2012), we get a slew of "age-defying advice." (Now, it pains me to proceed, as I am a serious Diane Keaton fan, and I'm hoping she may have hated this article as much as I did; after all, she didn't write it.) We learn that it's not even 10:00 A.M., yet the sixty-six-year-old Keaton has "practically run a decathlon." (At 10:00 A.M. I'm still trying to find my glasses. And my keys.) "Before dawn she was energetically typing at her computer, fine-tuning the afterword for *Then Again*," her best-selling memoir. At 6:15, she awakened her sixteen-year-old daughter and eleven-year-old son (I have experience with this; it's much safer to poke a grizzly bear in the eye with a stick) and got them both off to school. "Then I did a half-hour run with the dog, answered e-mails, [and] looked at designs for the house I'm building." She "has an architecture book in the works for Rizzoli New York. She is also a spokesperson for L'Oreal Paris, and late last year signed on as the 'face' for a line of clothes at Chico's." "Slowing down isn't something I relate to at all," Keaton adds.[60]

Really, having survived, throughout my life and not without

considerable guilt, anxiety, and ultimate failure, media exhortations on how to be rich and famous by the age of thirty, how to
become a size four in two weeks, how to be as perfect a mother
as Princess Diana, how to "have it all" (whatever "it" is), and how
to go through life poreless and wrinkle-free, now I'm supposed
to somehow still have the energy (and outlook) I did when I was
thirty-five, run like a gazelle with the dogs before dawn, and be
covered in envy because I don't have a clothing line?

It is in articles like these, and there's plenty more where that
one came from, where we learn about their clothing lines (Melissa
McCarthy), their multiple awards (Jane Fonda, among others),
their "almost poreless skin" (Cindy Lauper),[61] and how they show
"no sign of slowing down" (Jessica Lange).[62] It is easy to be inspired
by these women, and to welcome such profiles. But under the
guise of presenting positive images of older women is the message
that aging is something you should avoid at all costs, and that the
only successful way to age is through a stance of defiance. It also
goes without saying that Keaton's and the other stars' lifestyles
may indeed be possible if you are a wealthy, beautiful, famous,
white celebrity who hardly needs Social Security or Medicare. Or
maybe, despite this breathless portrait of ever-sprinting stamina,
Diane Keaton *is* getting just a tad weary.

It is hard not to have a love-hate relationship with aspirational
aging. Of course many of us who are not rich and famous are
still going strong; of course it is important for people to remain
active and engaged, and to take responsibility for their health, their
finances, and their lives—if and when they can. The alluring come-
ons of aspirational aging speak to our dreams and also to how
good many of us feel. There is a little bit of all of us, isn't there, in
aspirational aging? It certainly contains, on its surface, a welcome
break from the past—shiny, come-hither seductions, really. But it
also has lurking within it some nasty little serpents we would do

well to drive out. It traffics in conflicting media scripts about who should be applauded and who should be ignored. And in doing so, aspirational aging by turns supports—even advances!—and also can thwart the recasting we need of aging as dreaded to coming of age as fulfilling.

Given the rah-rah, take-on-new-challenges spirit in these pages, what are we lectured to avoid? Indulging in too much hammock time or watching daytime television instead of pursuing that second career can cast you as unproductive, not willing to work, or just plain lazy. Not actively engaging with others in those ballroom dancing classes or church outreach programs? Are you selfish, or lonely, or becoming a burden to others? Is not being in the peak of health or fitness or, worse, being sick or disabled somehow your fault because you didn't go to the gym four times a week and take fish-oil pills? And the flip side of being independent and self-actualizing— and who wouldn't want that?—is that being dependent on others (especially government programs) is a personal failure. This is the dark, normative underbelly of aspirational aging.[63]

Often embedded in this media framework are the never-ending anti-aging messages that are actually ageist. At times aspirational aging is condescending and sexist. And some of the advice is just preposterous. "Cross-train Your Brain" and "Take Up the Accordion" as a way to cultivate a "growth mind-set" are two of dozens of *O, The Oprah Magazine* imperatives.[64] "Buy some stylish shoes" exhorts *AARP* magazine; "Dye your hair a fun color!"[65] Just try to *find* some stylish shoes that fit and you can also walk in!

Yet, for the most part, elsewhere in the media—indeed, as we walk down the street—despite all the blaring megaphones from marketers over the last dozen years yelling "wait, wait, you're missing a huuuge neglected market," invisibility reigns supreme. "We are 100% invisible to marketers. That's pretty easy to establish," says marketing expert Marti Barletta. "You only have to look at what's online, what's on television, what's on radio."[66] As Linda Landers, CEO of Girlpower Marketing, put it in 2017, women over fifty "are the healthiest, wealthiest and most active generation of women in history who control half of the country's discretionary income and 75% of the country's wealth. That's a lot of spending power for one generation of women. It's a mystery why marketers ignore Boomer women . . . but ignore them they do." She adds, "All Boomer women are not grandmas or caregivers."

One entrenched assumption that remains is that older women are technologically illiterate (and thus never shop online and haven't heard of YouTube or Instagram). But as Landers notes (and as my credit card bills and the ceiling-high stacks of shipping boxes in our garage attest), boomers spend up to $7 billion annually online—more than millennials.[67] And while YouTube is especially popular among millennials, nearly a quarter of its monthly visitors are baby boomers or older (39 percent are millennials). Despite this, one marketing study showed that while YouTube advertisers are targeting millennials the most, they spend the least amount of money and, unlike older visitors, are the least likely to watch those ads.[68]

Except for that hunky salt-and-pepper-haired guy pitching Trivago or the obnoxious "Captain Obvious" for Hotels.com, we see very few images of people our age—let alone female ones—in ads for travel, wine, cars, laptops, clothes, or anything else remotely cool and disease-free. But there is one sector of the economy—the anti-aging industrial complex—that is aimed (like the proverbial laser beam) directly and relentlessly at us.

CHAPTER 4

The Anti-Aging Industrial Complex

WHENEVER MY THIRTY-SOMETHING DAUGHTER and I visit each other, we invariably end up at Sephora, where, in short order, the equivalent of a Lexus car payment is deposited into its coffers as we leave with all those seductive promises curled up in their cute black-and-white-striped bags. The bleacher-load of products accosting you in the store is overwhelming—there are more anti-aging, anti-wrinkle, firming, refining, restructuring, eye-puff-reducing creams, liquids, serums, masques, gels, cleansers, and exfoliators than fire ants at a Florida picnic. And they are not cheap. Plus, if you're of my vintage, they all whisper to you from the shelves, vying with each other, assuring you that they and they alone will remake you, while insisting you probably need, like, all of them.

But which ones? How to decide? They're all so persuasive; there is an absolute triumphalism in their tone and claims. Should it be Kate Somerville's $85 Retinal Firming Eye Cream that will "erase blatant wrinkles around the area" because it is "enhanced with a natural blend of *bidens pilosa* extract" (aka Spanish needles—you know those flat brown seeds you see in the woods with two barbs at the end that attack your shoelaces?) "and palm seed oil, as well as hyaluronic acid"?[1] What about Lancer's $210 The Method Nourish, a "highly potent balm loaded with avocado, olive fruit oils" and a convincing-enough-sounding but nonetheless mysterious "proprietary oxygen-boosting complex."[2] Or maybe the Dr. Dennis Gross C+ Collagen Deep Cream (a mere $72), an "intense concentration" that postpones wrinkles because it uses "sunflower, rice bran, and camellia japonica seed oils" to create "a skin barrier" on your face and is powered by its "proprietary energy complex, 3-O C vitamin C technology"?[3] Sunday Riley Good Genes All-In-One Lactic Acid Treatment could be a bargain at $158 since its formulation of "exfoliating lactic acid, licorice to counteract hyperpigmentation" (licorice does that?), "and lemongrass to improve radiance" will make "dark spots brighter and loose skin tighter" and "guarantees a plump, more youthful-looking complexion you'll want to show off."[4] Yes I will!

Dr. Brandt, who has a line labeled DNA (which stands for the simple yet impossible instruction "Do Not Age"), offers something called a Magnetight Age-Defier Magnet Mask ($75 for one third of a cup) that creates "tiny little fluxes to stimulate blood flow" through "electromagnetic interactions" that enable the skin to "rejuvenate itself."[5] You can then apply his $152 DNA Transforming Pearl Serum, which relies on "advanced DuoPearl technology,"[6] the mechanisms of which remain a bit unclear. Peter Roth Thomas has developed "Innovative bouncy Bio-Mesh Technology™" in its Cucumber De-Tox Bouncy Hydrating Gel (a steal at $48, but mysteriously unavailable now)[7] and his "liquid-to-frozen De-Puffing Eye-Cubes™" that "harness the skin-enhancing efficacy of 'cryotherapy'" and rely on frozen cucumbers plus, among other things, caffeine, chamomile, and arnica montana flower extract "that instantly diminish tell-tale signs of too much fun."[8] God, I thought I needed that too, until a Beautypedia review on YouTube showing the product revealed that you got freezer burn from it at first, until the eye-cubes began to melt, run, and sting your eyes, prompting a rating of "poor."[9] When I was last in Sephora, a helpful salesperson recommended a grape-infused cream produced, I believe, by a French woman who owns a vineyard and whose workers allegedly discovered that putting the remnants of grape skins on their faces made them look younger. If you step into a Kiehl's, for, say, their Powerful Wrinkle Reducing Cream, they up the ante by having their salesclerks dressed in white medical jackets, just like real doctors!

As you can see, several gambits are crucial here to have some-one like me fall under the hypnotic and self-delusional spell of their pitches, and abandon some, but not quite all vestiges of incredu-lity. First, there have to be ingredients that sound like they were developed by top chemists at the Lawrence Livermore Lab (Aging-Deterrent Department). At the same time, however, "natural" or, better yet, "organic" elements (preferably from mystifying plant life you've never heard of like the aforementioned *bidens pilosa*) must be coupled with the lab products so there is a perfect con-junction of science and nature. With publicity in the last several years about the toxic ingredients in some cosmetics—parabens, which are preservatives linked to breast cancer; synthetic colors derived from coal tar that are carcinogens; propylene glycol that can cause hives[10]—companies have gone on a horticultural hunting spree, harvesting exotic-sounding flowers, plants, seeds, and roots that they claim will exterminate wrinkles with extreme prejudice.

Here are some of the "natural" ingredients we are supposed to believe contain the fountain of youth: chamomile flower extract, noni fruit oil (go ahead and Google it: noni fruit looks like an engorged, misshapen lime-green caterpillar and is also known as "vomit fruit" because of its stench), willow bark, rose petals, sea-weed, cupuacu butter (naturally from the Amazon rain forests in Brazil), and the aforementioned cukes, avocados, and seed oils from sunflowers, rice bran, and camellia japonica (the state flower of Alabama). In its pitch to African American women featuring Vanessa Williams, L'Oreal boasts about its reliance on "Manuka honey," which is "uniquely sourced from New Zealand."[11] Urban Skin Rx, specifically for African American women, offers a product "inspired by Women's History Month" with glycolic, lactic, and salucylic acid.[12] Biopelle uses snail eggs (egg CellPro™ Technology);[13] Katie Holmes reportedly puts the snails themselves on her face, because, as *Glamour* gushes, the gastropods leave a trail of "mucus that's packed with proteins, antioxidants, and hyaluronic acid, which leaves the skin looking glowy and refreshed."[14] I don't know about you, but I think I'll pass on this particular treatment. Of course, the persuasive coup de grâce is to give the product a French name, like Eminence Organic Skin Care, "Crème rehaussement ultra pour le cou a l'hibiscus." And finally, have a gorgeous older celebrity who looks at least fifteen years younger than her age to be "the face" of the product.

So really, what are we to make of all this? How can women of all ages *not* succumb to these blandishments, even though we know, in our heart of hearts, that dodging aging is a fantasy? On the one hand, since I do want to forestall for as long as possible looking like Keith Richards, I want to believe that the latest skin creams containing these and other totally weird, allegedly miraculous ingredients will do the trick. On the other hand, I regard much of this as hucksterism of the highest order; I also know, absolutely, that they cannot possibly deliver on making me look twenty—or even five—years younger. At the same moment that I am considering buying the Ahava age-defying panacea I am holding in my hand, I am also reading "Dead Sea Osmoter™" and saying to myself, "Come on, really, WTF even *is* that??"

By becoming L'Oreal's brand ambassador in 2016, late-sixty-something Susan Sarandon (sigh, of whom I am a fan) implied that we can look as great as her curiously unlined face in a L'Oreal ad by just slathering on its products all day. We really want to believe you, Susan, even though L'Oreal seems to think we still believe in Santa. Let's recall that for several years prior to her ambassadorship, L'Oreal had been claiming that its emphatically French-named Lancôme Génifique was "clinically proven" to "boost genes' activity and stimulate the production of youth proteins" that would cause "visibly younger skin in just 7 days." At the same time, the company was also hyping its L'Oreal Paris Youth Code products by asserting that they enabled users to "Crack the Code to Younger Acting Skin" via "gene science."[15]

In 2014, on the basis of these ads, the Federal Trade Commission, whose mission is, in part, to root out misleading or fraudulent advertising, charged the company with deceptive advertising. Rejecting L'Oreal's boast that Génifique "stimulate[d] the production of youth proteins" and that its Paris Youth Code products "target[ed] specific genes to make the skin act younger," the FTC charged that L'Oreal's alleged "scientific studies do not prove the representations" about all those pumped-up, age-foiling genes.[16] L'Oreal was forced to enter into a settlement: it could no longer claim, among other things, that any Lancôme brand or L'Oréal Paris brand facial skincare product targets or boosts the activity of genes to make skin look or act younger, or respond five times faster to aggressors like stress, fatigue, and aging, unless the company had competent and reliable scientific evidence substantiating such claims. "It would be nice if cosmetics could alter our genes and turn back time," said Jessica Rich, director of the FTC's Bureau of Consumer Protection. "But L'Oréal couldn't support these claims."[17]

I think more of us are with Helen Mirren, who, as another brand ambassador for L'Oreal, admitted, and in front of the company's executives no less, "I know that when I put on my moisturizer, it probably does fuck all, but it just makes me feel better."[18]

Welcome to the anti-aging industrial complex, a behemoth that has metastasized over the past twenty years, whose sales globally are estimated to reach nearly $192 billion by 2019 and which includes, in part, skin- and hair-care products, spa services, Botox, cosmetic procedures, surgeries, and prescription drugs, and which has utterly colonized our media—and not just media geared to older women.[19] The mission of the anti-aging indus- trial complex, and its effect, have been to intensify to the level of air-raid sirens our anxiety about *any* signs of aging. It is stoked, in part, by the conquest of celebrity culture and the enormous pressure on female actors, television reporters, celebrities, and the like to look young to get and keep their jobs. With the exception of politicians and other public figures, white celebrities are the pri- mary older women we see on the screens of America. Most were gorgeous when they were twenty and are gorgeous now—some with "work," some without—setting an idealized and impossi- ble standard of beauty for older women, and one based on white standards. They embody what it means to defy aging, and if they don't, their career is usually over.

The pulsing heartbeat of aspirational aging, then, is another reigning and upscale media trend, the defiance mantra: we are commanded to defy aging itself. This drumbeat now surrounds women of all ages, who are accosted daily—in the supermarket, the drugstore, from magazines and online ads—by the anti-aging edicts of this industry. The defiance mantra tells young women they are supposed to cringe at turning thirty. Even women in their twenties who read magazines like *Allure* are being urged to begin "maintenance" of their youthful looks and will be assaulted by full- page ads like one for Clarins's Double Serum [Hydric + Lipidic Sys- tem] that is "[o]ur most powerful age control concentrate ever." It allegedly works because it includes turmeric, "distinguished for its exceptional anti-aging properties." The ad cites a "satisfaction test" that after only seven days, 88 percent of the 362 women who tried it felt they had "visibly smoother skin." If you Google "anti-aging turmeric claims" you'll get tons of hits about it being *the* latest miracle ingredient. You'll also find "Turmeric Isn't as Magical as We All Thought, Study Finds."[20]

Advertisers, of course, seek to make all of us, old and young alike, feel insecure about our current selves and envy the future selves we will become if we just buy their products. But what they've done with aging is pretty brilliant, especially with the ever-reliable "before" and "after" photos. Think about it: they insist that our now older faces are like a nasty disguise, a Halloween mask, misrepresenting the unchanging, essential identity inside us: it no longer matches who we feel ourselves to be, thus it must be changed. We have to declare war against our own faces and bodies. Because so many of us do feel younger than we look, it is extremely difficult not to buy into this notion, the insistence that our naturally older faces are not the "real" us when, of course, they are. Now that's a media effect!

To fix that mismatch, we can then buy some "face spackle," have the muscles in our faces paralyzed with Botox, or, of course, go under the knife. And what is especially shrewd about turning aging into a national phobia is that you can hook women starting in their twenties and you have a never-ending, always-replenishing market.

Better yet, deploying various anti-aging products and procedures draws from the language of feminism, and is now being sold as empowering. Take the 2018 Juvéderm campaign, for an injectable filler targeted straight to millennials, "created to empower the next generation of consumers to 'JUVÉDERM® IT.' "[21] Here, defiant, leopard-patterned and glitter-clad thirty-something-looking models, hands on hips, strut their stuff while the voice-over warns of possible side effects, including "injection site pain, lumps, bumps, bruising" . . . and that the "rare risk of injecting into blood vessels can cause vision abnormalities, blindness, stroke." Yet, via Juvéderm young women are exhorted to "Live it! Command it! Boss it!" like some really badass feminist dominatrix. Of course, these ads, with their high-end rhetoric (and prices) and mostly white models scream privilege.

This may be one of the most effective, long-lasting, and successful marketing campaigns ever: to make a natural process no one can avoid into a totally unnatural, thoroughly undesirable and allegedly preventable state of affairs. The sales, the sales, and the unending product possibilities! The ubiquitous anti-aging magazine headlines, ads, and marketing pitches have become so wall-to-wall that this obsession with youth does not seem remotely odd; it's part of our national common sense. And most women's magazines are rarely skeptical about new anti-aging and beauty products; they can't be, since those companies are often paying for so many of the ad pages. As Timothy Caulfield, author of the excellently titled *Is Gwyneth Paltrow Wrong About Everything?*, notes, "Publishers don't sell magazines by reminding readers that nothing works."[22]

In addition to swallowing the bait of the cosmetics industry, another anti-aging product we're supposed to consume, based on those moments when we can't quite remember the name of that movie or determinedly walk into the kitchen and then ask ourselves "why?" are memory supplements that, laughably, supposedly work because they come from jellyfish. The inescapable ads for Prevagen—with those pseudo-MRI-looking lime-green images of the brain, and what look like ganglia and all their chartreuse bloblike "proteins," followed by the charts showing over-the-top memory improvement—have colonized the nightly network news and CNN. Prevagen was taken on in 2017 by the FTC and New York's attorney general as fraudulent or, as the website Gizmodo put it, "bullshit." (Minuscule print in the ad says, "In a computer assessed, double-blinded, placebo controlled study, Prevagen improved recall tasks in subjects" followed by "these statements have not been evaluated by the FDA." That would be my guess.)

Complaints filed with the FTC charged that these supposed clinical tests were not scientifically conducted, and the FTC said that the tests Quincy Bioscience did actually fail to show any memory improvement. Quincy Bioscience aggressively defended the jellyfish pills and even derided the 2017 FTC as a "lame duck" agency, suggesting its suits were toothless with the antiregulation Donald Trump in charge.[23] Indeed, Judge Louis L. Stanton, a Reagan appointee and contributor to the Federalist Society, dismissed the suit in September of 2017, noting that some "subgroups" in the study did see improved function.[24] I'm sticking with Dr. David Seres at Columbia University Medical Center, since I really don't want to swallow jellyfish extrusions, who says "it is biologically inconceivable" that ingesting this stuff "would have any effect on memory."[25] Or, as Pieter Cohen of Harvard Medical School, an expert in the efficacy and risks of dietary supplements, notes, generally, "If I were looking for opportunities to make a lot of money while deceiving people, I think going into the brain supplement business would be real high on my list; you can make a lot of money, do something entirely legal, and you're good to go."[26]

What's wrong with this picture and how the anti-aging industrial complex makes endless lucre by hijacking what sounds like science while also burrowing so deeply into our fears, hearts, and desires? Sure, sunscreen especially (wish we knew that back in 1967 when we lay out in the sun slathered in baby oil and burning to a crisp), moisturizers, and makeup can protect our skin and maybe even make it look a bit better. But here's the sad truth, from eminent dermatologist Fayne L. Frey, who runs the truth-telling blog *FryFace*: "Science has not yet discovered a single product or ingredient that can slow or even reverse the aging process."[27]

So, what if instead of recoiling from our wrinkles, we said,

"OK, here they are. I've earned them and they are cool, testimony to my wisdom and the rich life I've lived so far"? One of our missions should be to regard the anti-aging industrial complex not unlike the Great and Powerful Oz, operating behind a curtain of illusion, a humbug who makes grandiose yet empty promises that he really can get us back to where we were. Because, in doing so, the anti-aging industrial complex urges us to expend too much time, mental energy, and money—often lots of it—to buy into attitudes about older women—that how we look equals how we should be regarded and treated—that seek to marginalize us and make us feel bad about ourselves.

Of course, women have been trying to forestall the visible signs of aging for millennia. *Harper's Bazaar* reported that Cleopatra took daily baths in donkey milk, a treatment I think I'd pass on, and that "Women of the French Court used aged wine on their faces," which would no doubt be more fun.[28] But when cosmetic companies started to go chemical in the early twentieth century, things got out of hand. A woman was hospitalized in 1933 with excruciating eye pain, and "doctors watched in horror as her eyes were eaten away as though by acid." She had used a product called Lash Lure, meant to darken one's eyelashes; it contained a toxic coal-tar dye. Gouraud's Oriental Cream (yes, the age-old appeal to the exotic), a "magic beautifier," contained the mercury compound calomel, and one woman, whose gums turned a bluish black and who developed dark rings around her eyes and neck, was discovered to be suffering from mercury poisoning.

It was in the wake of various scandals, especially the exposé on the filthy conditions in the meatpacking industry in Upton Sinclair's *The Jungle*, that the 1906 Food and Drug Act was established to ban adulterated or mislabeled food and drugs. The act was updated in 1938 to enable the FDA to take action against dangerous cosmetics. However, the law did not require that cosmetics be pretested before going on the market.[29] And it still doesn't. The FDA does not require that companies prove their products are effective, or even safe.[30] As the *New York Times* noted in 2019, "the F.D.A.'s oversight of the cosmetics industry remains astoundingly limited."

More recently, a massive biomedical armada has sailed in to intervene in this stage of life armed with all kinds of anti-aging weaponry. What the deployment of biomedical science has done is to target natural physical changes and rebrand them as invasive pathogens to be injected, shot at, scraped away, or just cut off. The countless pseudoscientific names and claims that the products have been "clinically tested," or, better yet, "clinically proven," make it sound like all kinds of scientific assays have been conducted on the products by people with white coats, test tubes, and microscopes, and that the claims pass muster. But the FDA, which is required to test drugs to ensure they are safe and perform as promised, barely ever checks the claims of anti-aging products. That's because if the promise is simply to improve your appearance, the product is a cosmetic, not a drug. But . . . if the promise is to affect or alter the structure or function of your skin, then it's a drug, or at least that's how the FDA sees it.

Now, this is where the battle between the FDA and the cosmetics industry gets into very tricky word choice. "Anti-aging" sure sounds like something that could delay, thwart, even stop a biological process: a drug. The industry counters that their products perform cosmetic functions, such as adding moisture to make you look better, so they're not a drug. The companies want their products to sound flat-out science-based so we'll see them as actually skin-altering, yet they don't want them to be regulated as a drug or have their claims examined too closely. Thus a hybrid has emerged: cosmeceuticals. Doesn't that sound like it could be from the Mayo Clinic (or NASA) and be medicinal? Sure, the front half of the horse comes from "cosmetic," but the back half is straight from "pharmaceutical." (This totally made-up marketing word is, by the way, meaningless under federal law; it has no regulations or standards behind it.)[31] What the anti-aging industrial complex does is tell the FDA their product is a cosmetic, but then tries to convince us it's a miracle drug that will architecturally restructure our necks, lips, frown lines, eye bags, and overall wrinkles.

For example, Clarins claimed in 2013 that its $82.00 1.7 oz. jar of Extra-Firming Day Wrinkle Lifting Cream "firms, lifts and tones—smoothing lines and wrinkles in just 4 weeks." How does it do this? The Lifting Cream contains a "powerful plant complex" that flexes its leafy biceps to physically "rebuild the bonds between collagen, elastin and cells, strengthening skin's architecture on every level." As one of my new favorite websites, the *Enviroblog*, of the Environmental Working Group put it, "This most certainly is a promise to alter the structure and the function of the skin. And yet the FDA has not taken action to stop the marketing of this product." Other products, allegedly or actually concocted by dermatologists, use words like "prescription for beautiful skin," tiptoeing around the drug/cosmetic divide. As the *Enviroblog* notes, "If a claim sounds too good to be true, it probably is." And if it's a claim made about a wrinkle cream, "the Food and Drug Administration probably isn't checking it out."[32]

Indeed, as of this writing, if you Google "bogus anti-aging skin care claims," you get over 675 million results in .75 seconds. In 2015, the FDA did take on a few companies, like StriVectin, which instructed readers that wrinkles get their start at a "place" called the "Dermal-Epidermal Junction (or DEJ)" (sounds like a rural train station from the 1940s), a bunch of "rolling, 'wave like' cells" that "control the structural integrity of your skin." I mean, how convincing can you get? It claimed its wrinkle creams were "clinically proven to change the anatomy of a wrinkle" and "restore the elastin architecture, providing noticeable lift" and (my favorite) "improving resistance to gravity."[33] It's those remodeling claims that will get you into trouble, so they had to go into revision mode and rephrased their claims to say "the visible effects of gravity *appear* reversed" (italics mine).[34]

Under the media radar have been the various lawsuits by every-day people—few and far between but there—accusing the "anti-aging" claims made by cosmetics companies of being fraudulent. A flight attendant in Florida took on Estée Lauder, stating that its Future Perfect Anti-Wrinkle Radiance Lotion didn't work. A California man in 2013 filed a class-action suit against pH Beauty Labs, whose products boasted that their "High Potency Plant Stem Cells" and "Apple Stem Cells" were "Clinically Proven" to "Reduce the Appearance of Wrinkles and Improve the Texture of Skin in Two Weeks." The plaintiffs hoped said products would work such miracles but, alas, they were "unacceptable" and "did not possess the benefits" that were advertised and thus were fraudulent.[35] Suits like these are typically dismissed.[36] The FDA in 2016 sent a warning letter to the Crescent Health Center, makers of Ageless Derma Stem Cell and Peptide Anti-Wrinkle Cream that supposedly "removes crow's feet" and "reduces the depth of wrinkles . . . by attenuating muscle contraction," charging that their claims violated federal law because they were unapproved drugs whose purported effects were unsubstantiated.[37] The company had to change all of the language on its products and websites suggesting that their anti-aging treatments could "affect the structure or any function of the human body."[38]

Based on the assumption that women will believe anything that promises to make skin look younger, DERMADoctor Inc. sold its Photodynamic Therapy Liquid Red Light Anti-Aging Lotion ("eye lift" cream too) that used the extract of the noni "vomit" fruit that it said captured "UV light and transform[ed] it into visible red light that" zapped aging skin. Sold in Nordstrom, Sephora, and Ulta for $85 an ounce, in 2014 the FTC forced the company into a settlement claim for making false and unsubstantiated claims. At the same time, the FTC busted them for selling something called Shrinking Beauty, a firming and toning lotion that—I love this— was based on "lobster weight loss inspired technology."[39]

So, what are some ingredients and assertions that should make us roll our eyes? Let's start with "hypoallergenic," used to pitch anti-wrinkle creams, which actually has no standard defini- tion, guidelines, or testing procedures and, according to the FDA, "means whatever a company wants it to mean." It's promoted to suggest that the product won't cause an allergic reaction, but, according to let's-get-real dermatologist Fayne L. Frey, such prod- ucts "often contain at least one ingredient, usually a preservative, that is known to cause skin reactions."[40] Cosmetic companies are not required to substantiate such claims with the FDA.

What about "clinically tested" or "dermatology tested"? Let's say I'm a dermatologist. And I rub some cream on pretty much any part of my body, maybe for several weeks, maybe just yesterday, and I don't break out in hives. I proclaim it to work (which would be especially helpful if I had a financial interest in the company) and, voila! Dermatology tested.[41] "Clinically proven" can mean that I give a product to a group of women telling them it improves the appearance of their skin, and some of them think it does (no "before and after" photos required). Boom, proven it is. More to the point, various dermatologists have either been brought on or paid by cosmetic companies as consultants or have started their own line,[42] to the consternation of some doctors in the field. In his profession's scholarly journal, an exasperated dermatologist Ernst Epstein asked, "Are We Consultants or Peddlers?" and made clear that most of the claims ballyhooed for the "magic rejuvenators of aging skin" are "scientifically . . . nonsense."[43] Or as one reporter summarized it, "Do anti-aging skin creams work? Mostly no, der- matologists say."[44]

Eye creams, meant to be especially weaponized to produce results, contain pretty much the same ingredients as facial moisturizers; there are no ingredients that work specifically on skin around the eyes—which, under a microscope, can't be distinguished from skin taken from your cheekbone.[45] The much-touted hyaluronic acid does nothing to eliminate wrinkles; applied topically, as various dermatologists have noted, its molecules are too big to get into the skin.[46] Ditto for collagen—which is what our skin is made of and does break down over time—but its molecules are also too large to penetrate the skin (unless it is injected, often with larger than expected lip-ballooning consequences).[47] And what about those "antioxidants" that protect skin cells from ballistic-sounding "free radicals"? While there has been fervent cheerleading for the benefits of antioxidants, as the dermatologist Dr. Richard Thomas notes, "There is still a great deal of hype for their use for skin."[48] Again, my new hero Dr. Frey advises, quite simply, that despite all the hype about green tea and coenzyme Q, "there is little scientific evidence proving their effectiveness in this regard." More to the point, because our skin is actually designed, as an organ, to "keep things out," it "does not readily absorb charged molecules, like most antioxidants," which would actually have to "penetrate through many layers of skin" and even lower to get to where the free-radical damage is having its way with us.[49]

Have you noticed how, in the past few years, we've gotten serums? The word's first meaning is a medical term for the protein-rich liquid that separates from a blood clot when it coagulates. So "serum" has a medical aura that makes it sound like it comes from beakers and test tubes. However, cosmetic companies now use this word in a way that has no connection to its scientific meaning. Serums, most of them quite expensive, are being pushed as yet another whole-wallet skin product one needs to slather on in addition to anti-aging wrinkle creams, because "the molecule is very small" so it penetrates the skin better.[50]

And then there are the retouched ads. A Lancôme ad featuring Julia Roberts and a Maybelline ad with Christy Turlington were banned in 2011 by the Advertising Standards Authority in England when it was revealed that their faces had been photoshopped. When Lancôme claimed that the image of Roberts realistically showed what the product could do, and the Advertising Standards Authority said "prove it" by producing a pre-retouched photo of her, Lancôme couldn't because her contract stipulated that "no un-airbrushed shots" of her could be released.[51] L'Oreal in 2012 had its Revitalift wrinkle cream ad banned in Britain for the same reason when it was revealed that there was a reason Oscar winner Rachel Weisz did not look forty-two in the ad; the close-up of her had been digitally enhanced.[52]

What has emerged, as gorgeous, successful, and admired actresses themselves have aged, is a powerful symbiotic relationship between some celebrities, nearly all of them white, and the cosmetics industry. (A few women of color, Kerry Washington, forty-two, and Vanessa Williams, fifty-five, have been tapped to pitch anti-aging creams.) In fact, given the dearth of roles for older female stars, one way to maintain their visibility is in the service of the anti-aging industrial complex.[53] I'm gratified to have women of my vintage, and not a twenty-something, as "the face" of certain skin creams and still celebrated for their beauty. But since they've been beautiful for forever, and some have had "work" done or their images photoshopped to boot, they become the yardstick for how our skin and faces are supposed to look and embody a standard impossible to achieve.

Emerging out of the anti-aging injunctions, and on top of everything else, older women—at least those with money—must now engage with what our mothers did not: face-lift politics and

the question "Do I?" or "Don't I?" Is having "work" done empowering, even feminist, or is it a retrograde copping out to patriarchal
dictates about beauty and age? And how has reality television and
celebrity culture helped to move plastic surgery out of the precincts of Beverly Hills and into our psyches as a norm that everyday
women must now contemplate?

In the early 2000s, the peddling of cosmetic surgery for all
began its procession through popular culture, and especially on
television. Starting in 2001 we began to get subjected to those insuf-
ferable commercials on the nightly news showcasing Debby Boone
(of "You Light Up My Life" fame) hawking the "Lifestyle Lift,"
the gift we were supposed to give ourselves. "When you look in
the mirror, is there someone else looking back at you?" demanded
the ad. We saw the "before" images of unhappy older faces (the
"someone else") and the "after" images of happy, ecstatic, wrinkle-
free women. Message? Old is ugly and not even who you really are
(even though it is); surgically modified is much better and is the
real you (even though you no longer look like you)! Want to feel
better about not having ponied up for this? Google "Lifestyle Lift
Class Action Suit." Over 64,000 hits as of this writing.

Indeed, the "Lifestyle Lift" company (once with forty cosmetic-
surgery centers around the country) shut down in 2015 in the wake
of "multiple malpractice suits, the company posting false patient
reviews, [and] overpromised results."[54] In 2009 New York's attorney general had exposed that the company's employees were
posing as satisfied customers and writing bogus positive reviews.
Then, in 2011, in an exposé titled "Cosmetic surgery gets cheaper,
faster, scarier," USA Today reported on one complaint filed by Joyce
Wooten, who threatened to sue after her surgery left her with lopsided ears and loose flaps of skin around her neck. "I began hid-
ing my face everywhere I went because people stared and some
gasped."[55] The suits started mounting up, with the company fac-

ing at least thirty of them when it filed for bankruptcy in 2015.[56] Extremely dissatisfied customers complained of infected burns, horrible scarring, and even lost earlobes.[57] One woman woke up to find an earlobe freakishly attached to her face. As one of the many complaints you can read online, Janet in Georgia noted that "2 weeks after the procedure I looked like I had been beaten. I was swollen and bruised for months. My face did not even feel real."[58]

This mainstreaming of the scalpel was also propelled by all those makeover shows that colonized our cable listings in the early 2000s. There was *Extreme Makeover* (2002–2007), in which the plastic surgeons, presenting themselves as totally altruistic and caring, implied they could change people's lives via liposuction, breast augmentation, brow lifts, and the like. Even more Frankenstein-ian was *The Swan* (2004–2005), in which "ordinary women" who hated their faces and bodies willingly went through "a brutal three-month makeover," sometimes undergoing up to fourteen different procedures; at the end, they were shown their new selves in a full-length mirror, where they proclaimed "Is that me?" or "I don't even recognize myself." It was rightly reviled by critics, like Robert Bianco at *USA Today*, who proclaimed it "hurtful . . . repellant . . . obscene," but the show nonetheless garnered 15 million viewers, perhaps aided by airing right after Fox's blockbuster *American Idol*.[59] Not to be outdone, MTV aired the utterly reprehensible *I Want a Famous Face* (2004–2005), in which young people, mostly women, had surgery to make them look more like Pamela Anderson, Britney Spears, or Jennifer Lopez.

Not surprisingly, from 1997 to 2006 there was a 446 percent increase in the number of cosmetic procedures, despite the Lifestyle Lift mutilations. And by 2004 even the American Society of Plastic Surgeons (ASPS) was getting nervous about people's "unrealistic, unhealthy expectations about what plastic surgery can do." A 2007 survey they conducted found that four out of five cosmetic-surgery patients reported that they had been "directly influenced to have a procedure by the plastic surgery reality television shows they watch."[60]

At the same time, in the first decade of the twenty-first century, celebrity culture was conquering so much of our media that, by 2005, *Us Weekly*'s paid circulation increased 24 percent over 2004, and *People*'s circulation (not counting all those "pass-along" readers in dentists' offices) hit 3.7 million. By 2005, entertainment or celebrity news took up more space in magazines than any other topic, and new, snarky websites like PerezHilton.com, Pink Is The New Blog, and TMZ.com added to the glut. But snarky is the key term here—unlike PR-planted or semi-reverential pieces elsewhere, various of these websites delighted in taking stars down a peg.[61]

Here we see how aging is absolutely central to celebrity culture, with women's value specifically tied to how well they are or are not doing it.[62] These websites delighted in skewering aging celebrities, and trained their mockery on midcareer or older women whose cosmetic procedures had produced unfortunate, even disfiguring, results. Print media followed suit, and by the 2010s, stories titled "Plastic Surgery Nightmares," "Celebrities Who Look Worse After Plastic Surgery," and "Celebrity Plastic Surgery Disasters" proliferated. Poster women included fashion doyen Donatella Versace whose serial procedures led to jeering of her dirigible-sized lips, and La Toya Jackson, ridiculed for her paring-knife-sharp nose and chin. Rich socialite Jocelyn Wildenstein earned the moniker "cat woman" after reportedly spending $4 million on various interventions with deforming results. Jennifer Grey of *Dirty Dancing* fame said after her "nose job from hell" that she "went into the operating room a celebrity and came out anonymous."[63]

Speculation about who has had "work" and who hasn't has become something of an obsession in celebrity gossip; TMZ.com has its "Good Genes or Good Docs?" feature where it shows before and after images of stars and then invites readers to weigh in on the extent of the alleged surgical interventions. Female stars are supposed to remain attractive and ageless if they hope to ever get another role. Yet woe to those whose faces—the apple-sized cheeks, the sausage lips, that trapped-in-a-G-force-wind-tunnel look—betray how much attention, labor, and, most importantly, what is cast as rank narcissism and self-indulgence went into trying to escape the march of time. The gossip mongers especially strike when, in some stars' never-ending attempts to keep looking the same (or maybe even better), they stop looking like themselves at all.[64]

Hollywood too, then, and the celebrity gossip industry, are part of the anti-aging industrial complex. The entertainment business fetishizes slim, toned, youthful beauty, putting female stars of all ages under intense scrutiny ("Who Wore It Better?" "Best and Worst Beach Bodies!") with older faces and bodies brutally evaluated as unattractive, "washed up," no longer marketable. Yet it also distrusts, and often ridicules, women's efforts to efface the signs of age. Indeed, aging for women—who's done it well and "gracefully," who's been too vain or inept or obsessed and gotten too much or had a botched surgery—is a defining feature of celebrity culture, and thus a guidepost for everyday, nonfamous women. Older female celebrities must walk a very fine line between "maintaining youthful beauty" and "not appearing to try too hard for fear of seeming desperate."[65] It's OK, even glamorous and desirable, to take advantage of interventions that tame those wrinkles and jowls—just don't get caught!

Of course, like so much else that celebrities seem to get away with or vault over—a table at an impossible-to-get-into restaurant, no waiting in line for hours at the Department of Motor Vehicles—many try to get away with not aging. Some succeed, at least better than we do, and we envy them for this but resent them as well. So when the evidence of those efforts is both obvious and unfortunate—they actually look worse than if they had done nothing—it's really hard not to gloat.

Celebrity culture (as well as all those makeover shows) simultaneously promotes a beauty norm that has led to a more widespread acceptance and use of cosmetic surgery yet also contains multiple warnings about its perils. Why succumb to an aging face when the technology is available to refresh that Halloween mask? If as a star you don't maintain a youthful appearance you're doomed to oblivion, but if you're too obvious about it, you're desperate as well as self-obsessed and even pushy, trying to stake a claim to remaining in a line of work where you are no longer welcome. In a culture where older women are supposed to be invisible, those stars who refuse to give up the spotlight once the wrinkles appear, by having glaringly conspicuous interventions, are pitiful.[66] Some stars, like Sandra Bullock and Halle Berry, get the celebrity gossip stamp of approval because they either have apparently "employed the technologies of cosmetic surgery in 'acceptable' ways"—meaning you can barely see the evidence of "work"—or seem to be aging well, while others like Priscilla Presley and Melanie Griffith are ridiculed because their desperation to cling to youth and their failure to do so mark them as pathetic. These women sought to take control of the aging process in ways that suggested they were too vain, too obsessed, and not self-disciplined or savvy enough to do it well. Even worse in the eyes of celebrity bloggers are those whom the bloggers think have had work done—Nicole Kidman—and yet who insistently deny it.

Here again we are at a hinge moment culturally, where contradictions abound. It is especially on the terrain of celebrity culture that the "right" and "wrong" way of growing older for women is duked out.[67] The visibility, or lack thereof, of older female celebrities is dispiriting and retrograde one minute and empowering and affirming the next.[68] On the one hand, unlike men, it has seemed extremely difficult to reconcile female celebrity with aging: witness the multiple procedures Joan Rivers felt she had to have to stay in the spotlight—which, say, Robert Redford did not. And then there is the predictable, banal double standard of Hollywood casting, in which (to pick just a few examples) Jeff Bridges, sixty, was paired with Maggie Gyllenhaal, thirty-one, in *Crazy Heart*; Daniel Craig, forty-seven, with Lea Seydoux, thirty, in *Spectre*; Daniel Day-Lewis, sixty-one, with Vicky Krieps, thirty-five, in *Phantom Thread*; Tom Cruise, fifty-six, with Rebecca Ferguson, thirty-five, in *Mission: Impossible—Fallout* . . . you get the idea. In the summer of 2015, Maggie Gyllenhaal reported that a producer told her that, at age thirty-seven, she was "too old" to play opposite a fifty-five-year-old man.[69]

On the other hand, Helen Mirren, Meryl Streep, and Judi Dench continue to open movies, and Jane Fonda and Lily Tomlin have found a devoted following with *Grace and Frankie*. In 2015, eighty-year-old Joan Didion became "the face" of Celine, and ninety-three-year-old style icon Iris Apfel was selling Kate Spade bags and Hunter Thomas window treatments. Mirren and Dench, in particular, having the British knighthood title of Dame, have that "national treasure" aura about them and, with their continuing career successes and visibility, personify later life for women as still being dynamic and fulfilling.[70] This is progress! Nonetheless, because these women are beautiful, talented, admired, and stylish (and have access to trainers, spas, aestheticians, and designer clothes), do they become the rule, the models for who or what constitutes successful female aging? They are also white, rich, and, for the most part, "in possession of the kinds of trim bodies deemed aspirational by our culture whatever a woman's age."[71]

The intense pressure put on female celebrities to "age gracefully," the standards of beauty they are meant to adhere to and promote, and the outsized position they occupy as trendsetters and role models, shape our attitudes toward cosmetic surgery. Should we damn women who have done it, famous or not, because they can be seen as bending to the sexist edicts of a patriarchal culture? Or do we acknowledge that for women in the public eye, many have no choice but to head to the surgeon if they want to keep working? I was interviewed by a famous woman twenty years ago who, off camera, confided that she worried she would indeed have no choice about having work done even as she deplored the prospect of such procedures. As a feminist, I find it hard not to be torn between a woman's understandable desire—even economic need—to continue to be taken seriously because she "looks good," and the resentment that this is a double standard most men evade. One stereotype of feminists is that we all have a Stalin-like party line about fashion and beauty as sexist regimes of oppression, when in actuality many of us like nice clothes, color our hair, and spend too much (in vain, for the most part) at Sephora. So while I do deplore the democratization of cosmetic surgery as basically just another way to pit women against each other based on their appearance (while engorging the bank accounts of the overwhelmingly male plastic-surgery profession), who am I to judge what some women feel they need to do? I just wish more of us, especially the famous and prominent, would and could just say no, and push back against expensive and potentially risky interventions with which men do not have to have the same approach-avoidance relationship.

Because I have had inner-tube-sized eye bags since I was about twelve, I have to confess that I have fantasized about having the air taken out of their tires. However, since surgery terrifies me, I'd rather spend the money on travel, Planned Parenthood, and my daily wine habit. I also don't want to have that Kabuki mask thing happen (not to mention earlobes on my cheeks should the knife slip!), or for my family and friends to no longer recognize me, so I'm resigned to looking in the mirror and saying OK, I'll take it. Besides, I earned those eye bags, dammit (although, true, through some not highly recommended practices like drinking tequila shots with my brother and sunbathing with SPF 0 products, as SPF didn't exist when I was young). But I'm determined to think of them as my merit badges, for things like surviving rank sexism in grad school, a baby who did not sleep past 4:30 A.M. until she was about two, taking too many red-eye flights, and having (so far) a long and fulfilling career. As for Botox, I also don't want the muscles in my face frozen so I can't smile or frown, as scowling in particular is much more called for these days.

It turns out that I may not be alone. People are giving second thoughts to spending time, a ton of money, and the possibility of waking up to an unrecognizable face, on "work." In a 2016 Pew Research Center poll, 61 percent of respondents agreed with "People are too quick to use" cosmetic procedures "in ways that are not important." Only 36 percent agreed with "It's understandable that more people use them given the competitive advantage for those who look more attractive." But, the higher up you go in income, the more people agree that having elective cosmetic surgery is appropriate (78 percent for those making over $75K, 49 percent for those making under $30K). And while 82 percent agreed that cosmetic surgery has positive psychological benefits (without clear evidence), 71 percent also agreed that it could lead to "unexpected health problems" (I'd regard that earlobe situation as such a problem). When asked whether cosmetic surgery has more benefits, more downsides, or an equal amount of benefits and downsides for society, 61 percent of those who have had cosmetic surgery said either "more downsides" (12 percent) or "equal benefits and downsides" (49 percent), and 79 percent of those with a close family member or friend who had work said "more downsides" (18 percent) or equal amount (61 percent).[72] Clearly, many are torn about the merits of going under the knife, but as for me, I'm sticking with the eye bags.

In the United States in 2017, doctors performed more than 17 million cosmetic procedures, a 2 percent increase over 2016, and 92 percent of them were on women. However, the vast majority of these were not surgical but were "minimally-invasive procedures" like Botox injections or chemical peels.[73] And the American Society of Plastic Surgeons reports that in 2017 the number of people over fifty-five getting facelifts was down 5 percent.[74]

In 2007, Dove sought to go against the dictates of the anti-aging industrial complex by launching its line of Pro-Age products with an ad campaign featuring older women, some with gray hair and lines on their faces (including two women of color) who were not celebrities or professional models. They were, however, mostly slim and very attractive. The online "TV Ad" shows still and moving shots of four nude women with "too old to be in an anti-aging ad" superimposed on them. The spot finishes with the rejoinder that this is not an anti-aging ad, it's Pro-Age. The voice-over: "New Dove Pro-Age. Beauty has no age limit." The FCC banned the ads from U.S. television for showing too much skin, which some critics found laughable given how little some female performers wear, say, at MTV's music video awards.

"Dove seeks to create an attitudinal change in the anti-aging category—from negative and fear-driven to affirmative and hope-driven," said Kathy O'Brien, Dove's marketing director. "Pro-age is about looking great for your age."[75] Athena Uslander, fifty-one, who appeared in the campaign, asserted, "It really is time to change the limited view presented by the media and I'm proud to be part of it." *More* magazine jumped on the campaign, and within hours, according to its editor Peggy Northrop, the magazine's e-mailbox was overflowing with praise for the ads. "Our readers see themselves as happy, accomplished, optimistic women, and they don't necessarily see that image of themselves reflected anywhere else," Northrop noted. The ads prompted readers to challenge the magazine: "They were saying 'this is great—you should do more of that!'" given that most of the women featured in this magazine for older women were under the age of fifty.[76] Dove's website garnered "rapturous" e-mails from customers, some old—as in "I've been using Dove [soap] since I was 18"—and some who became Dove buyers because they loved the ads so much. While many lauded the much more positive images of older women, some critics did note that, at the end of the day, Dove was still trying to sell products.

Nonetheless, it sent a message. The cover of *Allure*'s September 2017 issue, featuring, of course, Helen Mirren, proclaimed "the end of anti-AGING: OUR CALL TO THE INDUSTRY." Editor Michelle Lee stated that the magazine would stop using that term because it reinforces the message "that aging is a condition we need to battle." She further added, "Growing older is a wonderful thing because it means we get a chance, every day, to live a full, happy life." Amen. And why Mirren? "Helen doesn't appear to be frightened of aging and taking her sexuality with her. And it kind of gives her female audience the right to say, 'Well, I can do that.' And we can do that too."[77] Of course, the issue remains filled with ads for products that will render you "ageless" and a Clarins ad for a serum with "anti-aging properties." And on the facing page of an article featuring a sixty-something woman with gray hair and lines on her face with the title "The Best Is Yet to Come" is a full-page ad for StriVectin (you know, the company the FDA cited in 2015 for deceptive advertising) and its "modern change agents" that "outsmart aging." A few pages later is a two-page ad for Botox. And in the November 2017 issue, there's a piece on injectable fillers "designed to make the skin look airbrushed," another on jowl lifts, and, of course, skin cream ads, including Reese Witherspoon promoting Elizabeth Arden's "anti-aging daily serum" with the tag line (allegedly in Reese's own handwriting) commanding "Own your future." So kudos to *Allure* for taking on the anti-aging mantra, but it is also exhibit A of the tenacious grip, financial influence, and continued seductive power of the anti-aging industrial complex.

Given these crosscurrents, might we be at a moment when we can reassess what we regard as beautiful? I recently met several friends for a drink—two women in their eighties and two in their early seventies—and as the rosy late-afternoon sunlight bathed their faces (yes, it is an especially flattering light), I reflected on how beautiful they all are. And not a pinprick of any cosmetic work among them. In fact, what I have been noticing on Facebook is how affirming people's friends are when older women post a new profile picture and the comments are "beautiful," "lovely," "gorgeous," "looking great!" Such postings might be only a minor riposte against Hollywood's standards of beauty, but maybe they are a start.

So here we are, on our puppet strings, poised between industrially produced fantasies of remaining ageless, and our knowledge that this entire industry promotes the very ageism that seeks to marginalize us. Mirren, Sarandon, Dench, Fonda, Keaton, Oprah, Streep—they all personify a model of older female beauty, achievement, and admiration most of us embrace yet can or will never achieve. It's an unattainable ideal that can police the rest of us for not coming even close to measuring up. They reinforce the desirability, even the necessity, of looking ten years younger or being slim and gorgeous in order to earn any respect as an older woman. Also, and ironically, as "the face" of whatever anti-aging elixir (sometimes their main way to maintain visibility), they promote products—and the defiance mantra—that perpetuate the very ageism that delimits the careers of female stars as they age.[78]

At the same time, though, there they are, claiming their visibility, their right to continue to work, have fun, and be outspoken (and yes, to use the word "fucking" as an adjective!) as nearly all of them are, especially about sexism and how the tentacles of ageism intersect with it. They have "disrupted [the] conventional patterns of female ageing," especially for celebrities.[79] One reason we love stars, at least certain stars, is the utopian, ideal images they embody, not just of ourselves but also of a different, more joyful future world. Some of them (although aside from Dench I'm hardly sure who) repudiate the notion that older femininity requires surgical intervention.[80] And women like Dench, Oprah, Mirren, Streep, and the others have come to be beacons, illuminating how women in their sixties and beyond can finesse the gap in the media between "failed" and "successful" female aging. Even though they are huge stars, they point the way to a middle ground, for how we can see ourselves and ask others to see us as well. They come across as "aspirational and down-to-earth, 'real' and glamorous, dignified and raucous." They acknowledge age while defying—yes, that word—that it necessarily involves irrelevance, dilapidation, and invisibility. They are, indeed, badass. For that, I think millions of us are grateful.[81]

So, yes, I'll probably still go to Sephora. I'll still sway to the siren call of rose hips (but not vomit fruit) infused skin cream. But, as Mirren notes, not for one minute because I think it will do "fuck all," because I don't. And then I think I'll go to Target and see about the low-priced spread.

CHAPTER 5

Visibility Revolts

MAY 2018. Amid the fusillade of Marvel comics, rampaging dinosaurs, and summer superhero movies aimed primarily at young men battling acne, a smoothie of a movie opened and grabbed the number-three box-office slot during its opening weekend; two weeks out, *Book Club* was a hit for Paramount.[1] I went to a matinee (of course), and the theater was filled with gray- and white-haired women, many coming together in groups to see this vintage female version of *Sex and the City*. They laughed their asses off and seemed to love every bit of the lip-glossed fairy tale laid before us. Although a major appeal is that we have known and followed these iconic stars for decades and, since aging is a democratic process, they are getting older right along with us, none of us (that I could see), including (especially) myself, looked anything like Diane Keaton (seventy-two), let alone Jane Fonda (eighty). Indeed, we initially see Fonda zipping up thigh-high black-leather stiletto-heeled boots (how can she still walk in those?) over her impossibly slim legs as she wraps up a sexual liaison with an attractive older man who loves her "independence."

This movie was, pure and simple, part of the still small but growing number of visibility revolts on behalf of older women. These have been staged intermittently over the past twenty-five years, primarily by certain white female celebrities, writers, and directors who, because of their fame, beauty, accomplishments, and ongoing clout (however circumscribed), have a platform that the rest of us don't have from which to raise their fists against the intertwining of ageism and sexism powerfully coursing through Hollywood. In our celebrity-obsessed and -driven culture, it is stars, as opposed to activists or politicians (Hillary Clinton and Nancy Pelosi being especially vilified), who get to—but also need to—be at the vanguard of this insurgency. It is an insurgency that is gaining momentum.

The media, of course, have always been one-way turnstiles, letting certain kinds of people onto the screens of America, keeping others out. They are mechanisms of inclusion and exclusion. And the turnstiles have been especially rigged when it comes to older women. For decades, and with a few notable exceptions, only a few stereotypes got past the metal bars: the doting, kindly, asexual, cookie-baking grandma; the meddling, fearsome battle-ax; the dying hospital patient; the crime victim; the evil crone. But now, more of the older women still in the entertainment industry—and with us as their fans—are pushing against the turnstile or trying to jump over it. They are pushing for the visibility and respect that await on the other side. And we are cheering them on. This too is a demographic revolution, however incipient, happening in Hollywood, further affirming our sense that we may be on the cusp of a cultural turn.

These revolts by certain actresses—uncoordinated and across many media platforms—are emphatically feminist and anti-ageist, depicting older women as feisty, strong, funny, smart, attractive, and, yes, even sexually active, despite aches and pains or forgetful moments. In addition to Helen Mirren and Judi Dench, other warriors include Jane Fonda, Lily Tomlin, Bette Midler, Kathy Bates, Rita Moreno, Charlotte Rampling, Sally Field, Susan Sarandon, Cicely Tyson, Diane Keaton, Candice Bergen, Meryl Streep, Oprah, Cher, Frances McDormand, and, of course, Betty White, with more about to join their ranks. And despite the entrenched "common sense" in Hollywood that people do not want to see older women headlining movies or television shows, many of these vehicles have been hits, sometimes massive ones. It goes without saying, given which women got to be movie stars in the early 1970s and beyond, that these visibility revolts remain mostly a white woman's game.

There are enormous pleasures here for us all, to see such aspirational figures—still!—making these biases visible, ridiculing them, and jettisoning them as relics from the past. These revolts, however frothy and fleeting, matter; they do important cultural work by pointedly calling out the creaky caricatures of older women. And our embrace of them challenges two other media caricatures: that women of a certain age are too old to be fans—that's for teenagers—and that fandom is the cotton candy of emotional attachment: artificial, superficial, lightweight, and feminine.

Anyone who has been to a David Byrne, Patti LaBelle, Joan Baez, Bruce Springsteen, or Mavis Staples concert recently (not to mention all the retro Motown shows), or seen the outpouring of emotion over the deaths of Prince, David Bowie, Anthony Bourdain, and Aretha Franklin, or tried in vain to get tickets to see Bette Midler in *Hello Dolly*, or visited the Facebook page for *Grace and Frankie*, knows that in our media- and celebrity-saturated age, fandom is a structuring element throughout our whole lives. We form strong emotional ties to stars we admire. Certain performers anchor us throughout our lives, sometimes even clarifying our sense of self, our hopes and dreams, connecting our past, present, and future as we go through life in tandem with them.[2] What they do as they age can validate our own mutinies against ageist shackles. And in the digital age, being the fan of an older female star can link us to a community of like-minded admirers who together can affirm a common set of values.

We were a generation of women perennially without role models—figuring out, without exemplars, how to be the first or only woman, let alone sole woman of color or lesbian—working; holding onto a job while pregnant; juggling work and family; dealing with sexual harassment; surviving divorce financially; managing as a single mother; coming out to family and friends without losing everything. Many of us, starting in the 1970s, had to write our own scripts or create them with friends as we went along. Now, facing the complexities, good and bad, of getting older, again in the absence of clear scripts, some female stars are serving, often deliberately and forcefully, as models for how to embrace our age positively, and, just as importantly, how to talk back to the ageism thrown at us. So, yes, fandom matters, as much and maybe even more for older women than for young people. But as we cheer them on, we also need to consider who and what gets left out when the media select and exalt some kinds of older women, but not others.

Book Club is a rom-com about four lifelong friends looking for love, sex, or both; all the characters are white, straight, and upper-middle class or rich. Jane Fonda portrays a luxury hotel mogul; Candice Bergen (seventy-two) a federal judge; Mary Steenburgen (sixty-five) a successful chef and restaurateur; and Diane Keaton, a recently widowed woman, lives in one of those opulent, *Better Homes & Gardens*, trumpet-vine-ornamented houses typically seen in Nancy Meyers movies (*It's Complicated*; *Something's Gotta Give*). All are physically fit and still gorgeous.

One of the movie's major (and very satisfying) goals was to tackle head-on the derisive stereotypes of older women as sexually unattractive, uninterested in sex, and deserving of ridicule or censure if they still have a libido. Indeed, given these stars (always beautiful, still beautiful), their appearance and their success in the world make such notions seem absurd. As Fonda's character notes, "Sex must not be taken off the table" for women of their age. Paraphrasing Dylan Thomas, she declares, "We shall not go gentle into the night." And they don't. The movie also celebrates the deep friendships of older women. (It does, however, pretend that seventy- [or eighty-] year-old women can find romantic partners as hunky as Andy Garcia or Don Johnson.)

Especially gratifying to the audience I saw this with was the sarcasm directed toward the widowed Keaton's two adult daughters, who treat her like a desperately lonely, physically frail, vulnerable woman in urgent need of a medical-alert button. (And since this is Diane Keaton, their eagerness to harness her to a walker is even more preposterous.) They demonstrate so many of the ways in which people try to infantilize older women. They insist she move in with one of the daughters, into a basement that they have redone for her safety with slip-resistant floors and the like. In her jailbreak scene (Keaton has met an airline pilot played by Garcia who owns a ranch the size of Nevada and is gobsmacked by her), she emphasizes to her daughters that she is still very much alive and vibrant, that there are things she still wants to explore, and that they should "save your parenting instincts for your children," a line my fellow theatergoers high-fived.

Not surprisingly, Bill Holderman, the cowriter and director of the film, said it was a battle to get the movie made: "Cast the movie younger" was a repeated response from the studios. He surmised that some may have been squeamish about a film involving older women actually having sex. "I do think [Hollywood] is male dominated and that [the subject of older women's sex lives] is still, sadly, taboo in our culture—particularly in America," he told the *Guardian*. "I think women after a certain point are relegated and put out to pasture, and that is reflected in a lot of male studio executives' mentalities. It's too bad, but hopefully this movie will start to shift at least some people's minds."[3] We'll see.

What's not to love? To see these four great actresses being mouthy, sarcastic, sexy, and full of energy, slamming back the wine as they trash the ageism directed at women, is like having a party with old friends, even role models, with whom we can say "Amen, sister." The movie's Facebook page is filled with enthusiastic, grateful reviews. However, this is also the comfy, Angora cat, seaside-bathed, sunshiny vision of aging for older women. It is *Grace and Frankie* territory, the Idealized Woman of a Certain Age. What are the pleasures, and the truly important advantages, of such celebrity-driven visibility revolts? What are the possible negative consequences? And what is the media trail that led us here?

Let's briefly review some of the mantles older actresses had to don in the 1950s and 1960s to get work, the mantles that Streep, Fonda, and others seek to consign to the used-clothing bin of history. What were their meager choices in trying to defy career obscurity? One was the deranged, evil crone, made insane by the fact that she was washed up. Indeed, in several iconic films featuring older women, the movies were about how aging itself is a warping, disfiguring, and horrifying process for female movie stars. (Of course, Disney gave us plenty of these too in the form of wicked stepmothers and malevolent, wart-covered witches whose mission was to destroy or murder the beautiful young things they envied.) *Sunset Boulevard* (1950) starred Gloria Swanson as has-been silent film star Norma Desmond, desperate to get back on the screen and utterly self-deluded about the prospects of doing so, given her age. In the ghoulish final scene, Desmond, who has shot the aspiring scriptwriter (William Holden) living with her after he tells her she will never have a comeback, imagines the police and newsreel photographers covering the crime as the crew shooting her new film. As she utters what came to be the immortal line of narcissistic derangement, "All right, Mr. DeMille, I'm ready for my close-up," she walks wild-eyed toward the camera, her coiling, Dracula-like fingers leading the way.

Bette Davis got her shot in a similar role as a pancake-makeup-encrusted fading child star rendered grotesque and mentally unhinged by the process of aging and the loss of the limelight in *Whatever Happened to Baby Jane?* (1962). She lives with her paraplegic, former film star sister (Joan Crawford), whom she basically imprisons, feeding her dead rats for dinner. The message was that older women, especially former stars, were supposed to willingly let go of the public attention they once had, get off the stage, and not force us to look at their wrinkled faces. Their refusal to acquiesce to these edicts turns them into monsters. At the same time, of course, such films did allow smart and persistent older actresses, like Davis, to use such roles to display their continuing talents and to dramatize the very shunning they were supposed to endure.[4]

HBO's *Feud* (2017), about the making of *Whatever Happened to Baby Jane?* with Susan Sarandon as Davis and Jessica Lange as Crawford, makes clear how both women struggled against and resented the ageism that hobbled their careers. "No one is looking to cast women of our age," laments Crawford. She felt she was "at the top of my game" as an actress and did not want to only portray grandmas. Studio head Jack Warner (Stanley Tucci) makes the bias quite clear: when women get older, he opines, "Their tits start to sag and they start having opinions," which is why "no one wants them." Davis's own daughter (played by Kiernan Shipka) upbraids her for not being willing to "step aside" now that her "spin on the carousel is over" and reaffirms that "no one wants you anymore."

Hugely successful, especially as camp, *Baby Jane* gave rise to imitators, more films featuring a formerly successful older woman, especially a star, whom the calamity and humiliation of aging has turned into a crazed, predatory monster. Indeed, this actually became a genre, referred to as—I can barely type in these terms, they're so awful—psycho-biddy, hagsploitation, or hag horror movies.[5] In addition to Davis and Crawford (let's remember, both Oscar winners and only fifty-four and fifty-seven, respectively, in 1962), other actresses slotted into "hagsploitation" movies in the 1960s and '70s (because those were pretty much the only roles they could get) included Olivia de Havilland, Barbara Stanwyck, Debbie Reynolds, and Shelley Winters. (Davis, who wanted to keep working, took on various of these roles rather than being forced to retire.) No wonder that Maggie Kuhn, and the thousands of women who joined the Gray Panthers, were hungry for something just a tad more affirming than older women as homicidal, soul-sucking Nosferatu types.

In the wake of Maggie Kuhn's and Claude Pepper's taking the networks out to the woodshed for their stereotyping or total neglect of older audiences, visibility revolts emerged in fits and starts in the late twentieth century. By the mid-1980s, a host of shows with older characters, although mostly male, premiered: *Matlock* with Andy Griffith (sixty) in 1986, *The Equalizer* in 1985 with Edward Woodward (fifty-five), *Jake and the Fat Man* in 1987 with William Conrad (sixty-seven), and *Murder, She Wrote* in 1984 with Angela Lansbury (fifty-nine). (It's unclear whether having the oldest person ever elected president, Ronald Reagan, also fueled this trend.) So it seemed that media activism against ageism on television had resulted in more positive, nuanced, and empowered images of older people than had existed before.

The foundational show here for older women, and the template for many future visibility revolts, was—and is—*The Golden Girls* (1985–1992). Even as a frothy sitcom, it remains one of the most progressive shows about older women ever aired. It featured Bea Arthur (sixty-three) as Dorothy, divorced because her husband left her for a younger woman after thirty-eight years of marriage; Betty White (sixty-three) as Rose, widowed and a grief counselor; Rue McClanahan (fifty-one) as Blanche, a widow; and Estelle Getty (sixty-two) as Sophia, made up to appear to be Bea Arthur's eighty-something mother. Reportedly, Brandon Tartikoff, the head of NBC, commissioned the show to reflect and tap into the growing population of older women, as well as changing attitudes about aging.[6] He may have also been trying to get Maggie Kuhn off his back.

It was the first television show in which all the characters were women over the age of fifty, and the only show up until then with an all-female ensemble cast. And it became a smash hit—in fact, it still is; *Golden Girls* has been in syndication for over twenty-seven years. It also won ten Emmys during its airing, including one for each of the four leads. As the television critic Tom Shales wrote at the time, "Encountering characters of an advanced age on a TV sitcom is so refreshing." Betty White recalled, "Few thought it would survive. It crossed generations. Half the mail the show got was from children and teenagers. For many young people, it was their first exposure to grandparents."

The show was groundbreaking—even revolutionary—on so many levels. Tellingly, we haven't seen its like since, with the possible exceptions of *Grace and Frankie* and *Hot in Cleveland*. Here was a nontraditional family—what Maggie Kuhn would have called a "family of choice"—living communally and sharing the trials as well as the pleasures of being older women. Here was happy, fulfilling aging with a powerful bond of love and friendship among women. These characters defied pretty much every stereotype Maggie Kuhn had railed against. No frumpy duds here, no pink floral-print "dusters" or muumuus, no Silly-Putty-colored support stockings rolled down to midcalf. These women sashayed around in fluttering bright red or gold silks, flowing scarfs, and big beads and earrings, fully made-up with their hair perfectly coiffed. They dated and had sex. Blanche, the southern belle, was especially proud of her ongoing ability to turn men into "putty in her hands." They were healthy, socially and politically engaged, thoughtful and funny. At times they took on issues of particular concern to older people, especially the truly dreadful, negligent treatment in some nursing homes.

The oldest character, Sophia, was the most spirited and sharp-tongued of the lot. Audience response suggested that people loved this irreverent, smack-talking, badass grandma. It was the young-est and most conventionally attractive character, Blanche, who was most anxious about losing her youth and beauty as she aged. When Blanche insists to Sophia that she is, in fact, not old, Sophia lets her have it, retorting that she refuses to indulge Blanche's "vain, nar-cissistic fantasy of still being in your forties." At the same time, Blanche personifies "many women's panic over becoming deval-ued in American society for what she cannot help: living life and growing older as a natural and inevitable process."[7]

As a harbinger of the emergence of aspirational aging, the show offered positive, affirming representations of older women as vibrant and empowered. They embodied female strength and independence. More to the point, at a time when conservative politics dominated the nation, Golden Girls showcased progressive values and attitudes and thus contradicted the conventional wis-dom that older women were stuck in their ways and impervious to new ideas. This was especially true in its politics about homo-sexuality and AIDS, at a time when the disease was ravaging the gay community and the Reagan administration refused for years to acknowledge its lethal impact, let alone fund research to find a cure. In "Scared Straight" from the 1988–1989 season, Blanche's brother comes to visit and struggles to come out to her, which he eventually does. At first, she's incredulous and thinks he's joking or trying to "get back" at her for something; "it can't be true, you're my brother!" But as she works through the revelation, showing audiences that this was a process, and a positive one, she assures him, "I'll get comfortable with it." The other women are initially surprised but supportive and accepting. The show also featured a friend of Dorothy's who was a lesbian, unheard of at the time on any television show.

The following season, Rose learns she has to get tested for HIV because of a blood transfusion from the early 1980s that might have been contaminated. As she expresses her terror at being HIV positive, the women discuss the wages of such a diagnosis—how people have trouble getting insurance or getting or holding onto a job, and how they become isolated as others shun them. When Rose shakes her fist at the cosmos, asking, "Why me? I'm a good person!" Blanche retorts, as if addressing every evangelical who smugly pronounced that the disease was divine retribution for being gay, "AIDS is *not* a bad person's disease. It's not God punishing people for their sins." They also rehearse—and dismiss— the myths about transmission, and, at one crucial moment, Sophia presents Dorothy with condoms for future use. Blanche admits to Rose that she got tested too and now makes sure that she and her partners take all the "necessary precautions" and practice safe sex.

Advocating condom use in a prime-time Saturday night sitcom was daring enough, but to have women in their sixties and older doing so was especially radical. For these and other reasons—like having a family of choice—the show was and remains very popular with gay audiences.[8] Betty White noted they heard reports that "when the show was originally airing, the gay bars on Saturday night would all shut off their music at nine o'clock, put on the show, and then start up the music and start dancing again afterwards. We always got such a kick out of that."[9]

The show was not without its critics. The women were all

white and straight (although, to be fair, having a central, ongoing lesbian character in a major role in 1985 would no doubt have been rejected by all three networks, and they developed only a handful of roles featuring women of color). The women were also afflu- ent, sharing a sprawling, well-appointed ranch house in Miami, so, yes, they were idealized women of a certain age. And while Blanche's robust sex life countered myths about older women being asexual, the jokes about her having "a welcome mat at the foot of her bed" also contained elements of ridicule that a woman of her age could be so lusty, and so should be seen as a slut. Also, much of the humor came from self-deprecating or mutually insult- ing barbs about appearance, personality, and behavior. The series ended with Dorothy leaving the group to get remarried, thus, for some, lapsing into a conventional, Cinderella-style, saved-by-the- prince ending, betraying the show's seven-year insistence on the primacy of female friendship.[10]

Nonetheless, there hasn't been a show like it since on any of the networks, or cable for that matter. Nor has there been a show that has taken this template and included older women of color, older lesbians or trans women, or older working-class women.

The other breakthrough show featuring an older female lead was *Murder, She Wrote*, which premiered in 1984 and lasted for twelve seasons. Within a year it was number three in the Nielsen ratings and stayed in the top ten to top fifteen until its last season. Aside from its overall strong ratings over the years, the show was especially popular among older viewers. The show utterly contra- dicted industry wisdom that viewers would not watch a show with an older female lead. With Angela Lansbury (fifty-nine to seventy- one during the series' run) as the mystery writer Jessica Fletcher, she invaded the overwhelmingly male turf of television detectives and crime solvers. The opening sequence showed Fletcher (in her cute coastal Maine town) riding a bicycle, carrying fishing tackle, jogging, and typing away, as an active, engaged older woman. Like the *Golden Girls*, her clothes violated the visual codes that screamed "stodgy old lady"; they were brightly colored and stylish, her hair perfectly teased and sprayed. Fletcher's special skill was finding and reading clues. She was logical, used deductive reasoning, and was very empathetic with her clients, countering the stereotype of women as irrational and overly emotional, as well as the notion that professional women were cold or unfeeling.

And the show never betrayed its lead character. Here's one telling example. Back in the sunset years of the network era, we sometimes got "crossover shows" (we sometimes still do), in which the cast from one popular program intermingled with those from another popular program to further boost ratings for both. Someone at CBS in 1986, maybe having passed the bong one too many times, decided to pair *Murder, She Wrote* with, of all things, that bastion of homosocial (and homoerotic), hairy-chested, short-shorts wearing manhood, *Magnum, P.I.*, and made it a two-parter.[11] Higgins, the British-issue khaki-clad "manservant" who runs the estate he and Magnum share, is driving several women there when someone tries to run them off the road. Obviously, Higgins wants Magnum to help figure out who and why. But one of the women is dubious that Magnum has investigative skills, so she decides to bring Fletcher in on the case. Magnum is noticeably irritated and keeps referring to the mystery detective as "he."

When Fletcher appears, Magnum is eye-rollingly contemptuous of her because she's not a "real" investigator (no mention is made of her age or gender, but those are implied as defects too). Instantly we know where this is going: Fletcher will prove her mettle and Magnum will have to eat crow. Not surprisingly, Fletcher notices various clues that Magnum has missed; we then see her determining the exact trajectory of a bullet fired into the estate. Of course, her "hunches" (female intuition) as well as her analysis of the clues matter. What was noteworthy about this episode is how it obviously sought to ridicule men who intertwined ageism and sexism to dismiss the talents and value of older women.

However, despite the success of shows like this, by the spring of 1992 the tide had changed, and they were given the whack-a-mole treatment from the networks. NBC announced it was canceling three mainstay shows with older characters, including *The Golden Girls*; the others were *Matlock* and *In the Heat of the Night* starring Carroll O'Connor, then sixty-eight, as a police chief in Mississippi. (*Murder, She Wrote* got the boot in 1996.) The networks, and the country, were coming off a recession, and despite a slight increase in ratings, NBC and CBS reported losses. They were also facing competition from the upstart network FOX, which was aggressively going after a younger audience with shows like *Living Single*, *Beverly Hills, 90210*, and *Melrose Place*. The conventional wisdom was that younger viewers, the eighteen-to-forty-nine demographic, spent about three times as much on consumer goods as those over fifty-five, so that's who the networks began doing battle over.

The result was what advertisers labeled a "granny dumping strategy" and coincided with the rise of niche programming and the eventual Ahab-like pursuit of millennials.[12] Having a core audience that skewed older was now deemed anathema. In the late 1990s, advertisers were paying two and a half times as much to reach eighteen-to-thirty-five-year-olds as they were to reach those over thirty-five.[13] By 2005, one researcher found that there were fewer older characters on television than there had been in 1985.[14]

Older women did get roles in hit shows like *Seinfeld* and *Everybody Loves Raymond*, but they inhabited another pervasive caricature: the meddling, prying, domineering, overly intrusive mothers or mothers-in-law who drove their children crazy, the archetype known as the battle-ax (usually played by very good actresses). In *Raymond*, Ray's mother Marie (Doris Roberts) typically walks into the house unannounced, rummages through Ray's mail, forces herself, uninvited, into dinners and parties, and is critical, either explicitly or implicitly, of how Debra, Ray's wife, is raising their children. Sharp-tongued and querulous (although of course good-intentioned), Marie also bickers constantly with her husband Frank (Peter Boyle). The parents in *Seinfeld* are similar, with George's and Jerry's mothers overbearing and interfering.

In both shows, these mothers were contrasted with another, maybe even worse kind of older mother: the elitist, art- and theater-loving, cold fish of a snob who looks down on less-cultivated older women and is not adequately maternal. These were warnings against *not* properly inhabiting the main role meant for older women: the nurturing, selfless grandma. In *Raymond*, this is Debra's mother Lois (Katherine Helmond), who visits a few times and seems to take little interest in her grandchildren; in case we've missed the point, Marie self-servingly emphasizes "she's not motherish." In *Seinfeld*, it's the mother of Susan, George's fian-cée. Played by Grace Zabriskie, she is beautiful and slim, and cold as ice. She condescends to George's parents in between insult-ing her husband. Then, of course, there was *The Sopranos*, with Tony Soprano's murderous, betraying mother Livia (played by the always amazing Nancy Marchand), who was voted by *Rolling Stone* in 2016 as #3 of their "40 Greatest TV Villains of All Time."

Despite these, in most hit television shows and movies in the early twenty-first century—*Friends*, *Frasier*, *ER*, *Desperate House-wives*, the *Law & Order* and *CSI* franchises—older women were either invisible, crime victims, or hospital patients. One exception was *Boston Legal* (2004–2008), in which Candice Bergen (fifty-eight to sixty-two during the run of the show) played senior partner Shirley Schmidt.

And in the mix of *Boston Legal*'s cast was the beloved televi-sion star Betty White, *the* pioneer of visibility revolts. In 2014, the

Guinness World Records book awarded her the title of "Longest TV Career for an Entertainer (Female)" for her more than seventy years in show business. (She tied with the British star Bruce Forsyth, who won in the male category.)[15] Although she started in television in the late 1940s, it was her role as Sue Ann Nivens, "The Happy Homemaker," on *The Mary Tyler Moore Show* that made her a hugely popular actress. White (ages fifty to fifty-five during the run of the series) was a brilliant admixture of simple syrup and snake venom as the two-faced Sue Ann, who was perky and wholesome on her show but sardonic, backbiting, male-obsessed, and sexually voracious off camera. It was here that she honed her trademark double-edged persona of the lusty older woman: it came off as inappropriately avid, yet also delicious because it challenged the forbidden. Since then, White has never stopped working; she appeared on *30 Rock*, the soap *The Bold and the Beautiful*, and *Hot in Cleveland*, in addition to various cameos and television commercials, most notably in a 2010 Super Bowl commercial for Snickers, in which she was tackled in a game of touch football.

By 2012, White was, according to the Q Score rating service (self-proclaimed as the "industry standard for measuring consumer appeal of personalities"), the most appealing celebrity in the country, tied only with Tom Hanks.[16] What made White *the* icon of a totally cool older woman, the one so many of us want to be when we grow up? Her characters embodied everything "little old ladies" were not supposed to say or do. She was the opposite of the kindly, ever-nurturing, selfless, polite, asexual grandma type that older women are expected to morph into: a personal rebellion against ageist confinement. In various of her roles she has combined sarcastic, wise-cracking, even biting humor with empathy and vulnerability. In particular, White has been on the vanguard of puncturing the taboo that older women do not and should not care about sex. White and her characters have glided through the aging process—and the stereotypes about it—with humor, sass, and confidence.

White had played the character Catherine Piper on the legal drama *The Practice* (1997–2004). When David E. Kelley created the spin-off *Boston Legal*, he brought her character to the new show, where she appeared in sixteen episodes. At the very same time that trade journals like *Ad Age* were warning advertisers that they were missing a bet with older audiences, *Boston Legal* in 2008 aired an episode in which one of the firm's lawyers, Carl (John Larroquette), agreed to represent Catherine in a lawsuit against the networks for ageism. White was eighty-six at the time. This was clearly tilting at windmills. As she lists the various injustices older people deal with—the high cost of prescription drugs, how Social Security doesn't keep pace with inflation, that some jobs still have a mandatory retirement age—she adds, "We're just shoved aside as a nuisance, I can't even watch television shows, for God's sake, because the networks consider me irrelevant; they don't program for anyone over fifty." She notes the irony that "you people invent all these medicines to keep us alive, even thrive and then you don't know what to do with us." Carl thinks she may be onto something, as the networks are supposed to serve the public. "I'm over fifty myself and I want something to watch." He takes her case to court.

Overseeing the case, Judge Clark Brown (Henry Gibson, seventy-three at the time) yells at Carl that you can't sue the networks, but Carl counters that they're a public trust, which is why they're regulated. He insists that the networks should have an obligation to program for everyone, and emphasizes, à la *Ad Age*, that people over fifty make up the fastest-growing market, adding that baby boomers over fifty earn two trillion dollars in annual income. The lawyer representing the networks says they want viewers with discretionary spending money, to which Carl counters that people over fifty account for half of that too. He then adds, "We have more money, spend more money, watch more television, go to movies, we buy more CDs than young people do, yet we're the focus of less than ten percent of all the advertising." Carl casts this discrimination as "bigotry . . . to intentionally exclude a class of society."

Warming to his task, he asserts that mature viewers should be able to turn on their TVs and see something other than "reality shows aimed at fourth graders" or television shows featuring "dimwitted sex-crazed twenty-somethings running around in suits or doctors' scrubs; old people with intelligence don't want to watch that crap, we're fed up, the networks might think we're dead, but we're not, we're very much alive with working brains, give us something to watch, dammit!" He then emphasizes that young people watch three hours of television a day while multitasking on their phones, while older people watch six hours and actually pay attention, so why program only for the young?

Although the judge is unsympathetic at first, he comes around, acknowledging that "ageism is one of the last socially condoned bigotries, and it is rampant in this broadcast network business. . . . How is it that we are not part of the target demo when we spend the most money and watch the most television?" Because he has come to see this as discrimination, he rules that the case can stand. But, of course, this is the fantasyland of the law as portrayed on television.

To illustrate how deluded this *Boston Legal* episode was, let's take *Harry's Law* (2011–2012), another David E. Kelley creation, starring the ever-fabulous Kathy Bates (sixty-three at the time) as a former patent attorney reinventing herself as a criminal defense lawyer. As Harriet "Harry" Korn, Bates was acerbic, funny, smart, and neither slim nor conventionally beautiful; she looked the way a lot of women in their early sixties look. And viewers loved it. In the spring of 2012, *Harry's Law* was NBC's first- or second-most-watched network drama (depending on whose numbers you read), beloved by its 7–11 million weekly viewers, very good numbers as audiences became ever more carved up into tiny niches. (At its average of 8.8 million viewers a week, it topped *Law & Order: SVU's* 7.6 million, and was nearly double other beloved NBC shows like *Parks and Recreation*, 4.4 million, and *30 Rock*, 4.5 million.)[17] But NBC canceled the show because, as one NBC executive said, "Its audience skewed very old and it's hard to monetize that,"[18] meaning that only 1.8 million viewers were in the eighteen-to-forty-nine demo.[19] So NBC actually aired a show that resonated with nearly 9 million viewers, most of them fifty or older, and then dumped it for that very reason. As one television critic noted, in the wake of the cancellation, "No other industry except television really works this way. A senior citizen's money counts just as much at the box office as Snooki Ipod's does. Restaurant patrons aren't shown the door because they look too old. On the contrary, they're often prized for being better tippers with more disposable income."[20]

A Facebook campaign sought to restore the show, but to no avail. As one blogger noted, "Racism, sexism, ageism. No TV network worries in the least about being accused of the latter."[21] Pissed-off comments on the *Los Angeles Times* site included: "Oh right, because it's my broke kid who spends all the money, not her older mom . . . brilliant, NBC"; "You really think over 49'ers aren't consumers? Wake up! Take a REAL POLL and find out how many parents and grandparents are supporting their children and grandchildren in this economy. If it weren't for our generation there would be a lot more people on the streets. You cancel a great show to support what?"; "Talk about age discrimination!! So if your [sic] over 50 it doesn't matter what you watch! NBC you suck!!!"; "Come on this is such bull. Guess people over 49 never buy anything and are withering away in a cave somewhere."

Nonetheless, despite the overwhelming shift to younger audiences, sporadic roles for older women began opening up after

2000. They stand out because they were both still rare but also unprecedented. Charting the ups and downs of such vehicles over the past fifteen years looks like an EKG run amok, but the upward clicks started to become more frequent. One early signal of this trend was *Something's Gotta Give* (2003), when a fifty-seven-year-old woman, Diane Keaton, actually got to play the lead female love interest in a romantic comedy. (And had a younger man, played by Keanu Reeves, thirty-nine, totally smitten with her.) In 2009, Meryl Streep (sixty at the time), got to do the same in *It's Complicated*. (Streep told *Vanity Fair*, "It's incredible—I'm 60 and I'm playing the romantic lead in romantic comedies. Bette Davis is rolling over in her grave.")[22] Then there was Helen Mirren's (then sixty-one) Oscar-winning performance as Queen Elizabeth (2006). And *Philomena* (2013), starring Judi Dench (seventy-nine at the time), for which she was nominated for an Oscar, as well as her role as M in seven James Bond movies up through *Skyfall* (2012). The 2012 miniseries *Political Animals* cast Sigourney Weaver (sixty-three) as the secretary of state and Ellen Burstyn (eighty) as her irreverent, booze-swilling, pot-smoking mother.

More recently, the trend seems to be accelerating, with more actresses getting through those turnstiles. At the vanguard here have been some cable channels and especially streaming services, some of which seem to care less about the eighteen-to-forty-nine demo. We've gotten TV Land's *Hot in Cleveland* (2010–2015), Netflix's *Grace and Frankie* (2015–present), *Book Club* (2018), yet another *Mamma Mia* (with Streep, sixty-eight, Cher, seventy-two, Julie Waters, sixty-eight, and Christine Baranski, sixty-six), and a 2018 reboot of *Murphy Brown* with Candice Bergen (seventy-two). Baranski is also the lead in the critically acclaimed *Good Fight* (2017–present), and Emma Thompson (sixty) the lead in *Late Night* (2019). The writer and producer Ryan Murphy, creator of *Feud*, has routinely featured older actresses like Jessica Lange, Angela Bassett, and Kathy Bates in *American Horror Story*. Multiple-award-winning Rita Moreno (eighty-seven) portrayed the self-loving, outspoken, flirtatious grandmother Lydia Riera in Norman Lear's remake of *One Day at a Time* about a multigenerational Cuban American family. Moreno told Lear she didn't mind playing an older woman at all, but she insisted that Lydia be sexy and sexual, which she was. (As of this writing, Netflix has canceled the show after three seasons, to the fury of devoted fans who find it one of the smartest shows on television and one of the few Latinx representations in the media.) And probably most important, the 2018 documentary *RBG*, about the kick-ass accomplishments of Ruth Bader Ginsburg (eighty-five), became Magnolia Pictures' highest-grossing domestic release of all time.[23]

All of these—and there have been others—constitute rebellions against Hollywood's deeply rooted and tenacious gendered ageism. Given the stereotypes and conservatism of the networks (despite the age of their most consistent audiences), it has been a few cable channels and streaming services (as well as some movies) that have provided platforms for this ongoing insistence on visibility. In 2010, TV Land, departing from its nostalgia-driven rerun lineup, premiered its first scripted show, *Hot in Cleveland*, with Betty White (then eighty-eight). It was the highest-rated telecast in the cable network's fourteen-year history; the premiere episode was the most watched show—nearly 5 million viewers—the entire day on American cable.[24] (In Canada, it aired on a mainstream broadcast network, CTV, where it became a major hit, the #1 ranked new import show of the year.)[25] In its first season, the show delivered 4.7 million total viewers in the United States, very impressive given that it was on an obscure channel at 10:00 on a Wednesday night.[26]

The preposterous premise was that three single LA career women, Joy (Jane Leeves, fifty), Melanie (Valerie Bertinelli, fifty), and Victoria (Wendie Malick, sixty)—are on a flight that makes an emergency landing in Cleveland. As they decide to pass their time in a local bar, several men make passes at them and offer to buy them drinks. "We appear to have landed in a dimension where men hit on women their own age," Joy says. "We owe it to science to investigate." And with that, they decide to move there, allowing for the re-creation—a full twenty-five years after *Golden Girls*—of a show with an ensemble cast of women fifty and older. They move into a house where the tart-tongued Elka (Betty White), smelling slightly of pot smoke, is the caretaker.

The show was another broadside against how women of a certain age are usually depicted in the media. The scripts revolved around the dating dramas and love lives of all the stars, especially Elka, who ended up having the most love interests of any of the women; the show specifically showcased her romantic relations, which always involved sex. When the other women take her to a bar, three men slip her their phone numbers, and she quips, "I had to wait until I was eighty-eight to find out I have game." Building on her bawdy Sue Ann Nivens character, White was expert in delivering sexual double entendres (including, in an especially beloved episode, about oral sex, or "going downtown," which supposedly women of her vintage were not supposed to even know about) to the delight of the live studio audience. As one writer put it, White was the show's hammer, "which means she comes in and nails the scene."[27]

While the show did feature jokes about older people (especially men) needing walkers, being hard of hearing, and wearing medical-alert bracelets, and the three younger, model-thin women at times worried too much about their weight and looks, it also routinely critiqued the media's consignment of older women to geriatric preserves. Victoria, the aging soap-opera star, ever eager to hear from her agent, primarily gets offers to pitch adult diapers or to play grandmother roles, even though she is slim, fit, and beautiful. When Joy (Leeves) says she is worried about getting older, Elka responds, "You shouldn't worry so much about getting old; there's a secret that nobody tells you, you don't feel old, you feel like yourself." She does add that "obviously the woman looking back at me from my mirror isn't young; she bugs me sometimes," emphasizing how our older faces can feel like a false mask, misrepresenting who we are and how we feel. For Elka (and White), age was a barrier to nothing.

Jane Fonda and Lily Tomlin picked up the visibility torch with a vengeance in May of 2015 with Netflix's *Grace and Frankie*. By 2017, it was one of the streaming service's most popular shows (although Netflix does not provide specific numbers) and had, in 2019, been renewed for its sixth season.[28] Thrown together after their longtime husbands announce their love for each other, Grace (Fonda)—an uptight, stuck-up, vodka-Martini-swilling, slimness-obsessed retired cosmetics executive—and Frankie (Tomlin)—a pot-smoking, incense-burning, Om-chanting, vision-quest hippie—who are anything but mutual fans, have to move in together in their jointly owned La Jolla ocean-view home.

While this is a pretty rare scenario for older women to face, having the rug pulled out from under you by loss is not. Co-creator Marta Kauffman (fifty-nine) explained, "We were searching for a way to explore aging and coming into your own at a certain point in your life."[29] In addition to not having to deal with the nine minutes of commercial breaks on most broadcast and cable channels, Kauffman knew there were taboo topics about women and aging that only pay cable or a streaming service would allow. And she didn't just want to make broad jokes about aging, but to deal with its pleasures and its pains. Older viewers are "a very marginalized segment of the population," Kauffman noted. "They're smart. They live long lives. They have great histories." Executive producer Marcy Ross noted simply, "There's a lot of people out there with nothing to watch for them. There are no characters that look like them on television, and if there are, they're the brunt of a joke"; Grace and Frankie "will not be the brunt of the joke."[30]

The show repeatedly calls out the intersections between ageism and sexism and shines a spotlight on the various indignities and dismissals older women face without lapsing into ageist humor or insults. In one memorable scene, Grace and Frankie are in a grocery store and, despite calling to several of the clerks asking for service, are ignored. Finally, one young man comes to the checkout line only to wait on a just-arrived twenty-something blonde at another register. Grace loses it and starts yelling and banging a grocery basket against the counter. "Do you not see me?" she yells at the cashier. "Do I not exist? Is it OK to ignore us because she [pointing to Frankie] has gray hair and I don't look like her?" [pointing to the twenty-something]. The ever-proper Grace admits her outburst lacks decorum, "but I refuse to be irrelevant." Any older woman, especially out on her own, trying to get served at a bar has been through this scene at least once.

The two women—vibrant, mouthy, and energetic—do have their aches and pains, trouble hearing (Frankie), difficulty reading fine print without glasses, and finding their phones. But they are not ready to be treated like Mrs. Fletcher in the infamous LifeCall commercials. When, in one episode, after Grace and Frankie literally fall down and can't get up because of back spasms, their children get each of them panic-alert buttons. Grace regards hers as radioactive, and both insist they are totally unnecessary. As Grace's son adds insult to injury by telling her she shouldn't wear high heels anymore as they're too dangerous, she agrees, takes one off, and smashes one of the panic-alert buttons with her spike heel.

The show's most audacious and courageous story lines confront, more explicitly than any other show, the taboos about older women and sex. Indeed, given how sex-saturated our media are, the show's ongoing confrontation of this subject still comes across as somewhat scandalous. As Grace braves the new world of dating, Frankie asks her if she's worried about vaginal dryness, a topic you could never mention on the networks, despite the wall-to-wall (or bathtub-to-bathtub) Cialis and Viagra commercials. Frankie has her own homemade yam lube that she urges Grace to try, but Grace reacts squeamishly, dramatizing many women's—and also our culture's—association of shame and repulsion with older women's bodies and their sexuality.

Grace does get to the other side of shame, and she and Frankie try to get Grace's daughter Brianna, who has taken over Grace's firm, to market the lube. First they have to admit they both use it, which Brianna cannot deal with, and we're not sure whether that's because it's her mother talking about having sex or the thought of older women doing so, or both. Grace explains to Brianna that "eighty-four percent of postmenopausal women experience pain during sex" and that Brianna's company, which is pursuing a younger consumer, is losing out on a "huge" market that needs such a product. Eventually, Brianna comes around, pitching the idea to her company because "there are twice as many dry vaginas out there as wet ones." This is totally forbidden territory. Indeed, in June 2018, the *New York Times* reported that drug companies have quietly and steadily, over the past five years, doubled the price of drugs that treat the condition (which some insurance companies refuse to cover) with little outcry because "the topic—women's sex lives and their vaginas—is still pretty much taboo." As one doctor noted, "Unlike EpiPen, women are not going to be rising up and saying, 'My vagina is dry and I don't want to pay $2000 to $3000 a year.'"[31]

Later in the series, after Grace has sprained her hand using a vibrator, she and Frankie decide to make an ergonomically correct one for older women, which includes glow-in-the-dark controls and large-print instructions. When they announce this new venture to their ex-husbands and adult children, everyone is aghast. So they seek to shock them even more. "Oh, grow up, older women masturbate too!" exclaims Grace. "And we have vaginas," adds Frankie. Grace's daughter asks, "How do I explain to my children that their grandma makes sex toys for other grandmas?" This scene in particular really drills into the shared cultural horror of thinking about older women as still sexually desirous and active. It also drills into the anathema topic—especially for women—of masturbation; it's so taboo that everyone acts as if it's completely abhorrent. Now the formerly uptight Grace proclaims, "We are sick and tired of being dismissed by people like you," to which Frankie adds, "Mic drop," and they stride out of the house like homeys in slow motion to rap music.

Grace and Frankie then try to get a bank loan for their vibrator business, but the loan officer turns them down, not because they're selling a sex toy but primarily because he thinks they're too old. Grace calls it "ageist bullshit," and Frankie adds, "Jeez, I was blasting Drake all the way here!" to deflate the notion that the last music that boomers knew about was Sam the Sham and the Pharaohs. "Do we look like we're about to die?" demands Grace. "Do we look like we're senile and can't remember anything?"

As they seek to market their product, they have to confront these cultural prohibitions about older women, and about their sexuality. They know that one of the obstacles is the very word "masturbation": "how do we get people to try a product no one will admit they want or need?" asks Grace. When they explore partnering with a company that specializes in erotica, the marketing team unveils packaging featuring Grace and Frankie, except that they have been photoshopped to look decades younger. An incredulous Grace says, "We look twelve years old in those pictures." They insist they want to reach out to older women, and the head of the company insists she does too, "But that's not how you sell it. The research is overwhelming; no one wants to see older women on a vibrator box and nobody wants to see older women with anything sexy, not even older women."

In the life-imitates-art department, Tomlin told one reporter, "Every TV show we've been on [to promote *Grace and Frankie*], we'd been cautioned not to say 'vibrator,' to say 'sex toy.' On the 'Today' show, we talked about it anyway, but they were on the discouraging side."[32] Back in the fantasyland of La Jolla, Grace and Frankie market the device on their own, and their online sales go through the roof. As one friend of their age reports after trying the Vybrant, "It awakened something in me I thought was long dead; you two are doing God's work." This is a major mission of the show, to transform the seemingly taboo into something normal.

I confess I love this show, in part because I love Tomlin and Fonda, especially together, but also because of the heroic demolition it is seeking to aim at gendered ageism. The characters' love for each other reminds me of my deep, often lifelong, friendships with women my age. And I have a lot of company. One look at the *Grace and Frankie* Facebook page (approximately 540,000 likes and followers as of this writing) reveals not only an emotionally intense and grateful engagement with the show, its characters, and plotlines (people give recommendations about what should happen in the next season), but also a powerful sense of community among the fans, who exchange comments with each other as well. As they discuss particular episodes or seasons, they participate in discussions about how aging is viewed, and how it should be viewed. Beachfront property aside, fans see the show as "true to life," a "real show for mature women" that "takes up real life issues." They see themselves in the characters and have a gratifying sense of recognition in the dilemmas Grace and Frankie face. What these viewers especially value is how the show depicts the physical indignities of getting older and how ageism is structured into so many taken-for-granted aspects of everyday life (like trying to get attention from a sales clerk), yet at the same time shows two assertive, outspoken women pushing back against it all. "You ladies have been a lantern in my life," posted one sixty-two-year-old woman.[33] On top of this, both Fonda and show creator Kauffman report that many younger women are fans of the show, saying it makes them less anxious about getting older, especially given the fun (and the sex) Grace and Frankie get to have.

At the same time, however, there is the aspirational aging problem. In one scene, when Jane Fonda is about to have sex with her love interest, she puts on a body-hugging, spaghetti-strapped, floor-length nightgown and she looks amazing. Hardly any of us look like that in a nightgown! (How many of us looked like that when we were twenty?) So there is that. In a scene from season four that has gone viral—13 million views, over 100,000 shares, and over 6500 comments—Grace confronts her love interest Nick (Peter Gallagher, at sixty-three years old nearly twenty years younger) about their relationship, saying she can't compete with younger women anymore. When he insists she doesn't have to, she contends that "once you see the real me, you're going to run for the hills." As she asks, "You think you can handle this?" she pulls off her false eyelashes and hair extensions, wipes off her makeup—all the trappings of youthful femininity—and says there's only one direction she goes from here, "and it's not prettier." Nick kisses her and affirms, "I'll take it!" Viewers loved that, once Grace exposed and stripped off elements of her youthful masquerade, Nick was not taken aback at all by her unvarnished appearance; it was Grace the person he wanted. While this scene exposes how many older women feel they must participate in the regimens of the beauty industry (and many enjoy doing so), Fonda—no makeup and all—still embodies an impossible model of aging that few of us can achieve.

So, while it is thrilling to see these negative stereotypes about older women's sexuality punctured, the flip side is how being sexually active—more to the point, enjoying "hot" heterosexual copulation—might be coming to be a key indicator—almost a compulsory one?—of successful aging.[34] With stories and headlines blaring "Energize Your Sex Life," "Better Sex than Ever," "How to Stay Hot," or, more insidiously, "The more sex you have now, the lower your risk for dementia," if you're not wrecking the sheets on a regular basis, you are not tackling this stage of life properly or valuing your health.[35] Women's sexuality, what we should or shouldn't feel or do, is still being dictated to us after all these years.

Older age—just like adolescence—is being increasingly sexualized in the media, with still being sexually active or, even better, still sexy as *the* way to distinguish yourself as not old.[36] How did being sexy become a damn lifelong project? With all the things older women have done and achieved, they're still reduced to how their bodies look. As per usual, we confront another double-edged sword of the media binaries presented to women: svelte, Jimmy Choo–wearing cougar on the prowl versus L.L.Bean-clad asexual grandma who may be repeating herself too much because she's not getting laid enough.

Well, at least we get Frankie, Lily Tomlin's dashiki-wearing, bong-toting, free-spirited character. Tomlin, not conventionally beautiful, has always had an elastic, animated face able to convey so much irony and skepticism about cultural norms that she has been, to many of us, magnetically attractive. And just as *Grace and Frankie* was picking up steam, we got *Grandma* (2015), Tomlin's tour de force portrayal of Elle, a broke, feminist, lesbian poet approached by her pregnant granddaughter who needs to find $600 in a hurry to pay for an abortion. In what becomes an intergenerational road trip, Elle and her granddaughter (Julia Garner) try to get money from the baby's ne'er-do-well father, whom Elle smacks in the balls with his hockey stick, and a tattoo artist who owes Elle money but is also broke, so she gives Elle a tattoo instead. Elle—mouthy, sardonic, defiant—who indeed succeeds in helping her granddaughter get the abortion—is unlike nearly every grandmother we've seen on the screen. And as Frankie, Tomlin's character does not shy away from staking her claim to visibility: she sports big jewelry, harem pants, and bold-patterned, dressed-to-kill floor-length dresses, when she isn't in her ripped-knee denim overalls or Led Zeppelin T-shirt. Frankie does not obsess about being thin or about fashion trends; she has her own flamboyant look that she owns. In these two roles, Tomlin has given us a different aspirational model, legitimating older women's moxie and happy embrace of who they are.

A related and growing visibility revolt, especially but not only about older women claiming fashion and a look of one's own, is happening online and on Instagram—you know, those platforms we supposedly know nothing about. Women like Lyn Slater (age sixty-four, 537,000 Instagram followers), fashion designer Jenny Kee (age seventy-one, over 33,000 followers), former Playboy Bunny and fashion blogger Dorrie Jacobson (age eighty-three, over 36,000 followers), Sarah Jane Adams (age sixty-three, 177,000 followers, whose hashtag is #mywrinklesaremystripes), and others post images and comments and write blogs about fashion and loving yourself, and being cool as you age. They and their devoted followers commiserate about the body's betrayals while also affirming the right for those bodies to be visible and out in the world. While Dorrie Jacobson, slim, gorgeous, and pictured in a sleeveless black dress, confesses, "I hate my arms. I think most women do," she continues that, nonetheless, it's hot and she has decided to talk back to her "inner critic . . . that little voice inside my head [that] shames me into covering up my imperfections." She then asks, "Do we need to be more accepting of our flaws?" Comments thank her for her frankness, admit to the same doubts, with posts affirming, "Get it Girl! Freedom for us all!!," "My HERo," and "I am 72 . . . I bare my arms and don't care what others think. Totally into comfort!! You go girl!"

These women and their followers, in voices most of the media ignore, also rail against gendered ageism and are evidence of the rebellion that's begun among women. In one post (over 2000 likes), Jacobson proclaims, "Dear World Media: Please Stop Calling Me 'Grandma.' At the age of 83, I'm so much more than that." As a model, a writer, and a pro-aging activist, Jacobson's mission is to "work tirelessly to promote the idea that older women can remain cool, stylish and relevant . . . that we don't have to fade into the background or become a side note in a youth obsessed society." Like so many older women, she too is searching for a more expansive vocabulary "to include more age positive language. Sorry, but 'Granny' just isn't cutting it anymore. What are your thoughts?" This post produced an outpouring of comments, especially among women who had never had children, but also among those who insist that "a woman is much more than her reproductive history" and hate the reduction of all older women to "grannies." Again, most of these Instagram stars are slim and conventionally attractive and have the resources to buy very hip, often high-end clothes. Nonetheless, that they are staking fashion out as an acceptable, fun, even audacious mode of expression for older women is being embraced by other women who may not be as slim or gorgeous, but who feel powerfully affirmed that they have every right to remain visible and, not as trivial as it sounds, to convey who they are through their clothes.

Then there was a visibility revolt sadly gone awry. I say sadly because truly vile off-screen attitudes and politics deep-sixed a show that, despite its problems, was trying to do something new and important. In March of 2018, ABC launched a reboot of the hit series *Roseanne* (1988–1997). The show soared to the top of the ratings with over 18 million viewers for its early episodes—1980s numbers unheard of in this age of micro-niche media and time-shifting viewing. According to the *Hollywood Reporter*, it was "the highest-rated regularly scheduled scripted show of the last few seasons . . . as well as the highest-rated sitcom broadcast in over three years."[37] Because Roseanne Barr had gone from outspoken feminist and progressive working-class advocate in the 1980s and 1990s to rabid and toxic Trump supporter on Twitter (where she promoted various bonkers conspiracy theories, like "Pedogate," which accuses some Trump opponents of being part of a secret pedophile ring), massive critical attention to the series was inevitable. Was this some long-awaited show about "the heartland" finally speaking to those previously ignored in flyover country? Did the success of the show speak to a new cultural power for Trump supporters? ("'Roseanne' Reboot Viewers Came from Republican States," reported *Broadcasting & Cable*; "Red States, Ratings Gold" proclaimed *The Today Show*.)[38]

Lost in the show's instant cancellation due to its star's offensive tweets was the fact that there was something else different about the series besides its politics: the ages of the top three stars: Roseanne Barr (sixty-five), John Goodman (sixty-five), and Laurie Metcalf (sixty-two). So, while *Roseanne* was cast by many in the media as a visibility revolt on behalf of the underrepresented Trump voter, not mentioned was that it was also part of the escalating visibility revolt that older actresses with clout were enacting in all types of entertainment venues. Notably, given the age of its top stars, hardly any of the commercials aired on the show for products such as Chase Mobile Apps, NexGard flea and tick protection, Laughing Cow cheese, Duracell batteries, the Lincoln MKX, or Ramada Inns featured an older woman. The two exceptions were a line-free, poreless Nicole Kidman (fifty) pitching Neutrogena

Rapid Wrinkle Repair and a Diet Pepsi ad saying it was what your mom drank when she was young and showing a young blonde hippie dancing. It then cuts to an attractive, silver-haired older woman sitting with a younger woman by a pool outside a swanky house as the voice-over says, "and drinks now that she's . . ." The silver-haired woman cuts in and warns the male voice, "Don't you dare," because he's about to say "old."

Roseanne (reported net worth, $80 million)[39] has admitted to having multiple cosmetic procedures that the working-class woman she portrayed on the show could never afford.[40] That aside, the show sought to deal with some of the challenges older working-class Americans might face while also taking on some ageist stereotypes. Because of crappy or minimal health insurance, Roseanne and Dan are seen in the first episode sharing their medications: statins, anti-inflammatories, pain meds, and antidepressants. (One fails utterly to understand how this depiction squares with Barr's support of Trump's obsession with dismantling Obamacare.) Yet the show makes it clear that Dan and Roseanne love each other and have an active sex life. They're both still working: Dan in construction and Roseanne driving an Uber part-time. And the show captures how many sixty-five-year-old women feel about themselves. Roseanne has a bad knee, so Dan installs a chair escalator for her to more easily get upstairs. She initially refuses to use it, denouncing it as something "for old people" and declaring that she's "young and vibrant" (although she eventually accepts it).

In one episode, played for both shock value and laughs, Roseanne and Jackie's mother (Estelle Parsons at ninety) gets kicked out of her retirement home because "apparently at my age I'm not supposed to enjoy a healthy sex life." She reports to them that she had sex with "multiple partners in multiple parts of the facility," and asks if it is "so difficult to imagine" that she still might want to have sex. Maggie Kuhn would have loved it. Nonetheless, in a subsequent episode, Roseanne's daughter Becky, who has taken her grandmother into her home, runs into Roseanne's house to announce with horror that her grandmother is having sex in her apartment and Roseanne and Jackie have to get her grandmother out of there. So just when the show acknowledges that one's sex drive does not wither and die as your wrinkles proliferate, it also casts sex among older people as appalling.

I wish the Roseanne of 2018 was still the progressive, feminist Roseanne of 1988, because that Roseanne could have fought for a kind of visibility we hardly ever, ever see: that of the older, working-class woman dealing with Social Security, Medicare, attacks on health care, and a government hostile to pretty much all of her needs.

So, what are we to make of these escalating revolts? Does it matter in the real, everyday world of ordinary women when female celebrities use their fame to amplify their protests against ageism? Given the rampant celebrification of American culture, one of the main ways—often the only way—that older women and their specific issues, their defiance of ageist stereotypes, and their ongoing aspirations get acknowledged in the mainstream is through the visibility of older actresses who can still get roles, open movies or television shows, and use those roles to speak out. *Book Club*, *Grace and Frankie*, and the like are so welcome because of how emphatically they insist on the coming-of-age process as affirming and full of life. This particular enactment of celebrity feminism, however embedded in the real-estate-porn beach houses of Santa Monica or La Jolla, may be candy-coated fluff, but as the feminist writer and activist Andi Zeisler notes, "An important part of social change is shifting public perceptions with images."[41]

These images remain a very important start, because when beautiful, fashionable, active, opinionated, and outspoken women make it clear that aging is not a disaster—far from it—it begins a conversation about how destructive and obsolete the age-phobia endemic in our culture really can be. Their on- and off-air insurgencies can validate our own desires for change and buttress our aspirations and self-esteem.

Unfortunately, these visions of cool, sex- and romance-filled aging have, so far, been restricted to traditionally beautiful, highly privileged, primarily straight white characters. (As one reviewer noted about *Book Club*, "Welcome to an L.A. where no people of color live, work or even qualify as background players.")[42] These visibility revolts fail to depict how the added strain of being a woman of color, lesbian, or without such financial resources can intersect with ageism to complicate not only how one is regarded but also how one must live. And while it is indeed feminist to repeatedly call out, with however much humor, how ageism disproportionately affects women, a rom-com like *Book Club* is far removed from the folding chairs and wood-paneled rooms where older women organize politically, and push for change, or simply seek to preserve the few programs and policies still left that serve us. What remains to be seen is whether these feminist-informed and defiant critiques of gendered ageism can lead to a greater awareness of its consequences, which might in turn inform policies that affect older women, including those not as cushioned from the financial and other vagaries of getting older.

Thus, while these revolts matter a lot, and are deeply satisfying, they are mostly, probably even deliberately, depoliticized, as they are cultural and social revolts, primarily on behalf of upper-middle-class white women. Visibility revolts so far are the protestations of the privileged. Roseanne showed, until her bigotry got the better of her, that people would indeed watch a television show about older working-class people. In 2017, Frances McDormand (sixty), Laurie Metcalf (sixty-two), and Allison Janney (fifty-eight) all took on difficult and partially or totally unappealing working-class characters in *Three Billboards Outside Ebbing, Missouri*; *Lady Bird*; and *I, Tonya*, in which they transgressed the normative expectations about femininity and motherhood. All three movies were critically acclaimed, all three actresses were nominated for Oscars, and McDormand and Janney won. Who says viewers won't watch movies featuring older women in prominent roles, and not just ones where they are dolled up?

Despite the exclusions and narrow focus of most of the visibility revolts, they need to expand and continue. Why? Because guess who's watching television and going to the movies? People aged fifty and older make up 31 percent of all moviegoers over the age of fourteen and are more likely to go to the movies than the general population. They account for nearly a third of all domestic cinema visits, and they go to the movies approximately two percent more than the general population. They see, on average, 6.8 movies annually, and those over sixty-five see an average of 7.3 annually. Older moviegoers are especially crucial to the success of independent movies, making up 75 percent of all those ticket sales.[43]

Visibility matters. And visibility revolts matter. On August 26, 1970, when women who lived far from New York, LA, Boston, or Chicago turned on their TVs and saw the massive demonstrations for women's rights, they learned of the bourgeoning movement called women's liberation that, if they embraced it, might change their lives. They also learned that their own personal indignities and injustices might actually be political issues. Indeed, most women learned about the women's movement from the media which, despite its often-condescending coverage, gave feminists a national platform.[44]

The media—the news, of course, but also entertainment—can help make people aware of social movements and how some groups in our culture have been marginalized. Joe Biden's comment that "I think *Will & Grace* probably did more to educate the

American public [about gay rights] than almost anything anybody's ever done so far," was hyperbolic and ignored other multiple, earlier media examples of gay visibility, but it wasn't wrong.

Betty White, Jane Fonda, Lily Tomlin, Rita Moreno, Helen Mirren, Meryl Streep, and others have staked their claim, often on behalf of the rest of us, to be seen, heard, and regarded with fresh eyes. And for that we are completely grateful. But within the guiding framework of aspirational aging, with its class and racial biases about who deserves the spotlight and who doesn't, and its insistence on personal responsibility, a lot of women are left out. More to the point, these women are the targets of an unspoken, never-acknowledged war against them and, indeed, against all older women. It's time to name and call out that war.

CHAPTER 6

The War on Older Women

FAR AWAY FROM the bougainvillea-draped precincts of southern California, and in the less-friendly, Corinthian-columned, gilt-embellished, white-male-dominated U.S. Capitol (where of the one hundred statues of dignitaries in its collection, only nine are women), a very different drama has been unfolding, especially over the past thirty years or so: the determined effort to eliminate, or at least claw back, some of the so-called entitlements that support millions of older Americans. This has been happening at the state level as well. It has been one of the most lusted-after goals of neo-conservatives, the bull's-eye target of market fundamentalism. The great and obvious irony here is that these efforts to relegate older people to living on cat food and never seeing a doctor again coincide with the increasing graying of America; talk about one arrow going up and another going down!

In all the talk, much of it hypocritical and dishonest mansplaining about what this means for "our seniors" (God, *when* can we get rid of that term?), an immensely important yet totally unacknowledged core of the campaign has not been called out, and it needs to be: this is a war against older women. To track it, we need to look at a different medium, the news, and the role it has played in abetting the war while also rendering its gendered consequences invisible.

Here is the basic takeaway: neoconservatism, the avid belief in the free market, is not only sexist, it is also ageist, and racist, and has women of a certain age—especially those not basking in the sun in Malibu—directly in its crosshairs. Yes, while gutting Medicare or Social Security will affect everyone over sixty-five (and some much younger), women live longer than men and typically have less saved up in Social Security because of lifelong lower salaries, work interruptions to care for children (and others), or minimal to no savings because they did not work outside the home (or, like domestic workers, were paid under the table, so have nothing). Nearly 55 percent of Social Security recipients are women.[1] Medicaid is also crucial to them. African American and Latina women have been especially concentrated in lower-paying jobs that typically lack pensions of any sort. They are also less likely to have any home equity or lifelong investments.[2] The number of Native American women over sixty-five has increased dramatically since 2000, yet they remain completely unnoticed and confront an even more fractured infrastructure of care.[3]

So millions of women enter this stage of life with fewer resources than men, yet our system of support has not even begun to catch up with this situation, to make sure older women are not further penalized for earning lower salaries or for their work as often-unpaid caretakers earlier in their lives.[4] While most older women are usually unseen on the screens of America, everyday middle-class women, working-class women, and poor women are rarely seen, except, occasionally, as disaster victims. This invisibility—what they are going through and what they need—powerfully enables their neglect in the very political precincts that should be attending to them. At the same historical moment when there are more women over fifty than ever before, our public policies lag woefully behind the demographic shift, with right-wing politicians seeking to make matters worse.

How far we've come from the 1960s and 1970s, when middle- and upper-middle-class white women, however blindered some were to their own race and class privilege, organized and marched and protested in demonstrations and rallies with those discriminated against, unable to vote, living in poverty, or sent off to war. Thousands joined the Peace Corps in what they felt was a mission to improve the lives of others. The social-justice movements back then might have been overly idealistic and naive, and there may have been insensitivities and stupidities within them, but despite their unfinished business, and even rollbacks, they tried to—and often did—change the country for the better.

These movements were individualistic—we women, for example, did want barriers knocked down for ourselves—but they were also communal and cooperative, in that many of us—including national leaders—truly believed that we needed to work together to expand social and economic benefits for as many people as possible. There was a sense that we had obligations to each other, and especially to those with fewer resources than we had. In addition, girls and women have historically been socialized to value, build, and sustain relationships. We did not believe that the care of others should be left to "the market," where people must fend for themselves. Of the many assumptions market fundamentalism sought to throttle, this belief in fairness, in justice, and in fellowship had to be strangulated, replaced by an "I've-got-mine-and-too-bad-about-you" mind-set.

While the rich get richer—the DeVos family and their ten yachts, Jeff Bezos and his five homes plus 290,000 acres of land in Texas, Larry Ellison (Oracle CEO) and his very own Hawaiian island (Lanai), plus "a flood of new millionaires around the world who like showing off"[5]—condo and McMansion builders, handbag companies, watch makers, Gucci fur slippers ($1800; you look like you have Chewbacca's scalp on your feet), all promote their wares as the enviable, barely attainable consumer goods that are supposedly an orgasmic thrill to own. Being rich, especially filthy rich, despite—and no doubt because of—massive income inequality, continues to be promoted as the most intoxicating state of being one can achieve. As images of Louis XIV–level opulence—from celebrities to athletes and tech billionaires—colonize the screens and dreams of Americans, being middle-class, let alone financially insecure, has become even more abject and reviled. Media imagery is supposed to be aspirational; it's supposed to make us happy and eager to buy more stuff. People without money, especially if they're older and female—well, who wants to see that? So, we don't.

If we are to reinvent the road ahead, those of us sipping our Pinot Noir need to put our goblets down for just a minute and focus on this war against older women. It is actually a war against us all, but some of us are and will be much more brutalized by it than others. To fight back, we need to revive that suffocated notion of collective responsibility, or what we used to think of as the common good. Just like reproductive rights, sexual harassment and assault, the lack of decent and affordable childcare, pay disparities, and LGBTQ rights (to name a few), the economic insecurity and overall discrimination facing older women must be a front-and-center feminist issue. This is not just a war on people's mothers, grandmothers, aunts, friends, former teachers, mentors, and the like; this is an assault that will affect younger women as well if we don't fight it now. This mission is foundational to lifespan feminism.

Income inequality, which has become a major political issue—with the United States having one of the largest gaps between the rich and the poor in the world—powerfully affects older women. The median income of people sixty-five and older in 2016 was just over $31,000 for men and an impossible-to-live-on $18,000 for women.[6] For African American women, the average Social Security income in 2014 was $12,640.[7] In 2016, the average annual Social Security income that women over sixty-five received was a shocking $13,891, way below what twenty-eight countries as diverse as Turkey, Denmark, Iceland, France, and Estonia pay in public pensions.[8] For 61 percent of older beneficiaries, Social Security is the majority of their cash income; for a third, it provides 90 percent or more of their income.[9] For older single women, the reliance on the program is even greater. Almost half of women over seventy-five live alone, so do not have anyone sharing living expenses. Older women are 80 percent more likely to wind up in poverty than men, with women of color having the highest poverty rates.[10] And as baby boomers approach retirement, only 55 percent have money saved. It makes sense, then, that 65 percent are worried about changes to Social Security.[11]

Social Security, which for decades was pretty much politically untouchable, has become a bête noire of neoconservatives who loathe social welfare programs, and more and more they are finding it safer to attack. Their gambit is to accuse those who must rely on Social Security for the bare basics of somehow ripping off hard-working American taxpayers. No one—well, except for some truly ideologically straitjacketed right wingers—would have dared to try to take these benefits away from "the Greatest Generation," those who survived the Depression and won World War II. But baby boomers? Those narcissistic, self-indulgent bloodsuckers? Now that's a different story.

An ongoing, relentless trend in public commentary, pioneered almost exclusively by seemingly self-loathing baby boom men, has emerged that weaponizes this war: the genre of baby boom bashing. The trashing of baby boomers by their elders as spoiled and entitled brats (as well as immoral and unpatriotic hedonists) goes back to the late 1960s when millions protested against the Vietnam War and became dedicated to various social movements challenging the status quo. But *self*-flagellation started ramping up in the early twenty-first century. Sample article and essay titles by male boomers themselves include "The Greediest Generation," "The Worst Generation," and "Baby Boomers: It's All Your Fault."

Boomer, political consultant, and adviser to the first boomer president, Bill Clinton, Paul Begala asserted in 2000, "The Baby Boomers are the most self-centered, self-seeking, self-interested, self-absorbed, self-indulgent, self-aggrandizing generation in American history." They "can't grow up . . . women who once eschewed lipstick are now getting liposuction. . . ."[12] Not to be outdone, boomer writer and editor Daniel Okrent proclaimed a year later, "There is so, so much to loathe about the boomers," insisting that they were "fatuous, self-important and lazy," as well as "preening, self-congratulatory, caviling solipsists," which was why they aroused so much resentment from Americans in their twenties and thirties. That same year Joe Queenan published *Balsamic Dreams: A Short But Self-Important History of the Baby Boomer Generation*, characterizing his generation as "a whiny, narcissistic bunch of paunchy, corporatized losers."[13] In his takedown, Queenan wrote, "We were appalling. We had appalling values." The "horrid truth" was "we had threadbare values . . . we became crass and self-absorbed . . . we stopped caring about anything except money and food."[14]

Alex Beam, protesting in an op-ed piece, "No! No! I'm Not a Baby Boomer," asked "How does one loathe the boomers? Let me count the ways." Aging boomers were "graying spongers, bent on retiring early, living forever and enjoying the 'good life.'" They were determined to bleed "entitlement payments out of their own children, consequences be damned."[15] Nicholas Kristof of the *New York Times* surmised that "we'll be remembered mostly for grabbing resources for ourselves," and for "preying on children" by ballooning the national debt, which was nothing less than "fiscal child abuse."[16] This is just a partial sampling of this bile-filled genre. These think pieces cast all boomers as feckless, unprincipled, self-serving, self-promoting leeches who never really cared about social justice or the common good; it was all a pose; they all sold out.

I must be part of the wrong crowd, as I don't personally know and have never known baby boom men who have hated their own generation. But baby boom women? Like *all* baby boom women? Greedy? Spongers? Crass and self-absorbed? Lazy? Corporatized losers? The women who pioneered the "second shift," taking care of the home and family after a full day's work outside the home, thus often putting in something like seventy-hour workweeks? (That was called, playfully, "juggling.") The African American, Latina, and working-class women who scrubbed floors after working eight hours as a cashier at Toys"R"Us so their kids could go to college? Women who worked in those really self-centered, self-aggrandizing jobs like teacher, nurse, day-care worker, secretary, sales clerk, guidance counselor, beautician, social worker, community organizer, nursing-home attendant, or waitress? Women who stayed at home to raise their kids and tend to their families, sacrificing their own income and enduring the "so what do you do?" questions that often made them feel small? Women who worked their butts off to become the "first female" whatever—store manager, law partner, college president, editor in chief, firefighter—paving the way for the women behind them?

OK, so not all baby boom women are Mother Teresa, but not *all* baby boomers are any one thing. And sure, there are baby boom women indulging in $1000 fringed and blaringly branded handbags. But this kind of monolithic generational stereotyping is moronic as well as false. (The poor millennials are faring no better. Type in "millennials are" in a Google search and two of the top words that pop up are "lazy" and "entitled," both of which, in my own experience, do not describe the millennials I know.)

But let's note something else important here: these stereotypes are sexist and completely erase baby boom women's contributions over the decades to the workplace, educational institutions, the law, our culture, their children, and their families. And the problem is that these stereotypes can enable punishing changes in public policy while masking how they disproportionately affect women. With words like "onslaught" or "tsunami" used to describe the growing number of retiring baby boomers, "reformers" want Social Security and Medicare to appear to be overwhelmed, about to be washed away. Plus, why sustain these programs anyway, when their recipients are self-centered, avaricious, entitled, and, most important, undeserving freeloaders? More to the point, why waste good money on people who are in their final innings? And let's not forget the edicts of aspirational aging, where older women who are aging successfully don't need help from the government, and those who aren't—the ones on the floor groping for their medical alert—should pull themselves up and assume some responsibility, or just become bag ladies. If older women are stereotyped on the one hand as self-empowered, independent, and rolling in dough, and on the other as forgetful, sexless, unattractive, frail, dependent, and irrelevant, who would want to support government policies on their behalf either way?

How and why did we get here? Social Security can be traced back to the New Deal and Franklin Roosevelt's presidency. But it was an older woman, Frances Perkins, fifty-three at the time, who proposed the reforms that became "the cornerstones of the New Deal." When Roosevelt invited her to become his secretary of labor, making her the first female cabinet member, she told him she would accept on the condition that he backed her plans to support women and families. These plans included abolishing child labor, pushing for a forty-hour workweek, creating unemployment compensation, establishing public-works programs that would hire workers and improve the country's infrastructure, and creating an "old-age pension."[17] This last program became Social Security, established in 1935. Various widespread and highly publicized activist movements had been agitating for some kind of guaranteed income for older people, in response to the fact that during the Great Depression, over half of older people did not have enough money to support themselves, with two-thirds living in penury. Widows left with nothing were especially poignant examples of indigence.

Social Security consisted of two parts: it provided the states with grants to immediately provide "old-age assistance," and it inaugurated a program that taxed people's salaries while they worked and stashed it in a "social insurance" plan they could draw on when they retired. The point was to have people contribute to their own future pensions.

Social Security, and other New Deal programs, rested on a new, caring, mutually supportive common understanding, made stark by the Depression, that it was the responsibility of the state to provide for the welfare of its citizens and to see the welfare of older people as a collective responsibility. (Or at least some of them: It is crucial to note that Social Security excluded agricultural and domestic workers—at the time about half the workers in the country, many of whom were African American.)[18] Extending this ethos, and as part of his goal to eliminate poverty, President Lyndon Johnson enacted Medicare in 1965, noting that in the 1930s, "the American people made a basic decision that the later years of life should not be years of despondency and drift." A study during the Kennedy administration had revealed that 56 percent of people over sixty-five had no health insurance; Johnson proclaimed that Medicare would now free older people "from the fear of financial hardship in the event of illness."[19]

Republicans have been vilifying Social Security from the moment it was proposed, never acknowledging what it meant to older women. Hyperbole was their favorite weapon of choice. The program would "impose a crushing burden on industry and labor," they warned in 1935. "Never in the history of the world has any measure been brought here so insidiously designed as to prevent business recovery, to enslave workers and to prevent any possibility of the employers providing work for the people," was one fulmination. Roosevelt's 1936 opponent, Alf Landon, castigated Social Security as "a fraud on the workingman" and "a cruel hoax"; Roosevelt crushed him in the election (Landon got eight electoral college votes). Over the years, various Republicans have pushed to limit benefits or gut the program, efforts that Republican President Eisenhower in 1955 labeled, simply, "stupid."[20]

These attacks remained somewhat quiescent in the 1960s and 1970s, not surprising given the turmoil of the Vietnam War and the civil rights, feminist, gay rights, and environmental movements. But they reemerged with the election of Mr. anti-governmentspending himself, Ronald Reagan, and the rise of what was called neoconservatism. Its basic principles were to slow or eliminate government regulations on businesses, constrain or undo social welfare programs, and have the distribution of as many goods and services as possible handled by the "free market."

To advance these and other goals, the neocon movement shrewdly established, with corporate funding and help, conservative think tanks to issue policy papers and press releases to promote all these goals in the media.[21] As part of this market fundamentalist mantra, Reagan warned that Social Security was "teetering on the edge of bankruptcy," but he did not end up dismantling it, much to the chagrin of the neocons. So the recently founded think tanks— such as the Heritage Foundation, the Cato Institute, and others— pioneered a revised, more corrosive, under-the-radar, long-term campaign to "prepare the political ground" to achieve the "radical reform of Social Security." Their goal? Privatization, or substituting the program with "individual accounts," into which people would invest their own money, which would then be subject to the vagaries of the stock market and dependent on the everyday person's knowledge—and lack of—about investment strategies. In their plan, a guaranteed and reliable program would give way to one subject to the ups and downs of bull and bear markets, just like a 401k. The true beneficiaries here? If instituted, privatization would be a boon to financial advisers, banks, and Wall Street.

How to sell this clawback? Stuart Butler and Peter Germanis of the Heritage Foundation coauthored a manifesto—really a deeply cynical propaganda blueprint—in which they argued that, given the program's huge popularity, what was needed was nothing less than "guerilla warfare against both the current Social Security system and the coalition that supports it."[22] It was crucial to drive a wedge between the old and the young, and to "cast doubt on the picture of reality" the coalition presents to the public: that Social Security was solvent and a still-necessary program. One "myth" requiring particular debunking was the notion that it "is an 'insurance' program financed by 'contributions' that provide an 'earned annuity'"—even though that is exactly what it is! Thus it was important to tarnish the term "entitlement," from something people merited, because they had paid into it, into an undeserved, unearned handout. An "education campaign" had to be launched to "weaken support for the present system" using the support of "key individuals in the media." The "present system" had to be recast as "welfare," which the GOP, with its inflammatory, fraudulent stories about "welfare queens" and recipients driving Cadillacs, had slammed as a corrupt program giving away taxpayer money to no-account cheats.

Especially vital was pitching the "private alternative" to young

people, "its most obvious constituency," in part by telling them
that the system was so bankrupt they'd never get a penny out of it.
Because they recognized that "the elderly represent a very powerful and vocal interest group," and because, politically, they couldn't
take away benefits from those already receiving them, they devised
a plan to "detach, or at least neutralize" the potential objections of
older Americans. They would leave Social Security as is for seniors,
but phase it out for younger people, thus nicely sowing generational resentment and divisions. By separating the two groups,
they could cast older people as parasites sucking Social Security
dry while offering young people what sounded like a rational, proactive solution to the alleged bankruptcy. This will be "a long campaign," they admitted, because "the next Social Security crisis may
be further away than many people believe."[23]

When George W. Bush, another conservative, got into office
in 2001, baby boom bashing was shifting into overdrive. The time
seemed ripe to advocate for the "privatization" of Social Security.
But that word became somewhat radioactive, as it made clear that
a benefit guaranteed for over sixty years could go away. "Banish privatization from your lexicon," warned Republican pollster Frank
Luntz in 2004; now the phrase was Social Security "choice" and
"personal accounts." "Younger workers should have the opportunity to build a nest egg by saving part of their Social Security taxes
in a personal retirement account," Bush proclaimed. "We should
make the Social Security system a source of ownership for the
American people." "Opportunity"; "nest egg"; "ownership"—who
doesn't like those?

Bush claimed that Social Security was "in crisis" and about to
run out of money. He then went out on the road in 2005 to multiple
hustings to pitch Social Security "choice." The Democrats yelled
"pants on fire" to the crisis claim. The opposition to privatization
grew loud and passionate. As the Brookings Institute reported,

"Observers noticed that the more the President talked about Social Security, the more support for his plan declined." Gallup reported that public disapproval of President Bush's handling of Social Security rose by 16 points from 48 to 64 percent—between his 2005 State of the Union address, when he pitched it fervently, and June, when the idea was on life support.[24] Republicans had to back away from any efforts to "reform" Social Security.[25]

However, by 2010, when the midterm elections gave Republicans control of the House of Representatives, and they began screaming about the allegedly disastrous deficit (without noting, of course, how Bush's tax cuts, the Iraq war, and the Great Recession had ballooned it), Social Security was back on the chopping block. (Also not noted was how devastated millions would have been, in the wake of the Great Recession, had their retirement funds been in the stock market instead of in Social Security.)

That year, former senator Alan Simpson (R-WY) interwove the negative attitudes toward baby boomers with a condemnation of Social Security, adding a soupçon of rank sexism. He derided older women seeking to protect Social Security as "Pink Panthers," which Ashley Carson, executive director of the National Older Women's League, denounced as sexist and ageist. Simpson responded, in an instantly notorious email, that she was babbling "into the vapors about 'disgusting attempts at ageism' and all that crap." But the kicker was his feminizing of Social Security itself as bovine, "like a milk cow with 310 million tits," implying, idiotically, that the entire U.S. population was "milking it to the last degree."[26] (After the outcry over the "tits" remark, he issued a lame apology.) Simpson, eighty-one, also had the chutzpah to smear those who were resisting raising the eligibility age for the program as well as proposals to privatize it as "greedy geezers." Because these attacks were inflammatory, they were newsworthy and thus widely reported, fueling the discourse about Social

Security as a welfare program engorging already privileged, entitled, undeserving resource hogs.

As this incident attests, the news media was, and has been, complicit in amplifying the message that Social Security had to be cut, yet rarely broadcasting what that would mean for women. Remember, nearly all the news media in the United States is corporately owned, commercially driven, supported by advertising, and in a constant quest for ratings. And in the 1980s and 1990s, with cuts to newsroom staffs in an effort to maximize profits, various outlets became more susceptible to position papers from think tanks that helped do their work for them. Given all this, it's not surprising that many news organizations, despite the ideal of objectivity, had a bias toward market-driven solutions to social and political issues, and this certainly has been true for coverage of Social Security. Because of their role in explaining policy issues to the public, the news media not only tell people what issues are important to think about but also how to think about them.

In the first three months of 2013, for example, the three largest broadcast and cable news networks dedicated nearly 70 percent of their coverage of Social Security to the alleged solvency problems that could only be fixed through cuts to beneficiaries. A scant 14 percent of the stories gave airtime to how the program might be strengthened, even though the agency's annual report released that year concluded that the program was not facing an immediate crisis and was able to pay full benefits until 2036. The report noted that various fixes, like more fairly taxing the rich, would extend the longevity of the program.[27] Thus the media could have emphasized that, by lifting the cap on income subject to payroll taxes (currently at $127,000), wealthier Americans would pay more of their fair share and would make Social Security solvent for decades.[28] Or they could have suggested other possible solutions, like taxing the income that the wealthy earn from capital gains and inheritances.

Instead, they chose the doom-and-gloom stories. The work of the Heritage Foundation and the Cato Institute, especially their cultivation of the media, was bearing fruit.

Trudy Lieberman, who covers Social Security for the *Columbia Journalism Review*, had already noted in 2012 that "much of the press has reported only one side of this story using 'facts' that are misleading or flat out wrong while ignoring others."[29] Words like "crisis," "insolvency," "running out of time," and "promises [the government] can't keep" all could have come out of the Cato Institute playbook, buttressed by sound bites from neocons from right-wing think tanks—although their conservative credentials were not identified as such.[30] As Theodore Marmor, an expert on Medicare and Social Security, bemoaned, "The elite press repeatedly quotes the commentary of the devoted opponents of social insurance retirement programs," which results in "supporting a strategic attack" on them by the right. Broadcast anchors and guests identified as "experts," but not neocons, emphasized that Social Security was the main cause of the federal deficit (again, unlike tax breaks for the wealthy). Rarely does coverage contradict the falsehood that Social Security is the main cause of the deficit. It is not.

The economist Dean Baker, in his book *Social Security: The Phony Crisis*, coauthored with Mark Weisbrot, emphasized how "generational warriors," using the ageist fears and resentments of "demographic determinism," repeatedly imply that money-squandering baby boomers are "laying waste to the potential savings of Generations X, Y, and Z."[31] Conservative columnist Robert Samuelson asserted in 2012 that Social Security had evolved into "welfare" and that "spending on the elderly is slowly and inexorably crowding out the rest of government."[32] The word "elderly," in referring to people from their mid-sixties on, conjures up people with one foot already out the red exit door—isn't that just pissing money away? And in articles like *Esquire*'s 2012 piece "The War

Against Youth," the descriptive copy reads, "The recession didn't gut the prospects of American young people. The Baby Boomers took care of that." The "biggest boondoggle of all"? Social Security.[33] When the AARP and others opposed cuts to the program, the *Washington Post* derided the "self-centered, shortsighted intransigence" of the "don't-touch-my-benefits purists."[34] But nothing is mentioned about where older women are supposed to find enough money to live on nor why they should give up the money taken out of their paychecks for Social Security year after year!

Why does this negative coverage matter, aside from affirming the fake "Social Security is broken" mantra? Because, with few exceptions, most people don't have any experience with Social Security until they're in their mid-sixties. When personal knowledge about an issue is limited, the news media can have a much greater impact on shaping public understanding about programs and policies. One 1995 study analyzed coverage of Social Security at the Associated Press from 1977 to 1994, along with mainstream news organizations like the *New York Times*, the *Washington Post*, ABC News, and CNN from 1992 to 1994, and found "clear cases of media distortion" with "disproportionate coverage" of the program's problems and "undercoverage of the program's strengths and contributions." The news media's "favorite topic"? Curtailing benefits (40 percent of the coverage), with "Republicans . . . more often used as sources than Democrats." Reporting about alleged problems was double that given to "statements favoring the status quo and maintaining the existing program," and "news stories overwhelmingly reported support for reducing benefits."

Defense of the program by groups like the AARP received "relatively little coverage." The study found that effects on public opinion were mixed. On the one hand, this coverage, alleging support for cuts, "sharply differed" from strong public support for the program and opposition to reducing benefits. On the other hand, when alarmist media coverage increased (in response to conservatives' agitation for "reform"), confidence in the future of the program declined. The study's conclusion? When it comes to Social Security, "no news is good news."[35]

In 2017, with Trump and the Republican Congress gaining control of the government, the survival of Social Security and Medicare seemed in jeopardy. Paul Ryan's fervent dream—by his own admission, something he started fantasizing about in college!—had been to cut Medicaid (which currently supports nearly 7 million people over the age of sixty-five), Medicare, and Social Security. (Ryan was a major proponent of privatizing Social Security.) And Trump (a boomer himself) seemed poised, despite campaign promises, to declare war on his own generation—or at least the ones who didn't live in gilt towers in Manhattan. Most Republicans argue, again, that these programs are bankrupting the country by bloating the deficit—unlike the 2018 tax cuts for the wealthy and corporations, which are projected to add anywhere from $1.9 trillion to $2.3 trillion to the national debt over the next ten years.[36] More to the point, these cuts also mean *less* money going into the Social Security trust fund. When, in the fall of 2018, the *New York Times* posed the question "Does Social Security Add to the Deficit," its response was "It depends on who you ask, but the simple answer is no."[37]

That's not what the allegedly liberally biased NPR had to say. Scott Simon featured Bob Bryan from *Business Insider* in February 2019 to explain how we got to "the biggest national debt ever." The major problem, Bryan observed, is that "we're spending a lot of money on an aging population." Reducing the deficit thus requires unpopular moves like cutting Medicare and Social Security. Simon then asked whether there will be a push to have such "entitlement programs" slashed (as opposed to, say, rescinding the Trump tax cuts), and Bryan reiterated that Social Security,

Medicare, and Medicaid are the "big, long term drivers of the debt."[38] But as Reuters reaffirmed in 2018, simply, "By law, Social Security cannot contribute to the federal deficit, because it is required to pay benefits only from its trust funds."[39]

Social Security is not bankrupt; however, around 2036, if no changes are made to strengthen the program, it will only be able to pay for 75 percent of scheduled benefits.[40] Thus there is time to make adjustments in how much is paid in, especially by those earning more than $127,000 a year, so that it remains able to pay the benefits people have earned.

Blanket attacks made by certain—although mostly white male—Republicans and their neocon think tanks on Social Security, Medicare, and Medicaid as "the driver of our [national] debt" (Marco Rubio [R-FL]) and as "liberal programs" prompting the country to "spend itself into bankruptcy" (Orrin Hatch [R-UT]) are lies. And they mask what their proposed "reforms" would do to the lives of older women. Also ignored and utterly irrelevant to these men is a 2015 report documenting that Social Security lifted more than 22 million people out of poverty, 15 million of them over the age of sixty-five. More than half of those are women. Without Social Security, 41 percent of those older Americans would live in poverty, and over 50 percent of older African Americans would.[41] (Interesting side note: if DACA [Deferred Action for Childhood Arrivals], which allows nearly 800,000 immigrants brought to the country as children to work here legally, is eliminated, that would also reduce money put into Social Security.)[42]

Despite the over-thirty-year right-wing campaign to discredit Social Security and convince people it should be eliminated or replaced, support for the program has remained rock solid, even among the young. The Pew Research Center reported in 2011 that "there is little evidence of generational resentment or friction over what government provides for seniors." In their survey asking whether Social Security "has been good for the country" over the years, 88 percent of boomers said yes, as did the same percentage of Gen Xers and 81 percent of millennials. Agreement about Medicare's positive effects was comparable or even higher. Most respondents agreed that maintaining benefits trumped deficit reduction. Another survey from 2014 found similar results, with nearly nine in ten Americans saying, "Social Security is more important than ever to ensure that retirees have a dependable income," with this support cutting across age and income lines. These respondents supported increasing payroll taxes to keep the program strong, and especially increasing the taxes paid by the wealthy.[43] In its 2017 report, "Few Americans support cuts to most government programs, including Medicaid," Pew Research found that 86 percent of Republicans and 95 percent of Democrats wanted to maintain or increase spending on Social Security.[44]

Where the Heritage-Cato campaign has borne fruit has been in young people's support for privatization, changing the system so that younger workers can invest their Social Security taxes in private retirement accounts.[45] Many young people have been convinced by the repeated media tales of crisis that they will pay into Social Security but get nothing in return.

What about two other benefits that older women rely on: Medicaid and Medicare? Medicaid, the health care program for low-income people, provides essential care for 7 million people over sixty-five, including nursing-home and home care; over half of these are women.[46] Medicare (Part A for hospital stays, Part B for doctors' visits and some medical supplies) is a crucial, although partial, source of economic security for older women; more than half (56 percent) of recipients are women. Republicans have been slavering to slash or eliminate these as well with, again, no acknowledgment of the gender biases involved. In print coverage of Medicare cuts, proposed or real, from 2001 to the present, the sources that people heard from were doctors and how the cuts might affect their practice, and rarely if ever from the recipients themselves. Older women were nonexistent in this reporting.[47]

In his efforts to cut Medicare, demolition plans that go back to at least 2012, Paul Ryan claimed—falsely—that the Affordable Care Act was bankrupting the program, when the opposite is true; Obamacare has extended the solvency of Medicare by over a decade.[48] But we know the truth is irrelevant to this crew. So beware of this user-friendly-sounding concept of "Medicare exchanges," which would convert Medicare from a government-funded single-payer program to a complicated system where private insurance companies would compete with government-run Medicare for customers. People would get "vouchers" (that word should always sound alarms) or, even more rhetorically reassuring, "premium support" from the government to pay for their insurance. If the vouchers aren't enough, well, too bad. Plus, we'd have to grab our magnifying glasses and try to make sense of a host of fine-print options that would make Facebook's "terms of service" seem like a See-Spot-Run book.

The Kaiser Family Foundation, a nonprofit organization focusing on national health issues, estimates that, under Ryan's plan, retirees would have gone from paying 22 percent of their Social Security benefits on health care to 49 percent by 2022.[49] His plan also rested on a cynical effort at generational warfare. To placate current recipients or those just about to retire, the proposal would not apply to anyone currently fifty-five or older; only those younger would be affected.[50] This should outrage everyone, including every older person. Are we really supposed to succumb to a bribe that will leave subsequent retirees impoverished?

Donald Trump's elephantine 2020 budget proposal, the most bloated in the country's history, includes a 5 percent increase in defense spending—more than the Pentagon asked for—and $8.6

billion for his hugely unpopular Mexican border wall, to be paid for in part by major cuts to benefits for older Americans. He would eviscerate Medicare by over $800 billion and Medicaid by $1.5 trillion. Current federal support to the states for Medicaid would be replaced by another caring-sounding program, "market-based health care grants," an idea Republicans themselves rejected in 2017, when they controlled Congress, because it couldn't possibly keep pace with rising health care costs. One hundred billion dollars would be cut from support to nursing homes and health agencies that care for people once they've left the hospital. As icing on the cake, Trump proposed spending $26 billion less on Social Security.[51] While Democrats proclaimed his budget dead on arrival, the fact that these efforts to throw older women to the wolves appear and reappear should be cause for alarm—and political action.

For millions of older women, even those with decent insurance prior to retirement, the uncertainties about what the country will do about health care in general, and for older people in particular, is a source of considerable anxiety and economic stress. Because older women have been poorer than men of the same age, Medicare has played an especially important role in keeping some out of poverty. But Medicare doesn't cover dental care, routine eye exams, hearing aids, home health services, or nursing-home care. Medicare participants need to buy a separate policy to cover prescriptions. As Medicare typically pays for only half of medical costs, older women need to turn to Medicare Advantage and other insurance plans to cover the gap, and some simply don't have the funds to do so.[52] Medicare needs to be strengthened, not have a stake driven into its heart.

All of this is part of the broader agenda of the right to off-load a slew of costs and financial risks onto the 99 percent, with large holes in the safety net for older people. There's just one problem with this. Deregulation, limits on state and federal governmental spending, the privatization of basic services, have been proven to be a massive failure, except for one group: the top one percent. Even a research wing of the International Monetary Fund, that bastion of market fundamentalism, in an article titled "Neoliberalism: Oversold?" admits that some neoliberal policies have "increased inequality." The top one percent in the world reportedly now has as much wealth as the rest of the planet's population combined. In the United States, the top one percent own 40 percent of the nation's wealth, and more wealth than the bottom 90 percent combined. When the other 99 percent can't buy as many goods and services as they used to, this stalls economic growth. One solution? "Policymakers should be more open to redistribution than they are" by relying on "taxes and government spending," especially to minimize the impact of such policies on "low-income groups."[53]

So let's revisit Alan Simpson's blanket greedy-geezer stereotype. It turns out that many older Americans, unlike the sun-dappled images in those Big Pharma ads, are having a tough time. Those who are sixty-five and older are filing for bankruptcy at a rate three times higher than those of the same age did in 1991. Soaring health care costs, vanishing pensions, and debt are some of the major culprits. What kind of debt? Well, some parents cosigned their kids' student loans, which can be hard to get discharged in bankruptcy court. One study found that a third of parents are on the hook for some or all of their children's student loans. Even worse, between 2002 and 2015, the garnishing of people's Social Security checks to pay for student loans, which used to be illegal, increased by a whopping 540 percent.[54] (The change came in 1996 under the soothingly named Debt Collection Improvement Act, designed to enable the government to collect money owed to it, like student loans.) As Deborah Thorne and her coauthors made clear in their 2018 study, "The Graying of U.S. Bankruptcy," "Older Americans' reported reasons for filing strongly suggest that they are experiencing the fallout from our current individualized risk society and the corresponding shrinkage of their social safety net."[55]

To reiterate first principles: neoconservatism and market fundamentalism are hostile to all women except the wealthy, and are particularly, and disproportionately, punishing to older women. Yet hardly anyone is raising this issue. And the most vulnerable women are not part of the target market that Nielsen and *Advertising Age* have been exhorting advertisers to pursue. We rarely see them in the news media or anywhere in popular culture, except for occasional, often negative, images. They remain invisible. Worse, they are made to feel that their financial precarity is not a pressing social issue or a concern of the government. Do we really think that in our country, some older women should be hounded by debt collectors or have to choose between food and medical attention? More women will join their ranks if Social Security or Medicare are reduced.

Those of us with more resources—who are supposed to feel that "there but for the grace of God go I"—cannot let our less-fortunate sisters get kicked to the curb by mostly white men with superior health care and retirement packages who benefit from government largesse but want to eliminate it for women (except perhaps for their wives). So, as feminists strap on our policy polygraphs, unmasking lies, what rhetoric should make those needles go into the red-danger, chicanery zone? Proposals to "modernize" Medicare, which usually means "annihilate." Ditto for neutral-sounding terms like "entitlement reform," "structural changes," and "saving," which should be immediately dismissed as mansplaining bunkum. One 2016 "reform" plan, put forward by Sam Johnson, the Republican head of the House Subcommittee on

Social Security, wanted to raise the eligibility age to sixty-nine, cut benefits by one third, yet, at the same time, give tax breaks to affluent retirees. Some estimates are that for retirees whose average annual incomes were quite modest—between $28,000 and $49,000—their benefits would decrease by 28 percent.[56]

Baby boom women have a major opportunity to redefine attitudes and policies that will be much friendlier not just to us, but to those who come after us. And the biggest challenge is how to change the imagery, the conversation, and the assumptions. Can we help to enable an historical reversal of the market fundamentalism project, given the inescapable allures of the meritocratic, self-actualizing individualism of aspirational aging?

Yes, we can. Because market fundamentalism, despite all its macho posturing, is also crippling the finances and aspirations of many young people. The Republicans have demonized increased taxes on the wealthy for decades as bad for the economy when the opposite is true. Indeed, most Americans believe that the wealthy should pay their fair share of taxes, and that "share" got even lower with Trump's much-ballyhooed 2017 tax cuts, even as they bloated the deficit—a Republican source of outrage only when the Democrats are in charge. By the summer of 2018, various polls showed that public support for that massive gift to our nation's corporations and plutocrats was hovering at just 34 percent of the population.[57] As Lynn Parramore, a research analyst at the Institute for New Economic Thinking, succinctly put it in 2018, "Current tax policy, then, has been instituted against the will of the people, and is in opposition to their health and wellbeing."[58]

So let's call out this political and economic war against older women as a major feminist issue. And instead of fake, media-fanned "wars" between millennials and boomers, compartmentalizing people into monolithic generational groups, it's time to build new alliances across the generations around a host of feminist issues. Economic issues, like income inequality, have a greater impact on women throughout the arc of their lives. Relegating debates about Social Security and Medicare as being of concern only to "seniors" cordons women off from each other by age and erases the profoundly gendered consequences of vilifying these crucial—and earned—benefits.

CHAPTER 7

Lifespan Feminism, Bridge Groups, and the Road Ahead

TODAY, WOMEN OF A CERTAIN AGE feel ourselves to be at another turnstile moment, poised between outdated norms that seek to render us irrelevant, voiceless, and invisible, and our own widening rebellion against such strictures. We are rejecting acquiescence and inequality, and, instead, are claiming our right to be seen, heard, and respected in the world. So much in our media and culture tell us the main thing we should feel about being older is shame, especially, because we are women, over how we look. They also erase from view women who cannot afford to personify the ideals of aspirational aging, buttressing the notion that most older women do not matter at all.

We are, in many ways, in a similar, contradictory place to where girls and women were in the late 1960s and early 1970s, corralled by dismissive and trivializing media stereotypes and retrograde, sexist public policies, while at the same time rebelling against being penned in simply because of our gender and, now, our age. Once again pulled in opposite directions—messages suggesting we should go sit in our rocking chairs and be quiet and invisible, versus the budding visibility revolts countering such tired assumptions—millions of older women, famous and not, are pushing for another liberation. When Ruth Bader Ginsburg, in her eighties, a deeply admired jurist, is a feminist pop cultural icon for women in their twenties and thirties, we can recognize a sea change: strong older women are becoming role models for younger women.[1] Bridges between generations are starting to be built. Women of all ages are finding it compelling when older women own their presence, their experience, and, yes, their age.

Remembering history and how we got to where we are matters. In the late 1960s and early 1970s, with that simple but electrifying phrase—"the personal is political"—women started to see that what had seemed like their own individual disappointments and losses were part of a national, legally ensconced pattern of discrimination. And they fought back. Much was accomplished—what millions of girls and women can do now that they were utterly prevented from doing, often by law, in 1968 has been revolutionized.

It has been work, and such work is often dispiriting, frustrating, and infuriating. It is also exhilarating, self-affirming, and fun to defy stereotypes and demand our rights. Women became less interested in pleasing the world than in changing it. They built on each other's advances, whether they were movement leaders and activists or, simply, striving on their own or with one or two coworkers. They told their bosses they would no longer make the coffee, left men who treated them like doormats, organized childcare collectives, and became professionals who pioneered major changes in health care, education, the law, journalism, and other areas.

What this activism did, what this defiance did, for second-wave feminists, if only in fits and starts, was to give many women a new kind of confidence, however still stippled with doubts and insecurities. What stoked that confidence was that we—particularly those from the white middle class—were still so visible, and so sought after, by the media and marketers that we remained convinced we mattered as a generation. Now, without such visibility, we must reclaim our confidence and chutz-pah, combine our strength and brandish it. In truth, despite so much media invisibility, in everyday life we are more visible than many of us appreciate. Even with inequality among our ranks, our generation contains the largest group of older women ever to have their own money and independence. And an overwhelm-ing majority of us see ourselves as kind, loved, happy, valued, and smart.[2] These are essential building blocks of confidence and, yes, activism.

There is, of course, much unfinished business from the 1970s, some of it from feminism's failures, some of it from a vigorous, brawny backlash trying and at times succeeding in overturning our accomplishments. What has become maddeningly clear is that a white male gerontocracy—out of touch with and hostile to older and younger women alike—is determined to dismantle this legacy, from ravaging women's health and reproductive rights, wiping out equal protections at work, increasing inequality, strip-ping away the rights of the LGBTQ communities, to dismissing sexual harassment, assault, and rape as something women make up, continuing to show that black lives don't matter, and further polluting the planet.

It's time to take strength and inspiration from our legacy, bol-ster it, and chart new, possible, and as-yet-unrealized futures for us, hand in hand with younger generations. We embody a huge demographic revolution, and we remain a force to be reckoned with. By advocating for lifespan feminism, the issues facing older women become a natural extension of the ongoing feminist fight for equity, fairness, and justice.

To Do: Embrace Our Coming of Age

We need to see that what we are doing, feeling, and saying about ageist assumptions, to ourselves and to our friends, in person and online, is happening all over the country and is emerging as a national movement. We need to recognize our collective coming of age for the demographic revolution that it is. Many of us are in the best place of our lives now, emotionally and financially, and are newly energized. But, as we learned in the 1970s, essential social and political change does not result only or even primarily from individual empowerment. It results from collective action. We need to see ourselves as allied with younger women, to listen to each other, and to work together. And we have much work to do. There are enemies we must resist, attitudes we must change, and alliances we must forge. And there are media images, advertising campaigns, political gambits, and public policies to talk back to, make fun of, and to revamp.

Some of the visibility revolts have given permission to older, mostly famous women to talk back to outdated, age-based restrictions, particularly about sexuality, fashion, media images, and public attitudes. I have no doubt that they seem more palatable coming from beautiful and admired women. Yet most of these revolts have been about lifestyle and prejudice, not about politics and policy. Our culture conflates being sexy with being empowered, which—just as for younger women who get the same line—is both a punishing and an apolitical version of empowerment.[3] And the goalposts keep being moved to where, even now, we can't relax a bit about what we eat or how we look but must keep striving toward impossible standards of thinness and beauty, just like those still-stunning stars.

Coming of age means we can refuse to be confined to the kindly, docile, feathered grandma nest we're supposed to roost

in. When we exhibit—or better yet, flaunt—our ongoing appe-
tite for life, our love of music, dancing, eating, drinking, reading, and going to the movies, we are enacting a way of being
in the world that not only refuels us but also kindles a beacon
for younger women to see their way forward. When we affirm
that we are still in our prime, younger people can see how our
younger selves and our older selves are not cleaved apart, but
instead are a continuum.

To Do: Talk Back to Gendered Ageism

It is everywhere. Gendered ageism is designed to take our hard-
earned confidence and grind it into submission. We need confidence to stake our place in the world and to talk back to those who
try to make us invisible. Like Nancy Pelosi, Maxine Waters, Helen
Mirren, Oprah, Jane Fonda, Lily Tomlin, and more, who exude self-
assurance, we have earned our confidence too. Let's take it and own
it, wrap ourselves in it like chain-mail armor. Because, really, what
is cooler than a confident older woman—Jane Goodall, Ruth Bader
Ginsburg, Glenda Jackson, Mavis Staples? Let's use that to talk back
to the double helix of ageism and sexism every chance we get.

In 1971, in what would count back then as "going viral," Jane
O'Reilly's *Ms.* article, "The Housewife's Moment of Truth," coined
an instantly embraced concept: the "click moment." It was that
"aha" instant when you suddenly, shatteringly saw the sexism in
your life: your husband nearly trips over toys in the living room
and asks why *you* didn't pick them up, you cook and serve dinner
and clean up afterwards and no one says thank you or even notices
the work involved. O'Reilly named lots of them. We all had them,
all the time, and they changed us.

Increasingly, I have comparable "click" moments about what it
means to be an older woman and how gendered ageism lurks just

beneath the surface in so many realms. Some are banal and some are serious, but they do intertwine. Let's start totting them up.

It's a Friday afternoon, around 4:30, and I need a drink. But I have just learned that there is a work-related event I must attend in a few weeks, the kind that calls, preferably, for a new dress. This means I need to put the drink on hold and trudge to the mall-on-life-support near me. Women of my vintage, millions of whom are still in the workforce, and have a presentation or client meeting or social obligation where a dress would be the ideal sartorial choice (weddings are the worst!), know that this is pretty much the impossible dream.

Because here's what happens when you get to the mall. As you walk past Aéropostale, Express, H&M, American Eagle, the especially dreaded Abercrombie & Fitch, places called PacSun, Buckle B, Dry Goods, and a Forever 21 the size of a bowling alley, all you see in shop after shop are spaghetti-strapped, plunging-neckline, halter-topped minidresses for nineteen-year-olds. For me, much of what's in Talbots, like skirts with a postcard motif featuring pineapples and sailboats, makes the clothing in the Plow & Hearth catalog look fashion forward. The anchor store Macy's (which may have closed by the time this book comes out) has devolved into something resembling a secondhand outlet in Uzbekistan. But at least they have Eileen Fisher, seemingly the only company besides J.Jill that thinks women of my age still like to buy clothes. Except, none of it is on sale (given the price point, a deal breaker for me) and there are no dresses. On top of this, the helpful salesclerk has called me "hon" in a tone of voice and elevated volume usually reserved for toddlers. As I leave, I notice that most women of my age aren't shopping; they're racewalking around the mall to keep fit. I blast home, empty-handed, but now there's that drink. However trite this failure in retail might be, with my wine in hand I see how the mall is a brick-and-mortar manifestation of the edifice of gendered ageism.

Here's another "click" moment, and this was hard to miss. In its 2017 skit about how difficult it was for "people of a certain age" to use Alexa, *Saturday Night Live* featured various of its regulars dressed up as older people struggling to use "Amazon Echo Silver," a version of the device designed for senior citizens. It's "super loud" and "responds to any name even remotely close to Alexa," as we see numerous names including "Alberta, Aretha, Excedrin" scroll across the screen. Cast members call the device Odessa or Alessandra and ask it questions they immediately forget. When they get an answer, they respond with "I don't know about that." The voice-over tells us it can be paired with other "smart devices, like your thermostat" and can play music "they liked when they were young." Speaking of its scanning feature "to help them find things," we see Aidy Bryant, phone in hand, ask "Amelia, where did I put the phone?" Alexa has to point out the obvious. The device also has an "Uh-huh" feature to deal with "long, rambling stories."

The skit is funny and, of course, as with some stereotypes, contains elements of truth. But it is ageist and dismisses older people as clueless half-wits. When I have shown it to my students, some note they had never thought about ageism as a form of prejudice and discrimination. They're hardly alone.

In "Gauging Aging," a 2015 study of attitudes about getting older based on interviews with people aged twenty-one to sixty-four, the researchers found that the public lacks an understanding of ageism and "of the prevalence of this discriminatory practice." They also found that the general public has a very negative view of aging: people don't want to get old, and they often pity or resent older people. (Just go to the birthday card section of any greeting card rack; every added year, starting pretty much after twenty-one, is a source of gallows humor.) Older people, like those in the *SNL* skit, were seen as "other," an "identity you must fight against," and activated an "us versus them mentality." As this study discovered, "The reality that many older Americans find themselves consistently marginalized from participation and opportunities—in employment, civic life, recreational activities, housing, commerce and other arenas—is simply not part of the public's thinking about aging and older Americans."[4] Or as Victoria Lipnic, acting chair of the Equal Employment Opportunity Commission (EEOC) declared, we would find "the horror and sarcasm about aging" that she's heard people express "repulsive" if said about race and gender.[5] Often, such ageism is implicit, without conscious awareness or control, but it can be quickly activated by stereotypes.[6]

Ageism is an embedded form of prejudice that suffuses our society and yet remains spectral, invisible. What this important study didn't do, however, was look at gender, to see how attitudes may be even rougher for older women. While some studies find that older people, not surprisingly, have more positive and nuanced views of their age group than younger people do, other studies find that older people themselves can be ageist, having just as negative attitudes toward their own age group as young people do, and actively refusing to identify with their own generation.[7] If we are doing this, we have to stop it.

Gendered ageism is everywhere, from the bar where five people (usually men) are served before you, to older women being forced out of their jobs, to medical research that skews heavily toward ailments experienced primarily by men. And as soon as you hit sixty-five and go to the doctor's office, you are bombarded with questionnaires about falling down, how good your memory is, and whether you've had a bowel movement in the last fortnight. While these protocols are no doubt medically responsible, even mandated, women I know who are sixty-five and older and typically put in a fifty- or sixty-hour week of working, volunteering, or caregiving, feel that such questions automatically assume a state of decline they find insulting. Some older women report being called "sweetheart" and "hon" by medical professionals, which they suspect would not be used to address men.

Several medical schools have sought to correct their students' often ageist attitudes. Dr. Ronald Adelman at Weill Cornell Medicine in New York, concerned that medical students only see older people who are sick or impaired, started a program to introduce students to active, healthy older people. One such woman, Elizabeth Shepherd, eighty-two, talked to the students in part about her ongoing sex life, noting, "It's important that they don't think life stops as you get older. . . . So I decided to be frank with them." Others told the students about being misdiagnosed, their symptoms attributed to being old instead of to the real cause, like an infection. Doctors report that some students formed friendships with the older people they met, while others became more interested in working with older people.[8] These are hugely important interventions. Indeed, recent studies have suggested that ageist attitudes among the young can be significantly reduced when they interact more regularly with older people.[9]

Gendered ageism can also cripple women financially. Around the country, some have been alleging age discrimination as the cause of getting fired, not promoted, or not hired in the first place. While age discrimination is illegal, it is very hard to prove. Nonetheless, women working as symphony musicians, secretaries, faculty, or in other careers have sued their employers, and sometimes won. Two female instructors at Ohio State in their late fifties and early sixties were forced to retire after being called "deadwood" and "hippos" and having their contracts cut. They sued and won a $765,000 settlement and got their jobs back.[10] A fifty-eight-year-old woman working for the Danaher technology company—whose website features an elegant gray-haired woman with a lab coat and beaker—won $31 million in damages after bosses repeatedly made remarks that she was "outdated," "part of the old culture," and a "dumb female."[11]

That's one way to talk back to gendered ageism. How can we stand up to the anti-aging industrial complex? First, we must appreciate how this industry has turned what used to be, in hindsight, a trickle of wrinkle cream ads into a blasting, pressure-filled fire hose of anti-aging merchandise constantly pummeling women with age-phobic messages. Our mothers, whatever their feelings about the lines on their faces, were not bombarded by ads for Botox, endless cascades of anti-aging products, and the insistent hawking of "momovers" and cosmetic surgery. We need to keep pointing out that Photoshop is a technology of duplicity, deployed to dupe us into thinking that skin creams that should evoke the term "highway robbery" instead will get us to liquidate our checking accounts to try to achieve aspirational images impossible to attain. For women working in the media, whether in news or entertainment, they confront a vexing dilemma. In the 1960s and 1970s, there were very few female on-air reporters or anchors; the women's movement helped change that. But the rub was that, to stay in television journalism after a certain age, cosmetic surgery was nearly a requirement to avoid getting put out to pasture. And the metastasizing of celebrity culture, even into the news, has only widened the gap between women who look one way at, say, age sixty, and those of us who, well, look another.

Ageism doesn't only affect how others look at and treat us. It powerfully affects how we internalize our possibilities and limitations. I imagine that those of us who succumb to the gravitational pull of Sephora or Ulta will not stop slipping in their doors (or their websites). But it might be fun to stand in front of, say, the Dr. Brandt "Do Not Age" shelf and note in a slightly elevated voice how, yeah, maybe we'll buy it, maybe not, but, channeling Helen Mirren, we know it "will not do fuck all," as stopping aging is, in fact, impossible. Some choice sardonic comments at the greeting card section of stores about all those "over-the-hill" jokes that mock our intellect, mobility, and appearance can call out how we are constantly urged to be unwitting and complicit participants in seemingly innocent yet derisive jokes about who and where we are in our lives. More collectively (and obviously more effectively), we can set our sights on offensive or misleading "anti-aging" products and campaigns by targeting them on Twitter, Facebook, and Instagram, and castigating the offending companies themselves.

Thus, as difficult as it might be, we need to try to stifle that voice that's been implanted in our brains since we were young that wrinkles are ugly and horrid. As Instagram fashion icon Dorrie Jacobson (eighty-three) advises, it is time to silence our unforgiving inner critic and tell her to shut the fuck up. However challenging, we need to say that to ourselves. Some of us seem to be already doing so: according to a 2014 Gallup poll, as women get older, especially once they hit sixty, they actually feel better about their physical appearance than women in their thirties and forties—and, get this, even women in their twenties.[12]

Gendered ageism can also seek to silence us politically. Too often, when older women march in demonstrations, organize rallies, lobby their representatives, or criticize the media, they are cast as crotchety, peevish biddies who complain for the sake of complaining and don't know their place. We have to confront and overthrow these caricatures. The more women get involved in politics to fight for feminist issues, not just as candidates but as campaign workers and volunteers, the more gender equality is advanced.[13] As more progressive older women, some of whom may have newly found extra time, work on campaigns to advance progressive goals, the more our role as legitimate political actors will be accepted, even welcomed.

Gendered ageism undergirds how people look at us, how we look at ourselves, how we're treated in the world, and how corporate and government policies shape our lives and the lives of girls and women who will come after us. It is not easy to expunge, but we must start. Our biggest weapons here will be confidence, talking back, and—as the late and very great Molly Ivins said—raising more hell. Central to lifespan feminism is to call out those "click" moments, share them with others, especially the young, and expose them for what they are.

To Do: Talk Back to the Media

It is time to raise our voices against gendered ageism in the media. Given where the population is, and how the media are leaving out about a third of it, it's time for older women to call out these truly discriminatory corporate practices against their main customers.

Despite increasing visibility revolts, older women still remain significantly underrepresented in the media. The Women's Media Center, cofounded by Jane Fonda, Robin Morgan, and Gloria Steinem, reported that, in 2016, "men still dominate media across all platforms—television, newspapers, online and wires—with change coming only incrementally. Women are not equal partners in telling the story, nor are they equal partners in sourcing and interpreting what and who is important in the story." It is even worse for older women where, in 2016 Hollywood hits, they were outnumbered by older men three to one.[14] Even with growing outrage over Hollywood's failure to recognize and promote female directors (*Lady Bird* filmmaker Greta Gerwig being only the fifth woman in history to be nominated for an Oscar), *Fast Company* pointed out that the 2018 Golden Globes failed to nominate any of the twenty-nine deserving women directors the magazine listed.[15] Only 5 percent of magazine covers that year featured models over fifty,[16] which is why one of the twelve covers of the October 15, 2018, issue of *New York* magazine ("Powerful Women Talk About Power"), showing a clenched-fisted, defiantly posed, majestically

groove-faced Glenda Jackson (eighty-two), was like a glove across
the face of the whole industry.

In the broadcast and cable news media (median age of cable
news viewers in 2017: sixty for CNN, sixty-five for MSNBC and Fox),
there are not enough older women on-air reporters, or pundits or
experts, especially when compared to all the white-haired men
dominating those split screens.[17] Some women have had enough:
In June of 2019 five anchorwomen, who range in age from forty
to sixty-one, filed a discrimination lawsuit against their employer,
NY1, New York City's local news channel. They alleged that the
cable giant Charter Communications, which acquired NY1 in
2016, systematically reduced their on-air time in favor of younger,
less-experienced hosts. As Roma Torre, sixty-one and one of the
channel's longest-serving anchors, put it, "We feel we are being
railroaded out of the place. Men age on TV with a sense of gravi-
tas and we as women have an expiration date."[18] On top of this,
we see very few stories about successful older women and what
they've accomplished, whether they are leaders in their places of
worship, business leaders, scientists, activists, you name it. When
Chris Hayes on MSNBC featured Morgan, Fonda, and Steinem at
a roundtable to discuss women's activism in the 2018 midterms, it
was a bracing reminder of the exception that proves the rule.

When will television, and the advertisers that support it, abandon the anachronistic eighteen-to-forty-nine demographic as the
gold standard for assessing the worth of keeping a show (or a
woman) on the air? It's older viewers keeping those cathode-ray
tubes (well, now, LCD screens) shining, yet advertisers—except for
Big Pharma—remain obsessed with millennials, many of whom
are watching less television. For those eighteen to twenty-four, the
decline has become quite steep: in 2017, they watched less than
two hours of television a day, the lowest figure ever. Between 2012
and 2017, according to Nielsen, traditional television viewing for

those twenty-five to thirty-four dropped from just over 30 hours a week to 18 hours a week; for the thirty-five-to-forty-nine age group, from 36 to just under 27 hours. Meanwhile, the viewing of people sixty-five and older has dropped a scant one hour over the past seven years.[19] So advertisers, and thus programmers, are pursuing millennials who aren't there and don't want them, while shunning their most loyal customers.

What's especially annoying here is that the few network shows seemingly featuring and geared to older viewers still must live and die by the dictates of the eighteen-to-forty-nine demo. The 2018 reboot of *Murphy Brown* starred Candice Bergen, seventy-two, Faith Ford, fifty-four, Joe Regalbuto, sixty-nine, and Tyne Daly, seventy-two, who spent much of their time trashing the Trump administration and its policies. FOX's *The Cool Kids*, about four feisty residents of a retirement community (its stars range from sixty-two to seventy-five), does deal out the de rigueur jokes about fading eyesight, seized-up backs, and attenuated hearing. But because its characters are also booze-drinking, trouble-making party people, it jettisons the stereotypes of older people—including those in retirement communities—as sexless, grumpy has-beens. *Murphy Brown* started out strong with 7.5 million viewers, but by week four that had gone down to 6 million. These days, that's still a strong showing, but for the eighteen-to-forty-nine demo, the numbers went from one million down to about 800,000, and that's what counts. Ditto for *Cool Kids*, whose Facebook page is filled with fan endorsements. It started with 6.8 million viewers in its first week, but quickly lost nearly 11 percent of the eighteen-to-forty-nine demo.[20] By comparison, *Man With a Plan*, starring Matt LeBlanc, was initially deemed a hit because, while it also had only about 6 million viewers, 1.1 million of them were in the younger demo. Why do younger people have to endorse shows about older people for such shows to have a chance of surviving?

Occasionally, advertisers dare to put an older face in their ads. In 2013, Procter & Gamble launched a series of ads featuring Lee Kaufman (she was ninety-one at the time) using a Swiffer because it is allegedly easier and safer to clean with when you're older. At one point her husband Morty (also ninety-one) says, "Be careful, babe." The ad, as of this writing, has had over 2.3 million hits on YouTube, with many comments loving that Morty still called her "babe." The two became famous, appearing on *The Today Show* and *The Ellen DeGeneres Show*. Here were older people, living in their own home still, vibrant and happy, *not* kayaking or learning the accordion, who became fleeting icons of a version of aging that millions of viewers loved. Why have other advertisers not followed this lead?

All those Big Pharma ads make us want to vaporize our TVs (especially because we have to sit through all the disease mongering while subsidizing it to boot), and a few politicians and the American Medical Association would love to deport them from our screens. Why don't we try to help? If the online chats and comments I've seen are any indication, the ads viewers hate the most are those for Big Pharma. One reason people give for flocking to Netflix and Hulu is they can't take any more of the "ask your doctor" ads. Given the mounting concerns about the future of health care in our country, and the role of Big Pharma in keeping medications and devices much too expensive, we can tell our representatives we want more regulation and would love to have the disease mongers leave our TV screens altogether. We can also take a few moments to ridicule those ads on Facebook (remember, it's for "old people"), Twitter, or Instagram. The networks and cable channels are complicit here too, profiting off of these commercials that inflate our health care costs; we can tell them we are, yes, sick of them.

We should give all of these outlets hell, just like Maggie Kuhn did in the 1970s. We should also praise them when they defy such practices. I love *Saturday Night Live* and Stephen Colbert, but when they rely on ageist jokes, shouldn't we object? Many networks have feedback websites as well as posted snail-mail addresses, all of which can be Googled in seconds. They are increasingly using Twitter and Facebook pages to court viewers, promote their programs, and get feedback. If we are fans of programs featuring older women, we should let the networks know, and tell them that the eighteen-to-forty-nine demo standard is irrelevant and discriminatory. We should let them know that we value seeing reporters like Barbara Starr, CNN's Pentagon correspondent (sixty-eight), or Elizabeth Palmer, CBS's intrepid senior foreign correspondent (age well hidden, but probably early sixties); and interviews with congressional representatives like Jackie Speier (D-CA, sixty-eight), Zoe Lofgren (D-CA, seventy-one), and Nydia Velazquez (D-NY, sixty-six), to name just a few. We should see more older women as commentators and experts on news and public affairs programming. And when they give more coverage to male candidates, or repeatedly refer to a female politician's clothes but not her policies, we should blast them.

So, while media visibility matters, we do not want to be addressed primarily as a market for commodities, particularly for wallet-gouging skin creams and prescription drugs. We want to be seen as the political, economic, and social actors that we are in our country.

To Do: Expose the Sexist Hypocrisies of Market Fundamentalism

It has been macho bluster and confidence—overconfidence, really—that has hyped and buttressed market fundamentalism all these years. But the ravages of this ideology are real, and it has nearly erased people's memories of what used to be, and what we used to be able to take for granted.

As we sought, and in so many ways succeeded, to change what seemed like our preordained mac-and-cheese-making futures in the late 1960s and early 1970s, we were doing so in a very different political environment than the early twenty-first century. Even with Richard Nixon, a conservative Republican president, there was still a general acceptance that the state had a responsibility to mitigate inequality, to provide basic services like decent public education or building and maintaining the nation's infrastructure, and—through a combination of monetary and fiscal policies—to even out capitalism's boom-bust cycle. It was Nixon who established the Environmental Protection Agency in 1970 and, that same year, signed the Occupational Safety and Health Act to provide basic standards of health and safety on the job for American workers. There were also major increases to Social Security, Medicare, and Medicaid benefits.[21] Nixon was no liberal (and he cruelly vetoed a bipartisan bill that would have established federally funded day-care programs), but enormous political pressure and, indeed, this notion of government responsibility, still held sway as common sense.

Women today, of all ages, confront a very different common sense in much of our nation's capital: the mantra of market fundamentalism. It is macho dogma, emotionally withholding, cold, uncaring, and callous. It assumes that everyone is, or should be, self-sufficient. This ideology asserts that it is naive and unsophisticated—that we are suckers, really—to think that we have a collective responsibility to care for each other, especially those who are poor, weak, or vulnerable. Market fundamentalism was sold as modern, innovative, and the way forward, with the quasi-welfare state cast as outmoded, out of step with the times and with people's desires. So even though it was the beginning of regressive economic policies for so many people, it was shrewdly pitched as enlightened.[22]

Well, experience has taught us that it isn't. "Trickle-down" economics—that the wealth and prosperity the rich and corporations hoover up through tax cuts and other benefits will dribble down into our wallets—has proven to be a complete sham. Economic studies show that when the rich engorge their financial tapeworm with more income, the gross domestic product (GDP) actually goes down, and when those at the bottom and in the middle have more money, GDP goes up.[23] As the Nobel Prize–winning economist Joseph Stiglitz affirms, conservatives' "almost religious belief in the power of markets . . . had no basis in theory or evidence."[24] Even the International Monetary Fund has said, flatly, that "benefits do not trickle down" and it further emphasized, "Widening income inequality is the defining challenge of our time."[25] Simply put, market fundamentalism is ethically bankrupt. As the distinguished philosopher Elizabeth Anderson has argued, it is equality that is the basis for a free society, and market fundamentalism is equality's enemy.[26]

It is crucial to remember that no common sense remains the common sense forever, especially when widely challenged, and market fundamentalism has left out a lot of people, young and old—some further out in the cold than others. And they know it. "There is widespread discontent in our land," observes Stiglitz in his urgently necessary *People, Power, and Profits*. But it doesn't have to remain this way, and he argues forcefully for a new, progressive capitalism that will reverse the toll taken on so many by market-driven inequality. "We got the economics wrong: we thought unfettered markets—including lower taxes and deregulation—were the solution to every economic problem."[27] Stiglitz too sees a desire and a desperate need for less hyper-individualism and more social solidarity.

Young people today have no experience of growing up and living in a country with our earlier mindset: government support and funding for broad-gauge social welfare. But during and after the 2016 campaign, when millions embraced Bernie Sanders's call for free tuition at public colleges and universities, and "Medicare for all" gained traction as millions feared they would lose the insurance they got under Obamacare, some began to reimagine and get a glimmer of what a renewed, more mutually supportive politics might look like.

It is time for seasoned women, who know and have lived through this history—arm in arm with younger people—to rip off the armor of market fundamentalism and expose the rotting corpse inside. This will take time given that it is firmly embraced by the rich and powerful, but the shift is already happening. And it relies, crucially, on new, stronger alliances between the young and the old.

Older women who are financially secure need to be better allies with those who are not—this too is part of lifespan feminism. Because, whatever invisibilities we experience, the erasure of older, financially insecure women is nearly total. Why should they be subservient to the interests of a more privileged, mostly white male class? Many of them live in impoverished neighborhoods or in rural areas with minimal health care. Older African American women face what has been described as "triple jeopardy," because the interlocked disadvantages resulting from racism, sexism, and ageism cause significant health declines. Although they typically live fifteen years longer than African American men, government policies fail to take their issues into account at all. We never see or hear about the trials confronting older Native American women, Latinas, and Asian American women of minimal means. A lifetime of discrimination, poverty, and hostile living and working conditions can, not surprisingly, lead to depression and despair.[28] On the website Justice in Aging (which accepts donations), there are moving video portraits of what women who face such issues put up with and suffer through. But where, where, in our media do we hear about this? Do the persistent stereotypes of African American women as, on the one hand, undeserving welfare queens and, on the other, sassy, hands-on-their-hips towers of strength and defiance further urge white women to avert our gaze from their plight? These are feminist issues.

More and more people are hungering for an antidote to self-ishness and inequality. They want policies built on a structure of care. They want the rich to pay their fair share of taxes so there can be investments in the future, like combating the peril of climate change (with significant majorities worried about it),[29] rebuilding our roads, highways, bridges, tunnels, and water systems as well as our public schools, increasing the wages of working- and middle-class workers, and dealing imaginatively with an aging population—to name just a few.

We need more women economists, and especially more feminist economists, at the decision-making table. A 2019 survey conducted by the American Economic Association found that nearly half of the female economists who responded said they had faced sex discrimination, and 46 percent said they had not asked a question or presented an idea at work or at conferences to avoid harassment and discrimination. Only 28 percent felt "included intellectually within the field of economics."[30] It's not clear whether creating a more female-friendly climate in the field would produce findings less chummy with market fundamentalism, but studies have found a gender gap among economists in Europe, with women "less likely than their male counterparts to favour market solutions over government interventions and more likely to favour environmental protection policies." The same is true in the United States, where women economists support policies that redress inequality and redistribute wealth, and also favor government over market solutions in doing things like allocating resources and protecting the environment.[31]

Market fundamentalism insists we're all on our own. But women, especially older women—many of whom are caregivers of one sort or another throughout their lives—know that is false. Lifespan feminism requires that we attack market fundamentalism every chance we get as being especially inimical to women, and that we advocate for a more compassionate, solidarity-based conception of what the government can and should do to promote people's well-being.

All of this calls for more political involvement and activism at the local and national levels, which, as many women discovered when they canvassed for progressive candidates in 2018, can be exhilarating and empowering. We need to make our voices heard, loudly, to those who represent us, telling them that we reject market fundamentalism and any policy that promotes it. We need to advocate for more citizen-friendly, supportive government policies, especially those that can buoy older women of minimal means, like strengthening and expanding Medicare, Medicaid, and Social Security, and building more affordable housing.

We will be told that it's impossible, that the country can't afford it. We will be told we don't understand numbers. Which leads me to the next To Do item.

To Do: Contradict Mansplaining Statistics

Here's why we need to get a better handle on numbers.

In 2005, Larry Summers, then president of Harvard, in an extensive address on why there weren't more women in science and engineering, and using as data the play habits of his twin daughters when they were toddlers, opined that socialization and discrimination played a minimal role in these disparities and "that people naturally attribute things to socialization that are in fact not attributable to socialization." Before acknowledging discrimination "as pervasive, and as the dominant explanation of the patterns we observe," he asserted instead that women may lack "intrinsic aptitude" in some fields like, well, math and science. As evidence, he cited the lower scores of girls on science and math tests in high school.[32] The suggestion was that there were basic genetic differences between males and females when it comes to math, which I guess is why John Glenn insisted that Katherine Johnson confirm the accuracy of the orbital calculations for *Friendship 7* before he had his butt launched into outer space. Because genetics contributes to the incidence of autism, Summers suggested that genetics may also explain why more girls don't rock their trig classes.

As you might imagine, a firestorm of outraged reaction ensued, and the Women in Science & Engineering Leadership Institute issued a blistering rebuttal. "Summers glosses over a vast body of research on gender differences in science and math tests," including how "expectations and stereotype threat" can influence performance. "To rely upon genetics as the explanatory factor is irresponsible and unscientific." They added that "Summers' comments on women's innate inabilities are insulting . . . to women in general and women scientists in particular." In a kicker, their denunciation added that "failure to engage with the scholarly work in this field should be an embarrassment to Harvard University."[33] Summers had to issue an apology.

However, I'd like to turn Summers's numbskull remarks into a call to arms for women of all ages who care about equality and justice. Because I don't think we use numbers nearly as much as we should to counter such biased mansplaining. Yes, there are lots of damning numbers out there that feminists cite about pay inequities, the prevalence of sexual assault, the escalating threats to women's reproductive rights—all essential data. But not enough statistics are out there about the status of older women. If you go to websites for the American Society on Aging, the National Committee to Preserve Social Security and Medicare, Justice in Aging, the Institute for Women's Policy Research, and the Pew Research Center, to name a few, you'll find data, studies, videos, and articles about what many older women confront and what their lives are like.

In order to counter the "we can't afford it" bromide about better supporting older women, we need additional, alternative numbers, the ones often hidden from us, the incriminating ones lurking in the shadows. Some we kind of know, but they are defended with armaments of misleading and fear-inducing rhetoric, like why the United States somehow needs to account for 35 percent of global military expenditures, "more than the seven next highest-spending countries combined."[34]

So, despite those equations with pi and beta signs, and mind-numbing phrases like "exogenous specification of advance in multifactor productivity (MFP)," basic economics is not rocket science. Men use numbers, often to keep us down. We need to use them more. And we need to do a better job of showing the connection between numbers and injustice, between numbers and everyday lived experience.

There is actually a school of thought that hasn't gotten much play outside of academic journals and conferences: feminist economics and gender-responsive budgeting. Who knew? This involves analyzing budgets and policy decisions to see how they help or disadvantage women, and it is part of "gender mainstreaming"— incorporating a gender perspective (and not just for women) into analyses of the impact of government policies. As the global studies scholar Keerty Nakray put it, "A nation may claim that its priority is achieving gender equality . . . but the real test would lie in studying the efforts in achieving the same with the appropriate budget allocations."[35]

You know how there are environmental impact statements on the consequences of certain policies? What if we had gender impact assessments, analyzing what budget priorities would mean for women? Japan, Canada, and France do just that.[36] What if the U.S. government was required to produce a gender impact statement that laid out what elements of the budget helped or hurt women of all ages, incomes, races, ethnicities? Gender-responsive budgeting has gained special currency in thinking about how developing countries can promote more and better health and education for girls and women, and how instituting these programs is tied to countries' overall productivity and wealth. Wouldn't the United States, and its female majority population, benefit from this too?

The national budget, as least those parts not designed to defund Planned Parenthood or deep-six the Violence Against Women Act, is supposed to be gender-neutral. But, often, members of Congress are simply gender-ignorant or, worse, they prioritize institutions and policies that overwhelmingly benefit men.[37] Sex- and age-based discrimination have become baked into the baseline of many public policies, sometimes ignorantly and other times willfully.

For example, when food stamps, the Children's Health Insurance Program (CHIP), Social Security, Medicare, or Medicaid are cut, the burdens of those costs fall disproportionately on women, especially low-income women (and their kids). Rebuilding infrastructure like our decaying roads and bridges, which is desperately needed, would create good-paying jobs, primarily for men. But what about building up our social infrastructure, like childcare and elder care, or public schools, which, true, do not pay women nearly what they're worth, but would create tens of thousands of jobs, many of them for women? With gender-responsive budgeting, we could support these workers to be paid more, and respond positively when they go out on strike. Ditto for expanding health care. Maybe then our infant-mortality rate would not be nearly double that of Japan, Sweden, or Austria, and also the highest of the nineteen developed countries in the world (in 2017, we ranked 40th in the world, behind Guam, Slovenia, and Wallis and Futuna, two volcanic islands in the South Pacific).[38]

There is also an obsession about GDP as a measure of the country's economic health: How big is it? Is it getting bigger? And is ours bigger than theirs? However, as feminist economist Heather Boushey pointed out to me, minimal attention is paid to how GDP is distributed; who benefits and who doesn't? A report she coauthored argued, "Adding a measure of how income is distributed would allow us to quantify inequality in our economy," and use statistics to document "how the economy is performing for subgroups of people," like women, or those of lower income. The report suggests that if GDP is growing but inequality remains rife for women, especially older women, we could "design policies that encourage more equitable and sustainable economic growth."[39]

I am not about to argue that women are inherently more nurturing or compassionate than men, although some might disagree. But we have been socialized or compelled to be caregivers; we have been told we have to be nurturing because our government will not. But what if that trait we're supposed to embody, compassion, infused how we as a nation spend our money? If the United States had more affordable and better childcare, not to mention paid maternity leave (we are one of only eight countries on the planet not to provide this and the only developed country not to do so),[40] maybe more women would have children—not unimportant in an aging society. In funding for health and medical research, does more money go to diseases or conditions that afflict mostly men? For universities getting state or federal support, do they have to have a minimum percentage of female professors, and do they have to pay them the same as men for comparable career achievements? Gender budgeting may sound crazy and impossible, but here's who's already doing it: Austria, Belgium, Finland, Iceland, Israel, Japan, Korea, Mexico, Netherlands, Norway, Spain, and Sweden.[41]

Feminists have at times pointed to the bloated defense budget as diverting money away from much more female-friendly social programs. We might do well to remind ourselves of what feminist scholars like Sheila Tobias advocated back in the 1980s: identify a particular weapon or set of weapons, like the F-14, each of which cost $50 million in 1985, and then demand why the navy needed 512 of them, instead of, say, 511, and have $50 million go to programs to prevent child abuse.[42]

Today we could ask why the military needs the littoral combat ship (LCS), at $362 million each, with one report totaling the program's ultimate tab at $67 billion. Plagued by cost overruns and mechanical failures, "unable to fulfill its core missions," susceptible to cyberattacks, and labeled a "floating garbage pile" by one military watchdog group, the navy may not even deploy them.[43] There's the F-22 Raptor (great name), which also cost the Pentagon $67 billion to design and deploy (and over $60,000 an hour to operate!) and was then terminated in 2009. Let's not overlook "Zombie Zumwalt: The Ship Program That Never Dies," the headline *Roll Call*, which covers the doings on Capitol Hill, gave to its story about the naval destroyers that "don't exactly work as planned." Initially funded in 2006, they were still not "ready to fight" by 2018, "lack a functioning combat system" (which really does seem like a somewhat fatal flaw in a weapon), and "are years from demonstrating even rudimentary capability." At a cost of $8 billion per vessel, the Zumwalts are "the most costly and time-consuming ship project . . . in recent memory," with the exception of aircraft carriers.[44] Those include the USS *Gerald Ford* carrier program, begun in 2005, at $38 billion, that by 2016 was $6 billion over budget and was referred to by Senator John McCain as "one of the most spectacular acquisition debacles in recent memory."[45] Then there's the Virginia-class submarine, at $2.7 billion a pop, with the navy wanting thirty-two of them. Could they live with twenty-eight, or thirty? Just asking.

Women are not urged to drill down into these numbers, and we should. Let's compare and contrast. For example, the Children's Health Insurance Program, which provides health insurance to low-income kids (nearly 9 million in 2016) and which Trump tried to cut in 2018, costs $13.6 billion, less than two nonfunctioning Zumwalts. The much-vilified Planned Parenthood, which serves anywhere from 2.5 to 4 million patients year—most of them low-income, and many in rural areas—gets a miserly $543 million from the government, primarily via Medicaid reimbursements.[46] Think how many more people could be served if we could redirect the budgets for four—only four—littoral combat ships (the ones that don't work) to programs supporting women and children. The feds spend an equally puny $2 billion to support home services for older Americans, like Meals on Wheels, in-home services, and transportation; with one less Virginia-class submarine, that amount could be doubled.[47] Congressional representatives with military contractors in their districts push for military spending because it creates jobs for their constituents. But what if they pushed for other kinds of spending that would do the same but would be focused on different, pressing wars, like the ones we need to fight against climate change and income inequality?

Expanding Social Security should also be a feminist issue. Little noticed in the $5 billion worth of free airtime given to the Donald in 2016 and the hyperventilating about Hillary Clinton's emails was her proposal to expand benefits for low-income widows and unpaid caregivers.[48] Congresswoman Nita Lowey, D-NY (eighty-one), in 2015 introduced such legislation, noting that women make up 66 percent of caregivers and, on average, lose $324,000 in wages and retirement benefits during their lifetime. She called unpaid caregiving a "financial emergency for millions of women."[49] We should push for women to continue to earn credits toward Social Security when they leave the paid workforce to care for others. The Family and Medical Leave Act needs to be updated to allow benefits to help those caring for an older relative.[50] Where to get some of the funds for this? Let's further comb that bloated Pentagon budget for starters.

Also, do we appreciate how many older women live alone, many more than men? Many of them need more affordable housing. Roughly 75 percent of men aged sixty-five to eighty-four are married; for men eighty-five and older, 60 percent are married. For women, in contrast, of those sixty-five to seventy-four, 58 percent are married, and of those seventy-five to eighty-four, 42 percent are married. Women eighty-five and older? Only 16 percent are married. And it's not only because women live longer, giving men a larger pool of women to choose from. It turns out that men are simply much more likely (maybe more inclined?) to remarry. Another burden is that women take a much greater financial hit from widowhood and divorce.[51] As the economist Dean Baker emphasizes, "Women living alone should be the targets of real Social Security reform."[52] What if we redirected some of the tens of billions in corporate subsidies (i.e., welfare) given to companies as diverse as Boeing, Amazon, Walmart, and Microsoft to this important feminist project? Think Social Security can't be strengthened? Go to strengthensocialsecurity .org, filled with information and an action page.

I could go on, but these are the types of equivalencies we'd do well to unearth. More to the point, I'd like to propose that numbers like these may be one very important tool in building a new bridge feminism between young and old, between white women and women of color. When we not only see but also quantify how girls and women are, still, so often screwed over from childhood to older age along very common lines—health; economic security; unpaid caring for family members; vulnerability to violence and abuse; objectification, stereotyping, or erasure by the media; and being told to not make waves about any of this and more—we can use numbers to unite us. By validating these lifelong inequities with statistics, we can expose market fundamentalism for the bankrupt, muscle-bound yet anemic ideology it is.

To Do: Building Bridge Feminism

This is a plea and a call to arms. I propose that it's time for bridge groups. Not the card-playing kind, but the talking kind, where older and younger women get together, share their stories, listen to each other, and forge intergenerational ties—bridges—that help construct a notion about, and policies for, a lifespan feminism. It's kind of an update on consciousness-raising. This may sound frivolous, or that spanning generational differences might be too challenging. But hear me out. Because, despite what the media might fail to bring into view, or outright misrepresent, these bridges are already starting to take shape.

I confess. When I was getting swept up by the women's movement in the early 1970s, I was of course gripped by issues of concern to young women: reproductive rights, quotas at professional and graduate schools, job and pay discrimination, older men's caveman treatment and dismissal of younger women. I gave little thought to what issues might be facing older women. We embraced "the personal is political," but that often meant that if something didn't affect you right now, you might not think you needed to care about it. Now I am hoping to persuade younger feminists that while being fifty, sixty, or older might seem light years away, you will someday be our age. I for one would like you to confront less bias and bullshit when you get there than we do now.

First, and crucial to the mission of lifespan feminism, we must confront the supposed "war" between millennial and younger feminists (the fourth wave?) and second-wavers. Actual article titles include "Feminism's Generation Gap," "Young Women Are So Over Hillary's Old-School Feminism," and "The New Feminist War: Young Women Vs. Old Women," where we read, "Social media is crackling with barely concealed inter-generational rage between feminists of different vintages."[53] It was the #MeToo movement that allegedly plowed this gap between women, with the *New Republic* observing that, as a result, "it has become an article of faith that there is a 'generational divide' between older and younger feminists."[54] As the caricature goes, older women think younger women should toughen up and learn how to say no better, while younger women think older women don't appreciate the extent and multiple forms of sexual abuse. It hardly helped when, at one end of the spectrum, babe.net writer Katie Way, twenty-two, bashed HLN anchor Ashleigh Banfield, fifty-one, as a "burgundy lipstick bad highlights second-wave feminist has-been" or, on the other end, when second-wave feminist Germaine Greer, seventy-eight, told Harvey Weinstein's victims that they should stop "whingeing" about the abuse and that they were "cashing in" on the #MeToo movement.

The media love this dissension—yay, another catfight—and use inflammatory, unrepresentative comments to stereotype entire generations of women and pit them against each other. But despite some very real differences—I mean, we did grow up in historically specific times with their particular pressures and sensibilities—these alleged intergenerational differences have been exaggerated, sometimes by women but especially in the media and the ever-pulsating digital ecosystem.

In a poll of more than 2500 women conducted by Vox.com and the media and technology company Morning Consult, the

#MeToo generation gap "is a myth." Founded by Tarana Burke in 2006, the Me Too movement sought to bring attention to survivors of sexual abuse and assault; the term went viral in 2017 when, just days after the Harvey Weinstein scandal broke, the actress Alyssa Milano urged women to tweet "Me too" if they had ever been harassed or assaulted. Within a few days, over 40,000 people had responded to Milano and more than 12 million had used the hashtag on other platforms.[55] This movement has remained robust and widely embraced by women, and indeed confirmed the revival of feminism that the 2017 Women's March signaled. According to the Vox poll, over two thirds of women of all ages support the #MeToo movement and share a broad agreement about what constitutes sexual harassment. While one distortion is that older women worry more than younger women about accused men being denied due process, Vox found that approximately 50 percent of both groups had this concern. The results indicated that the movement enjoys "broad support" and is "inspiring women, older and younger, to rethink their assumptions about work, politics, and the future."[56]

Sensationalized accounts of feminist warfare casts all generations as monolithic, but they have been especially quick to go to the ageist and sexist second-wave-has-been trope. The implication is, in part, that older feminists are simply jealous of younger feminists because, well, they're still young and wrinkle-free. In turn, younger feminists have no use for second-wavers because we're old. And what younger feminist wouldn't want to off-load those 1970s stereotypes of feminists as humorless, man-hating, anti-sex ninjas or as utterly blind (or, worse, hostile) to the additional oppressions brought on by the intersections of gender, race, sexuality, and bodily ability? Of course there are differences in the priorities of feminist activism fifty years ago and today—how could there not be? Feminism evolves, as it needs to, with the times. As does patriarchy. Today, enlightened sexism—a more subtle, sneaky form of sexism—coexists with a full-throated, war-whooping misogyny that seeks to keep women in their place and even reverse the rights they have won. Since each generation has experienced sexism and taken on patriarchy differently, there is not "one" feminism; there are many, including within generations. So, can we still forge alliances with each other?

Younger feminists, in addition to caring deeply about women's rights and equality, are seeking to construct a much more inclusive feminism that does a better job than the "second wave" did in forging ties among white women, women of color, and those in the LGBTQ community. Unfortunately, there can be a tendency—especially in the often nuance-free world of space-limited Twitter or Instagram—to paint the second wave with overly broad strokes. First of all, we were not all white and privileged. We were not all homophobic or racist or clueless about what working-class women of all colors put up with in the 1970s. We are not all "woke" now, but many of us are trying to expand our sensitivities and deepen our awareness of how differently positioned women experience sexism and patriarchy. And not all younger feminists fit the stereotype of being fragile and hypersensitive, interpreting every male compliment as harassment and dismissing what the second wave fought for and accomplished. Yes, there are and will be differing ideas about how to proceed, but sharing and debating them can be highly useful and productive.

The rise of Trumpism—not just as presidential practice but as a philosophy—has given us all, whatever our age, a profoundly dangerous and threatening ideology we oppose. We have way more in common, it seems to me, than what divides us. Feminists have much to share about winning and losing battles, about how to change politics and the law, about the ongoing daily, personal negotiations between feminism and the cultural dictates of femininity, and much more.

Nothing helps build common ground like face-to-face meetings. If we are going to begin to raise awareness about gendered ageism—a bias no woman will escape if she lives long enough—we need to reach out to younger women and forge an intergenerational bridge. Maybe I am overly optimistic about this possibility because I teach young women and feel very strong ties to them. But women of all ages joined together, in record numbers, during the 2017 Women's March and again during the 2018 midterm elections. We know each other through work, religious organizations, family, volunteer groups, or friendship networks. But how often do we get together to talk about what is going on in our lives, our communities, and our country, as women?

Hence the proposal for bridge groups. Over coffee, over drinks, over lunch, let's start to connect better to share our stories and to identify what we are confronting and what we need to fix. Because the list is long. Bridge groups can also counter the phobia about aging in our culture, which is increasingly imposed on women at ever younger ages. Much in the media tells us that you should measure a woman's vitality, her worth, her ability to be an active, productive agent in the world by whether she has lines on her face. In being more visible ourselves, more confident, more outspoken, and by actively reaching out to young people, we can become living rebukes to that snaking together of ageism and sexism. Younger women, in turn, sometimes dismissed as well because of their age, as being too inexperienced or naive, have been and will continue to be models for how to revitalize and expand a feminist politics to counter a newly emboldened misogyny. If together we work for and embrace lifespan feminism—which includes financially bolstering older women's lives—younger women won't need to fear the future.

Two or three women over the age of fifty could invite two or three younger women they know through work, friends, or family to get together with the purpose of sharing and exploring the gender-based challenges they face, how they might be addressed, and how women see and feel about gendered ageism. If the group clicks, invite more women in. If it doesn't, try again. Libraries, community centers, local feminist or senior organizations might be happy, even eager, to help coordinate and host such meetings. Groups might decide to do different things: connect with national feminist organizations and feminist websites; organize speaking events or teach-ins; let their politicians know about their existence and agendas; share their activities and agendas on Facebook, Instagram, and Twitter. This is a cross-generational synergy that we need right now to harness and propel our anger, our energy, and our hope for a better future.

To Do: Get Active, Get Political, Donate

Let's refuse to be silenced or sidelined. Let's refuse to be depoliticized. With the Internet, Facebook, Instagram, and Twitter—despite their not-inconsiderable failings and pitfalls—it has never been easier to get involved in local, regional, and national campaigns, not just for candidates but for issues. Many Democrats in Congress and at the local level support strengthening social programs for women, including Social Security, Medicare, and Medicaid, and they need our voices and support, including knocking on doors and helping them raise money when they run for office. People often don't know how fun and gratifying it can be, until they try it, to canvass for a candidate you believe in.

Without a notion of lifespan feminism, older women get segregated off as "seniors," their issues folded into organizations that advocate solely on behalf of retirees and aging Americans. While many of those organizations do important work, not all of them have a feminist orientation or underscore the issues of

specific concern to women. Feminist organizations like NOW—
between trying to preserve reproductive rights, protecting immi-
grant rights, advocating for pay equity, battling sexual abuse and
assault—have their hands full. But we can write and email them
and insist that feminism is a lifelong project, and push them to
foreground issues affecting older women as well, especially those
of lesser means. As of this writing, NOW, the Feminist Majority
Foundation, and UltraViolet, all crucially important, dedicated
activist organizations, do not highlight older women's concerns.
There needs to be stronger alliances between these groups and
those like Justice in Aging and the American Society on Aging,
dedicated to combating poverty among older women. Various
of these organizations need and accept donations. As does the
Institute for Women's Policy Research, "the leading think tank
in the United States applying quantitative and qualitative analysis of public policy through a gendered lens." Their website
features a host of studies about women and inequality that can
inform our activism.

It was this gap between activism and advocacy on behalf
of younger and older women, this generational partitioning,
that Maggie Kuhn sought to bridge. Might we need a new (and
renamed) version of the Gray Panthers to span this divide?

To Do: Celebrate Visibility Revolts

Yes, female celebrities are inspiring many of us to resist passé
notions about the place and role of older women. But so are many
other women, not quite as famous, who are successful and providing inspiration for how older women are remaining visible,
influential, and powerful. Here are a few of the many women I
could name: Jocelyn Bell Burnell, an Irish astrophysicist and co-
discoverer of radio pulsars (which the Nobel committee failed to

acknowledge in 1974 when it gave its prize for the discovery to men), in 2018 won a $3 million Breakthrough Prize established by tech entrepreneurs. She's proposing to use the prize money to create PhD fellowships for people from underrepresented groups in science.[57] Mae Carol Jemison, an American engineer and physician, became the first African American woman to travel in space when she served as an astronaut aboard the Space Shuttle *Endeavour*. She has established an international science camp for high school students. Elizabeth H. Blackburn, who has done pathbreaking research on DNA and chromosomes, is a Nobel laureate and continues to teach as a professor of biology and physiology at the University of California, San Francisco (UCSF). Christiane Amanpour, the intrepid international journalist, hosts public affairs shows on CNN and PBS. Cindy Sherman, the renowned artist whose self-portraits critique femininity as a social construction, is still making art, some of it focusing on women and aging. Guitarist Nancy Wilson, of the rock band Heart, continues to perform and has been ranked the eighth-greatest female guitarist of all time. Carol Lavin Bernick, CEO of Polished Nickel Capital Management, a private investment firm, launched Enchanted Backpack to provide the equivalent of $50,000 annually in school supplies and other resources to Chicagoland's most underserved elementary schools. Stacey Caywood, CEO of Wolters Kluwer Legal & Regulatory, an information, software, and consulting firm, was named the 2018 winner of the annual Stevie Awards for Women in Business. Martha Pollack, a computer scientist and professor, serves as the president of Cornell University. Amy Gutmann, president of the University of Pennsylvania, is an outspoken advocate for increased access to higher education for low-income and first-generation students. Her term has been extended to 2022. And Eileen Fisher is still going strong, designing clothes for women of all ages.

As we look around, many of us will see other women, some

of whom might not be as financially successful or quite as visible, who are powerful forces at their workplaces, volunteer organizations, and communities. It is not just certain movie stars who are shattering stereotypes. Millions of us, every day, are doing so, with dignity, determination, and optimism.

Reinventing the Road Ahead

Through all of this—talking back to gendered ageism and to male political orthodoxy, building bridges with younger people, becoming more politically active and engaged—we can and will pick up where the great Maggie Kuhn left off and reinvent the road ahead. It is time for us, everyday women, to enact our own visibility revolts. Our coming of age is happening at a very distinctive moment, when a resurgent feminism is crashing against a newly acceptable, even celebrated brew of racism, misogyny, and rank cruelty. Because there are so few media images out there of engaged, happy, gutsy older women who want to make the world a better place, we need to step into that role. Let's reclaim aspirational aging from Big Pharma and other carnival barkers who equate it with blowing bubbles with grandchildren or mainly focusing on ourselves. Aspirational aging is about staking our visibility in the world, being proud of and owning who we are, and making that confidence contagious. Then younger women today will be even less tolerant of gendered ageism, less willing to comply with its exclusionary edicts than we are, especially if we blow wind in their sails. It is time—individually and collectively—to rip off the invisibility cloak. It is time to talk back. It is time to hold hands. Let's do it now.

ACKNOWLEDGMENTS

All of my work on the representations of women in the media has been based partially on autobiography, on what I have experienced at different stages of my life as my lived experience has been shaped by—and against—what I've seen on the pages and screens of America. This book is no different. But now invisibility, ridicule, even derision governs much of what women of my age see—or do not see—in our mass-mediated environment. I did not see myself in most of this imagery, and I knew other older women didn't either. My friends and I kept taking note of this gap, and also celebrated when older female celebrities we loved and admired broke through the barricades of gendered ageism to gain acclaim on Broadway, in movies, on television, in music, and in politics. And seeing the thousands of older women passionately protesting against misogyny, racism, and homophobia at the 2017 Women's March, in solidarity with women and girls much younger than they, was dramatic, visible evidence that older women are a vibrant cohort of activism and influence barely acknowledged in our culture. Nor have their voices or issues been embraced as much as they need to be by the ongoing feminist movement. In my own field of media studies, where there is so much work about how children and adolescents are represented in and affected by the media, there is very little research and writing on the images of older women. All this I wanted to try to address.

My biggest debt is to my passionate, smart, and indefatigable agent, Elizabeth Kaplan. It turns out that ageism can grip sectors of the publishing industry as well, some thinking that no one would want to read a book about older women (including older women!). But Elizabeth believed in the project from the start, and helped me shape and reshape it from a somewhat irregular blob of Play-Doh into something a tad more structured. Her advice, her sense of humor, and her ongoing support for and enthusiasm about the manuscript has meant so much to me as I have gone through revision after revision. (And I owe a major debt to Paul Golob at Holt, who suggested that Elizabeth would be a terrific agent. He was right.)

At Norton, I had the privilege of working with Amy Cherry, an incredibly dedicated, astute, and meticulous editor, and one tough cookie. Amy pushed me to go in directions I was initially hesitant to pursue, and she made the book stronger as a result. And she tried to save me from myself: the repetitions, the shaky metaphors, the snarky asides. When she sometimes failed to do so is on me. (That Amy and Elizabeth are Michigan alums was icing on the cake!) Amy's trusty and efficient assistant, Zarina Patwa, helped expedite the editing process. Nancy Palmquist was a scrupulous copy editor. My enterprising research assistants, Monique Bourdage and Ellie Homant, provided me with crucial articles, documents, and sources essential to the manuscript.

Friends and colleagues at Michigan have had to listen to me go on about this book for several years now, and their thoughts, reactions, and support have been invaluable. Mary Kelley, Sidonie Smith, and Peggy Burns, separately and together, and usually over a happy-hour glass of wine, provided provocative insights, ideas, and endless encouragement. Mary Ann McDonald read the entire manuscript and offered a penetrating and gratifyingly enthusiastic response. Active, engaged, and very accomplished, they all defy every outdated stereotype about older women. The incomparable Paddy Scannell urged me to soldier on, knowing that so little has been written about how older women have been depicted in the media, as did Russ Neuman, who, whenever I saw him, was a constant font of boosterism for the project. Megan Ankerson's intellectual passion and support, and Katherine Sender's probing thoughts and sustaining friendship pushed me forward as well. Charlie Bright, Susan Crowell, and Sonya Rose have been important bedrock friends and listeners. Carroll Smith Rosenberg and Alvia Golden, who qualify as truly legit and awesome Grande Dames, not only offered suggestions and support but also have embodied for me how to age with dignity, humor, passion, and purpose.

I am also indebted to Barbie Zelizer at the University of Pennsylvania for inviting me to be a scholar-in-residence at the Annenberg School for Communication in the winter of 2016; her friendship and intellectual zeal have meant much to me. At Annenberg I was asked to present material from the book, and received important comments from Joe Turow, Emily Falk, and others. The most consequential help came from Kathleen Hall Jamieson, who had been asked by Rep. Claude Pepper's Select Committee on Aging in 1977 to head up two studies documenting how older people were represented in television programming and commercials. Kathleen had the original reports and generously lent them to me as part of my research, and also offered crucial, penetrating insights. I am so grateful for her help.

Andi Zeisler, the founder and head of Bitch Media, provided her astute observations into the state of feminism today and how its agendas are evolving. Heather Boushey, founding executive director of the Washington Center for Equitable Growth, offered indispensable material on feminist and progressive economic analyses of government spending. Bill Novelli, former head of AARP, shared his experiences about how the organization and its magazine sought to update and redefine how it combatted ageism. The Centre for Women, Ageing and Media at the University of Gloucestershire admitted me to its 2018 summer school, where I was able to present and get feedback on the project, and where I had the privilege of meeting amazing women, old and young alike, tackling the impact of gendered ageism.

Intergenerational friendships are so important to us all, and to the fabric of our society, and I have been especially blessed by these. To hear younger people reflect on—and reject—the shallowness of gendered ageism has been heartening indeed. Chaz Cox and I shared animated (and typically laughter-filled) discussions about this, as I did with Jake Prigoff, who made sure I knew about efforts to combat ageist attitudes among medical students. My endless and ongoing conversations with Chris Armstrong about the state of American politics (as well as so many other things) have been essential to my thinking. These friendships, and their ongoing interest in the progress of the book, have lifted me up, more than they may know.

As with everything I have written, I could not possibly have completed this book without the ongoing, patient, endless, and enthusiastic support of my husband, TR Durham, who listened, offered new ways of articulating points, suggested readings and concepts that might help, and read various drafts of the manuscript. And he has endured the bitching and moaning, doubts, and frustrations that often accompany writing. Our daughter Ella has been a constant source of pride and inspiration, and her love and pride in my own work sustains me every day. The support of my family has meant everything to me.

Finally, friendship is, of course, so crucial to our happiness and well-being, and there is something so precious about lifelong friends, those you have known since childhood. I have known Lynette Anderson, Margaret Bartiromo, and Jeffrey Golden since first grade, and we have remained close friends for over sixty years. Smart, funny, fun-loving, and accomplished, each in their distinctive ways, I can't imagine having traveled this road without them. I dedicate this book to our friendship, and to them.

NOTES

Chapter 1: Women Coming of Age

1. "NYC marathon's oldest runners: How'd they do?" CBS News, https://www.cbsnews.com/pictures/nyc-marathons-oldest -runners-howd-they-do/; https://www.tcsnycmarathon.org/about -the-race/results/finisher-demographics.

2. Dr. Nancy Etcoff, "Foreword" in "Beauty Comes of Age: Findings of the 2006 Dove Global Study on aging, beauty and well-being," September 2006, https://static1.squarespace.com/static/55f45174e4 b0fb5d95b07f39/55f45539e4b09d46d4847b60/55f45539e4b09d46d48 47c93/1255277563001/Beauty+Comes+of+Age+2006+Dove+Glo bal+Study+on+Aging+Beauty+and+Well-being.pdf, p. 4.

3. Women in elective office 2019, https://www.cawp.rutgers.edu/ women-elective-office-2019.

4. Weiyi Cai and Scott Clement, "What Americans think about feminism today," *Washington Post*, January 27, 2016, https:// www.washingtonpost.com/graphics/national/feminism -project/poll/.

5. This analysis is from feminist writer Sady Doyle, "It's Not (All) the Second Wave's Fault," *Elle*, January 22, 2018, https://www .elle.com/culture/a15841808/second-wave-feminism-sexual -harassment-generational-divide/.

6. "Beauty Comes of Age: Findings of the 2006 Dove Global Study on aging, beauty and well-being," September 2006, https://static1 .squarespace.com/static/55f45174e4b0fb5d95b07f39/55f45539e4b09 d46d4847b60/55f45539e4b09d46d4847c93/1255277563001/Beauty+

Comes+of+Age+2006+Dove+Global+Study+on+Aging+Beauty
+and+Well-being.pdf, pp. 14–17.

7. Monique Morrissey, "Women over 65 are more likely to be poor
    than men, regardless of race, educational background, and mar-
    ital status," Economic Policy Institute, March 8, 2016, https://
    www.epi.org/publication/women-over-65-are-more-likely-to-in
    -poverty-than-men/.

8. Nicole S. Dahmen and Raluca Cozma, eds., "Media Takes: On
    Aging" (International Longevity Center, 2009), p. 15.

9. D'vera Cohn and Paul Taylor, "Baby Boomers Approach 65—
    Glumly," December 20, 2010, Pew Research Center, https://www
    .pewsocialtrends.org/2010/12/20/baby-boomers-approach-65
    -glumly/.

10. https://www.usnews.com/pubfiles/USNews_Market_Insights_
    Boomers2015.pdf.

11. "Demographic Profile of the Older Population," https://www
    .un.org/esa/population/publications/worldaging19502050/
    pdf/90chapteriv.pdf.

12. Ben Steverman, "'I'll Never Retire': Americans Break Record for
    Working Past 65," *Bloomberg News*, May 13, 2016, https://www
    .bloomberg.com/news/articles/2017-04-28/your-money-in-trump
    -s-first-100-days-a-highlight-reel; Claire Cain Miller, "With More
    Women Fulfilled by Work, Retirement Has to Wait," *New York
    Times*, February 12, 2017, p. 1.

13. https://time.com/4464811/aging-happiness-stress-anxiety
    -depression/.

14. Monique Morrissey, "Private-sector pension coverage fell by half
    over two decades," *Working Economics Blog*, Economic Policy Insti-
    tute, January 11, 2013, https://www.epi.org/blog/private-sector
    -pension-coverage-decline/. See also Alicia H. Munnell, Kelly
    Haverstick, and Mauricio Soto, "Why Have Defined Benefit Plans
    Survived in the Public Sector?" Center for Retirement Research,
    Boston College, December 2007, https://crr.bc.edu/wp-content/
    uploads/2007/12/slp_2.pdf.

15. C. Lee Harrington et al., "Life course transitions and the future of fandom," *International Journal of Cultural Studies*, vol. 14, no. 6, 2011, p. 571; this is an excellent overview of the transitions facing older people in the twenty-first century.

16. Susan Sontag, "The Double Standard of Aging," *Saturday Review*, September 23, 1972, p. 31.

17. "Beauty Comes of Age: Findings of the 2006 Dove Global Study on aging, beauty and well-being," September 2006, p. 4.

18. Susan J. Douglas, *Where the Girls Are: Growing Up Female with the Mass Media* (New York: Times Books, 1994), pp. 8–10.

19. Petula Dvorak, "Hillary Clinton is a 68-year-old woman. And plenty of people hate her for it," *Washington Post*, October 6, 2016.

20. Deborah Jermyn, " 'Grey is the new green'? Gauging age(ing) in Hollywood's upper quadrant female audience, *The Intern* (2015), and the discursive construction of 'Nancy Meyers,' " *Celebrity Studies*, vol. 9, no. 2, 2018, p. 175.

21. Amanda Haboush et al., "Beauty, Ethnicity, and Age: Does Internalization of Mainstream Media Ideals Influence Attitudes Towards Older Adults?" *Sex Roles*, vol. 66, December 2011, pp. 668–76.

22. Jason Lynch, "U.S. Adults Consume an Entire Hour More of Media Per Day Than They Did Just Last Year," *Adweek*, June 27, 2016, https://www.adweek.com/tv-video/us-adults-consume-entire -hour-more-media-day-they-did-just-last-year-172218/.

23. C. Lee Harrington et al., "New Areas of Inquiry in Aging, Media, and Culture," in C. Lee Harrington et al., *Aging, Media, and Culture* (New York: Lexington Books, 2014), p. 2.

24. Dahmen and Cozma, eds., "Media Takes: On Aging."

25. Shyon Baumann and Kim de Laat, "Aspiration and Compromise: Portrayals of Older Adults in Television Advertising," in Harrington et al., *Aging, Media, and Culture*, p. 18.

26. Colin Milner et al., "The Media's Portrayal of Aging," in John R. Beard at al., eds., World Economic Forum, "Global Population Aging: Peril or Promise," 2012, p. 26.

27. Milner et al., "The Media's Portrayal of Aging," p. 25.

28. Ehud Bodner, "On the origins of ageism among older and younger adults," *International Psychogeriatrics,* vol. 21, no. 6, p. 1004.

29. Laurie Russell Hatch, "Gender and Ageism," *Generations,* Fall 2009, vol. 29, no. 3, p. 19.

30. Stacy L. Smith et al., "Inclusion or Invisibility? Comprehensive Annenberg Report on Diversity in Entertainment," Institute for Diversity and Empowerment at Annenberg, University of Southern California, p. 2, https://annenberg.usc.edu/pages/~/media/MDSCI/CARDReport%20FINAL%2022216.ashx.

31. "Hollywood's Glaring Gender Gap," *Time* Labs, October 6, 2015, https://labs.time.com/story/these-charts-show-hollywoods-glaring-gender-gap/.

32. Maria Coder, "Helen Mirren: 'Ageism in Hollywood Is Outrageous,'" https://www.people.com/article/helen-mirren-defends-maggie-gyllenhaal-hollywood-ageism-sexism-outrageous.

33. Martha M. Lauzen, "The Celluloid Ceiling: Behind-the-Scenes Employment of Women on the Top 100, 250, and 500 Films of 2017," Center for the Study of Women in Television & Film, 2018, https://womenintvfilm.sdsu.edu/wp-content/uploads/2018/01/2017_Celluloid_Ceiling_Report.pdf.

34. Martha M. Lauzen, "Thumbs Down 2018: Film Critics and Gender, and Why It Matters," Center for the Study of Women in Television & Film, 2018, https://womenintvfilm.sdsu.edu/wp-content/uploads/2018/07/2018_Thumbs_Down_Report.pdf.

35. Jermyn, "'Grey is the new green'?" p. 170.

36. "The Status of Women in the U.S. Media, 2015," Women's Media Center, https://wmc.3cdn.net/83bf6082a319460eb1_hsrm680x2.pdf.

37. Colin Milner et al., "The Media's Portrayal of Aging," in John R. Beard et al., eds., World Economic Forum, "Global Population Aging: Peril or Promise," 2012, p. 26.

38. Etcoff, "Beauty Comes of Age," p. 4.

39. Rance Crain, "Boomer boon: 'Crazy aunts and uncles' spend $1.7 trillion," *Advertising Age,* April 2, 2007, p. 15.

40. Jeanine Poggi, "What Will Life Be Like After Letterman for CBS?

Younger host may draw new viewers, but Eye Net's core demo is older," *Advertising Age*, April 7, 2014, p. 10.

41. Sarah Barry James, "The age-old question at CBS," *SNL Kagan Media & Communications Report*, March 21, 2013.

42. Lindsay Rubino, "Demo Doesn't Want to Sing 'Hope I Buy Before I Get Old,'" *Broadcasting & Cable*, April 15, 2013, p. 12.

43. Harrington et al., "Life course transitions and the future of fandom," p. 572.

44. Hilde Van den Bulck, "Growing Old in Celebrity Culture," in Harrington et al., *Aging, Media, and Culture*, pp. 65–67.

45. Dvorak, "Hillary Clinton is a 68-year-old woman."

46. Douglas, *Where the Girls Are*, pp. 194–96.

47. https://plus50.aacc.nche.edu/employers/popualation/Pages/default.aspxhttp://; www.nielsen.com/us/en/insights/reports/2012/introducing-boomers--marketing-s-most-valuable-generation.html.

48. Rebecca Traister, *Good and Mad: The Revolutionary Power of Women's Anger* (New York: Simon & Schuster, 2018), pp. xviii–xix.

49. Recent, important books about ageism include Ashton Applewhite, *This Chair Rocks: A Manifesto Against Ageism* (Networked Books, 2016); Jo Ann Jenkins (with Boe Workman), *Disrupt Aging* (New York: Public Affairs, 2016); Margaret Morganroth Gullette, *Ending Ageism, or How Not to Shoot Old People* (New Brunswick, NJ: Rutgers University Press, 2017) and *Agewise: Fighting the New Ageism in America* (Chicago: University of Chicago Press, 2011); Margaret Cruickshank, *Learning to Be Old* (Lanham, MD: Rowman & Littlefield, 2009); Todd D. Nelson, ed., *Ageism: Stereotyping and Prejudice Against Older Persons* (Cambridge, MA: MIT Press, 2002); Kathleen Woodward, ed., *Figuring Age: Women, Bodies, Generations* (Bloomington, IN: Indiana University Press, 1999).

50. Deborah Jermyn, "Introduction—'Get a life ladies. Your old one is not coming back': Ageing, ageism and the lifespan of female celebrity," *Celebrity Studies*, vol. 3, no. 1, March 2012, p. 2.

51. Jermyn, "Introduction—'Get a life ladies.'"

52. Alan Rappeport, "Gloria Steinem and Madeleine Albright Rebuke
     Young Women Backing Bernie Sanders," *New York Times*, Febru-
     ary 7, 2016, https://www.nytimes.com/2016/02/08/us/politics/
     gloria-steinem-madeleine-albright-hillary-clinton-bernie-sanders
     .html?_r=0.

53. Thanks to Caitlin Lawson for this. She notes, "This change is
     not noted within the article, but the original title is still viewable
     through the Way Back Machine web archive": https://web.archive
     .org/web/20160207220355/http://www.nytimes.com/2016/02/08/
     us/politics/gloria-steinem-madeleine-albright-hillary-clinton
     -bernie-sanders.html?_r=0.

54. Weiyi Cai and Scott Clement, "What Americans think about
     feminism today," *Washington Post*, January 27, 2016, https://
     www.washingtonpost.com/graphics/national/feminism
     -project/poll/.

55. Traister, *Good and Mad*, p. 250.

56. Dawn Davis, "This Is How Katie Couric Responds to People Who
     Think She Looks Old," *Popsugar*, July 25, 2019, https://www.popsugar
     .com/beauty/Katie-Couric-Aging-Interview-46419189.

Chapter 2: Why the Seventies Mattered

1. Roxane Gay, "Fifty Years Ago, Protesters Took on the Miss
     America Pageant and Electrified the Feminist Movement,"
     Smithsonian, January 2018, https://www.smithsonianmag
     .com/history/fifty-years-ago-protestors-took-on-miss-america
     -pageant-electrified-feminist-movement-180967504/.

 2. Excerpted from *Color Me Flo: My Hard Life and Good Times*, "The
     Miss America Pageant," Redstockings, https://www.redstockings
     .org/index.php/themissamericaprotest.

 3. Kathryn Schulz, "The Many Lives of Pauli Murray," *The
     New Yorker*, April 17, 2017, https://www.newyorker.com/
     magazine/2017/04/17/the-many-lives-of-pauli-murray.

4. History of NOW, "Founding: Setting the Stage," https://now.org/about/history/founding-2/.

5. History of the National Women's Political Caucus, https://www.nwpc.org/history/; Florynce Kennedy Biography, *Encyclopedia of World Biography*, https://www.notablebiographies.com/supp/Supplement-Ka-M/Kennedy-Florynce.html.

6. Janell Hobson, "Black Herstory: The Founder of the Feminist Party," *Ms. blog*, February 9, 2012.

7. Brooke Bobb, "As Gloria Steinem Prepares to Accept Her CFDA Tribute, 17 Feminists Share What She Means to Them," *Vogue*, June 1, 2017.

8. Cited in Susan J. Douglas, *Where the Girls Are: Growing Up with the Mass Media* (New York: Times Books, 1994), pp. 56–57.

9. Cited in Jerry L. Rodnitzky, *Feminist Phoenix: The Rise and Fall of a Feminist Counterculture* (Westport, CT: Praeger, 1999), p. 115.

10. "Patriarchal Views on women," https://blogparaprofesfeministas.files.wordpress.com/2015/10/workshoppatriarchalvisions.pdf.

11. Douglas, *Where the Girls Are*, p. 124.

12. Alice Kessler-Harris, *Out to Work: A History of Wage-Earning Women in the United States* (New York: Oxford University Press, 1982), pp. 313–15; "Equal Pay Act of 1963," *History*, https://www.history.com/topics/equal-pay-act.

13. "The Simple Truth About the Gender Pay Gap," AAUW, https://www.aauw.org/research/the-simple-truth-about-the-gender-pay-gap/.

14. Inez Robb, "Girls, Your Jobs Have Been Saved!" *Detroit Free Press*, April 10, 1963, p. A9.

15. Mitra Toossi, "A Century of Change: the U.S. Labor Force, 1950–2050," *Monthly Labor Review*, May 2002, p. 18.

16. Ari Kelman, "We are confronted primarily with a moral issue. It is as old as the scriptures and as clear as the American constitution," *Chronicle*, July 2, 2008, https://www.chronicle.com/blognetwork/edgeofthewest/2008/07/02/we-are-confronted-primarily-with

-a-moral-issue-it-is-as-old-as-the-scriptures-and-as-clear-as-the
-american-constitution/.

17. Gail Collins, *When Everything Changed: The Amazing Journey of American Women from 1960 to the Present* (New York: Little, Brown, 2009), p. 77.

18. https://www.aauw.org/2014/06/30/untold-civil-rights-act-story/.

19. Sascha Cohen, "The Day Women Went on Strike," *Time.com*, August 26, 2015, http://time.com/4008060/women-strike-equality-1970/.

20. For much more on the coverage, see Douglas, *Where the Girls Are*, ch. 8.

21. Lisa Hix, "Women in the Skies: The Birth of the Stewardess," *Ms. blog*, September 16, 2014, https://msmagazine.com/blog/2014/09/16/women-in-the-skies-the-birth-of-the-stewardess/.

22. Susan Erlich Martin and Nancy C. Jurik, *Doing Justice, Doing Gender: Women in Legal and Criminal Justice Occupations* (New York: Sage, 1996), p. 110.

23. Cynthia Grant Bowman, "Women in the Legal Profession from the 1920s to the 1970s: What Can We Learn from Their Experience About Law and Social Change?" *Maine Law Review*, vol. 61, no. 1, 2009, p. 10, accessed at https://scholarship.law.cornell.edu/cgi/viewcontent.cgi?article=1011&context=facpub.

24. Bowman, "Women in the Legal Profession from the 1920s to the 1970s," pp. 13–15; "Women in Law," Catalyst, https://www.catalyst.org/knowledge/women-law.

25. https://www.dol.gov/oasam/regs/statutes/titleix.htm.

26. "Women in Medicine," https://www.amnhealthcare.com/uploadedFiles/MainSite/Content/Staffing_Recruitment/Staffcare-WP-Women%20in%20Med.pdf.

27. https://www.nawrb.com/community/statistics-on-women-and-home-ownership/.

28. Gerald Eskenazi, "Title IX Rules Issued for Equality in Sports," *New York Times*, June 5, 1975, p. 29, https://www.nytimes.com/1975/06/04/archives/title-ix-rules-issued-for-equality-in-sports-title-ix-rules-are.html?searchResultPosition=2.

29. Marc Tracy and Tim Rohan, "What Made College Football More Like the Pros? $7.3 Billion, For a Start," *New York Times*, December 30, 2014, https://www.nytimes.com/2014/12/31/sports/ncaafootball/what-made-college-ball-more-like-the-pros-73-billion-for-a-start.html.

30. Stephen Douglas, "Ohio State Football Worth $1.5 billion," *The Big Lead*, September 21, 2017, https://thebiglead.com/2017/09/21/ohio-state-football-worth-1-5-billion-the-most-valuable-college-football-program/.

31. Jessica Bennett and Jesse Ellison, "Young Women, *Newsweek* and Sexism," *Newsweek*, March 18, 2010, https://www.newsweek.com/young-women-newsweek-and-sexism-69339.

32. Lynn Povich, "Women in the workplace: How 'good girls' fight back," *Los Angeles Times*, October 7, 2012, https://articles.latimes.com/2012/oct/07/opinion/la-oe-povich-newsweek-discrimination-gender-20121007.

33. "*Newsweek* agrees to end sex discrimination policy," *Eugene Register Guard*, August 28, 1970, https://news.google.com/newspapers?id=8JpQAAAAIBAJ&sjid=NuEDAAAAIBAJ&pg=5051,6088623&dq=eleanor holmes-norton&hl=en.

34. Jacey Fortin, "The Women Behind 'Good Girls Revolt' Think the Time Is Right to Revive the Feminist Show," *New York Times*, October 27, 2017, https://www.nytimes.com/2017/10/27/arts/television/good-girls-revolt.html.

35. Olivia Truffaut-Wong, "How Gloria Steinem & Dolores Huerta Championed Intersectionality in Activism," *Bustle*, August 22, 2017, https://www.bustle.com/p/how-gloria-steinem-dolores-huerta-championed-intersectionality-in-activism-video-77951.

36. Linda Gordon, "De-mystique-ing feminism," *Los Angeles Times*, July 27, 2003, https://articles.latimes.com/2003/jul/27/books/bk-gordon27.

37. https://womenemployed.org/milestones-1970s.

38. Sherie M. Randolph, "The Lasting Legacy of Florynce Kennedy, Black Feminist Fighter," *Solidarity Newsletter*, https://solidarity-us.org/atc/152/p3272/.

39. Ruth Hubbard, *The Politics of Women's Biology* (New Brunswick, NJ: Rutgers University Press, 1990), pp. 150–51.

40. Susan J. Douglas and Meredith W. Michaels, *The Mommy Myth: The Idealization of Motherhood and How It Has Undermined Women* (New York: Free Press, 2004), pp. 42–43.

41. Ana Swanson, "144 years of marriage and divorce in the United States, in one chart," *Washington Post*, June 23, 2015, https://www .washingtonpost.com/news/wonk/wp/2015/06/23/144-years-of -marriage-and-divorce-in-the-united-states-in-one-chart/?utm_ term=.d06b962bfb7b.

42. Douglas and Michaels, *The Mommy Myth*, p. 86.

43. Douglas and Michaels, *The Mommy Myth*, pp. 94–95.

44. Claire Cain Miller, "Mounting Evidence of Advantages for Children of Working Mothers," *New York Times*, May 15, 2015, https:// www.nytimes.com/2015/05/17/upshot/mounting-evidence-of -some-advantages-for-children-of-working-mothers.html.

45. Roger Sanjek, *Gray Panthers* (Philadelphia: University of Pennsylvania Press, 2009), p. 151.

46. Sanjek, *Gray Panthers*, pp. 151–52.

47. William R. Cash, "Gray Panther Due Here," *Boston Globe*, May 1, 1975, p. 48; Donna Schiebe, "Fiery Gray Panther Prods Oldsters to Start Fighting," *Los Angeles Times*, July 22, 1976, p. SF1; Michael Tackett, "Maggie Kuhn: At 75, a Pied Piper for aged," *Chicago Tribune*, July 13, 1980, p. 13.

48. Ellen Goodman, "Gray Is Beautiful, but . . . ," *Los Angeles Times*, February 22, 1978, p. D7.

49. Betty Liddick, "America's Older Citizens: Age of Activism," *Los Angeles Times*, October 26, 1977, p. F1.

50. Claudia Levy, "Gray Panthers Co-Founder Maggie Kuhn Dies at 89," *Washington Post*, April 23, 1995.

51. Levy, "Gray Panthers Co-Founder Maggie Kuhn Dies at 89."

52. Michael L. Hilt and Jeremy H. Lipschultz, *Mass Media, an Aging Population, and the Baby Boomers* (New York: Routledge, 2005), p. 6.

53. Francesca Lyman, "Maggie Kuhn: A wrinkled radical's crusade," *The Progressive*, January 1988, p. 29.

54. Bill Fripp, "The Gray Panthers," *Boston Globe*, June 23, 1973, p. 9.

55. Disengagement theory is discussed in Hilt and Lipschultz, *Mass Media, an Aging Population, and the Baby Boomers*, pp. 23–24.

56. Eleanor Hoover, "Gray Panthers Wage War on 'Wrinkled Babyhood,'" *Los Angeles Times*, March 24, 1975, p. C1; George Michaelson, "Maggie Kuhn: Gray Panther on the Prowl," *Boston Globe*, December 18, 1977, p. G6.

57. Levy, "Gray Panthers Co-Founder Maggie Kuhn Dies at 89."

58. Robert McG. Thomas Jr., "Maggie Kuhn, 89, the Founder of Gray Panthers, Is Dead," *New York Times*, April 23, 1995.

59. "Grey Panthers: Philadelphia woman organizing elderly to help them get a better deal," *Globe and Mail*, April 23, 1973.

60. "Hearing Before the Select Committee on Aging," House of Representatives, Ninety-fifth Congress, Second Session, January 28, 1978 (Washington, DC: U.S. Government Printing Office, 1978), p. 87.

61. Bill O'Hallaren, "Nobody (in TV) Loves You When You're Old and Gray," *New York Times*, July 24, 1977, p. D21.

62. Sanjek, *Gray Panthers*, p. 234.

63. O'Hallaren, "Nobody (in TV) Loves You When You're Old and Gray," p. D21.

64. Maggie Kuhn et al., *No Stone Unturned: The Life and Times of Maggie Kuhn* (New York: Ballantine Books, 1991), p. 162.

65. O'Hallaren, "Nobody (in TV) Loves You When You're Old and Gray," p. D21.

66. "Hearing Before the Select Committee on Aging," pp. 98–101.

67. "Hearing Before the Select Committee on Aging," pp. 3–6.

68. "Hearing Before the Select Committee on Aging," p. 2.

69. O'Hallaren, "Nobody (in TV) Loves You When You're Old and Gray," p. D21.

70. "Hearing Before the Select Committee on Aging," pp. 2–3.

Chapter 3: The Rise of Aspirational Aging

1. Bob Garfield, "The wrong icon, but the right tone for boomers," *Advertising Age*, November 20, 2006, p. 29.

2. Mya Frazier, "Locked in a cultural battle of the ages; Generation Gap: Age issues are often more about a power struggle," *Advertising Age*, February 5, 2007, p. 29.

3. Don E. Bradley and Charles F. Longino Jr., "How Older People Think About Images of Aging in Advertising and the Media," *Generations*, Fall 2001, vol. 25, no. 3, pp. 17, 19, 20.

4. Nancy Ryan, "Marketing to Older Consumers Still at an Immature Stage," *Chicago Tribune*, March 22, 1991; https://articles .chicagotribune.com/1991-03-22/business/9101260037_1_older -consumers-groups-for-older-americans-ad-agencies.

5. Anita Harris, *Future Girl: Young Women in the Twenty-First Century* (New York: Routledge, 2004), p. 4.

6. David Harvey, *A Brief History of Neoliberalism* (New York: Oxford University Press, 2007), p. 23.

7. Susan Jeffords, *Hard Bodies: Hollywood Masculinity in the Reagan Era* (New Brunswick, NJ: Rutgers University Press, 1993), pp. 4–5, 10–11.

8. Yvonne Tasker and Diane Negra, eds., *Interrogating Postfeminism: Gender and the Politics of Popular Culture* (Durham, NC: Duke University Press, 2007), p. 21.

9. See Rosalind Gill, *Gender and the Media* (Cambridge, UK: Polity, 2007); Tasker and Negra, eds., *Interrogating Postfeminism*; Harris, *Future Girl*.

10. Eric Lindland et al., "Gauging Aging: Mapping the Gaps Between Expert and Public Understandings of Aging in America," A FrameWorks Strategic Report, FrameWorksInstitute.org, pp. 22–23.

11. Lindland et al., "Gauging Aging."

12. James Tenser, "Ageless Aging of Boom-X; Latter baby boom, early Gen X want to be defined in terms of attitudes, not years," *Advertising Age*, January 2, 2006, p. 18.

13. James Tenser, "New Old Won't Go Quietly," *Advertising Age*, January 2, 2006, p. 20.

14. Rance Crain, "Boomer boon: 'Crazy aunts and uncles' spend $1.7 trillion," *Advertising Age*, April 2, 2007, p. 15.

15. https://www.marketingcharts.com/uncategorized/baby-boomers-control-70-of-us-disposable-income-22891/.

16. https://contently.com/strategist/2014/07/16/4-tips-for-marketing-to-baby-boomers-in-the-digital-age/.

17. George Chambers, "6 ways to market to boomers," *LifeHealthPro*, August 7, 2014, online.

18. Jim Gilmartin, columnist, "What We've Learned About Marketing to Baby Boomers—Part III," March 6, 2017, MediaPost, https://www.mediapost.com/publications/article/296442/what-weve-learned-about-marketing-to-baby-boomers.html.

19. Dan Barry, "Baby Boom Hits New Milestone of Self-Absorption: Age 65," *New York Times*, December 31, 2010, https://www.nytimes.com/2011/01/01/us/01boomers.html?pagewanted=all&_r=0.

20. Tim Arnold, "The Fifties, So Far," *Adweek*, June 12, 2006, online.

21. James Tenser, "Ageless Aging of Boom-X," p. 18.

22. Jessica Hawthorne-Castro, "The Art of Targeting the 'Boomer Consumer,'" *Response*, June 2015, p. 46.

23. Chambers, "6 ways to market to boomers."

24. Frazier, "Locked in a cultural battle of the ages," p. 29.

25. Andrew Adam Newman, "In AARP's View, Advertisers Need to Focus," *New York Times*, July 19, 2012, p. B4.

26. Jack Neff, "Unilever resuscitates the demo left for dead; Marketer spies goldmine in the over-looked baby-boomer consumer," *Advertising Age*, May 28, 2007, p. 1.

27. Mark Dolliver, "Having Bored You About the '60s, They'll Now Bore You About the 60s," *Adweek*, July 17, 2006, online.

28. Jack Neff, "Unilever resuscitates the demo left for dead."

29. "Marketers would be foolish to ignore boomer audience," *Advertising Age*, June 4, 2007, p. 26.

30. Carrie Whitmer, "The median audience age of the 10 biggest TV shows signals how few young people are tuning in," *Business Insider*, May 16, 2018, https://www.businessinsider.com/median -age-of-the-audience-for-10-most-popular-shows-on-network-tv -2018-5.

31. Abbey Klaassen, "Media players go after free-spending boomers; TV Land, host of websites try to cash out by building content for over-50 demo," *Advertising Age*, September 3, 2007, p. 3.

32. Klaassen, "Media players go after free-spending boomers."

33. Judann Pollack, "Boomers don't want your pity, but they do demand your respect," *Advertising Age*, October 8, 2007.

34. John Consoli, "Age-Old Question Remains: Why Not Target Boomers?" *Broadcasting & Cable*, March 31, 2014, p. 14.

35. Linda Landers, op-ed contributor, "Put Boomer Women on Your 'Nice' List This Holiday Season," October 26, 2017, MediaPost.

36. Bruce Horovitz and Julie Appleby, "Prescription drug costs are up; So are TV ads promoting them," *USA Today*, March 16, 2017, https://www.usatoday.com/story/money/2017/03/16/prescription -drug-costs-up-tv-ads/99203878/.

37. Shyon Baumann and Kim de Laat, "Aspiration and Compromise: Portrayals of Older Adults in Television Advertising," in C. Lee Harrington et al., *Aging, Media, and Culture* (New York: Lexington Books, 2014), p. 14.

38. C. Lee Ventola, "Direct-to-Consumer Pharmaceutical Advertising, Therapeutic or Toxic?" *Pharmacy & Therapeutics*, October 2011, vol. 36, no. 10, https://www.ncbi.nlm.nih.gov/pmc/articles/ PMC3278148/.

39. Michelle Llamas, "Selling Side Effects: Big Pharma's Marketing Machine," *drugwatch*, https://www.drugwatch.com/featured/big -pharma-marketing/.

40. Austin Frakt, "Why Are Drug Costs So High? Problem Traces to the 1990s," *New York Times*, November 13, 2018, p. B4.

41. Carolyn Y. Johnson, "Why America pays so much more for drugs," *Washington Post*, February 25, 2016, https://www.washingtonpost

.com/news/wonk/wp/2016/02/25/why-america-pays-so-much
-more-for-drugs/?utm_term=.0e86bc636bfe.

42. Jeanne Whalen, "Why the U.S. Pays More Than Other Countries
for Drugs," *Wall Street Journal*, December 1, 2015, https://www
.wsj.com/articles/why-the-u-s-pays-more-than-other-countries-for
-drugs-1448939481.

43. Bill Allison, "Big Pharma Lobby Group Spent Record Amount as
Reform Push Grows," *Bloomberg News*, January 22, 2019, https://
www.bloomberg.com/news/articles/2019-01-22/big-pharma-lobby
-group-spent-record-amount-as-reform-push-grows.

44. Whalen, "Why the U.S. Pays More Than Other Countries for Drugs."

45. Dylan Scott, "The untold story of TV's first prescription drug ad,"
STAT, December 11, 2015, https://www.statnews.com/2015/12/11/
untold-story-tvs-first-prescription-drug-ad/.

46. Ana Swanson, "Big pharmaceutical companies are spending far
more on marketing than on research," *Washington Post*, February 11, 2015, https://www.washingtonpost.com/news/wonk/
wp/2015/02/11/big-pharmaceutical-companies-are-spending-far
-more-on-marketing-than-research/?utm_term=.947f4d6fd69d.

47. Julie Liesse, "A Healthy Ad Market," in "Healthcare Marketing,"
Advertising Age, 2016, https://gaia.adage.com/images/bin/pdf/
KantarHCwhitepaper_complete.pdf; Horovitz and Appleby, "Pre-
scription drug costs are up."

48. Bob Watson, "McCaskill aims to end tax breaks for pharma industry ads," *News Tribune*, https://www.newstribune.com/news/
local/story/2018/mar/03/mccaskill-aims-end-tax-breaks-pharma
-industry-ads/715834/.

49. Baumann and de Laat, "Aspiration and Compromise: Portrayals of
Older Adults in Television Advertising," p. 22.

50. https://www.healthline.com/health/psoriasis/facts-statistics
-infographic#prevalence2; Maurince M. Ohayon et al., "Epidemi-
ology of Restless Legs Syndrome: A Synthesis of the Literature,"
https://www.ncbi.nlm.nih.gov/pmc/articles/PMC3204316/.

51. Rob Walker, "The Beast Under Your Toenail: Lamisil's stomach-

turning ad," *Slate*, July 4, 2003, https://www.slate.com/articles/business/ad_report_card/2003/07/the_beast_under_your_toenail.html.

52. Ned Pagliarulo, "Animated drug ads prompt FDA study into effect on consumer behavior," *Biopharm Dive*, March 2, 2016, https://www.biopharmadive.com/news/animated-drug-ads-prompt-fda-study-into-effect-on-consumer-behavior/414896/.

53. Horovitz and Appleby, "Prescription drug costs are up."

54. Llamas, "Selling Side Effects: Big Pharma's Marketing Machine."

55. Scott, "The untold story of TV's first prescription drug ad."

56. Katie Thomas, "Bayer and Johnson & Johnson Settle Lawsuits Over Xarelto, a Blood Thinner, for $775 Million," *New York Times*, March 25, 2019, https://www.nytimes.com/2019/03/25/health/xarelto-blood-thinner-lawsuit-settlement.html.

57. "AMA Calls for Ban on DTC Ads of Prescription Drugs and Medical Devices," press release, November 17, 2015, https://www.ama-assn.org/content/ama-calls-ban-direct-consumer-advertising-prescription-drugs-and-medical-devices.

58. Hilde Van den Bulck, "Growing Old in Celebrity Culture," in Harrington et al., *Aging, Media, and Culture*, p. 68.

59. Ken Budd, "New Adventures, New Risks, New You!" *AARP* magazine, June/July 2012, p. 57.

60. David Hochman, "Life's a Kick When You're Diane Keaton," *AARP* magazine, April/May 2012, p. 44.

61. Judith Newman, "Still Having Fun," *AARP* magazine, August/September 2016, p. 40.

62. Kenneth Miller, "Jessica Lange Can *Finally* Relax," *AARP* magazine, August/September 2017, p. 44.

63. These "dark sides" of the more positive imagery are also emphasized by Connie Zweig, "The perception of 'old' boomer, versus the reality!" on Boomer Café, February 19, 2019, https://www.boomercafe.com/2019/02/19/the-perception-of-old-boomer-versus-the-reality/.

64. *O, The Oprah Magazine*, September 2016, pp. 123, 132.

65. "How to Own Your Own Age," *AARP* magazine, June/July 2016, p. 38.

66. "Baby Boomer Women Remain Invisible to Marketers," American Marketing Association, Plus Media Solutions, October 8, 2016.

67. Landers, "Put Boomer Women on Your 'Nice' List This Holiday Season."

68. Jack Loechner, "Pay Attention to the Baby Boomers," September 8, 2017, MediaPost, https://www.mediapost.com/publications/article/307056/pay-attention-to-the-baby-boomers.html.

Chapter 4: The Anti-Aging Industrial Complex

1. https://www.katesomerville.com/anti-aging-products-retinol-eye-wrinkle-cream.

2. Yolanda Rosales G. De Al Baiz, "Skin Care Products You Should Start Using in Your 40s," *Fine Magazine*, September 2018, https://www.finehomesandliving.com/Skin-Care-Products-You-Should-Start-Using-in-Your-40s/; see description on its website for a smaller supply; https://www.lancerskincare.com/nourish#tab-description.

3. De Al-Baiz, "Skin Care Products You Should Start Using in Your 40s"; see also their website, https://drdennisgross.com/c-collagen-deep-cream.html?gclid=EAIaIQobChMInOOj3LP74gIVk8JkCh1HkwHjEAAYASAAEgKc6PD_BwE.

4. Julia Horniacek, "15 Anti-Aging Wrinkle Creams That Will Make You Believe in Miracles," June 13, 2017, https://www.bestproducts.com/beauty/g146/anti-aging-wrinkle-creams/.

5. https://www.drbrandtskincare.com/products/magnetight.

6. https://www.drbrandtskincare.com/products/do-not-age-with-dr-brandt-transforming-pearl-serum?rmatt=tsid:1027636|cid:210254619|agid:10748337339|tid:kwd-64408188819|crid:341350862307|nw:g|rnd:13890782141586633192|dvc:c|adp:1t1|mt:e|loc:9016851&gclid=EAIaIQobChMIyeXtxrX74gIVT77ACh3BnA3wEAAYASAAEgK_kvD_BwE.

7. https://www.macys.com/shop/product/peter-thomas-roth
   -cucumber-de-tox-bouncy-hydrating-gel?ID=2390848.

8. https://www.influenster.com/reviews/peter-thomas-roth
   -cucumber-de-tox-depuffing-eye-cubes.

9. Beautypedia Reviews: Peter Thomas Roth De-Tox De-Puffing Eye
   Cubes, https://www.youtube.com/watch?v=Ey8YczD5dxo.

10. Vanessa Cunningham, "10 Toxic Beauty Ingredients to Avoid," *Huff-
    Post*, November 12, 2013, https://www.huffingtonpost.com/vanessa
    -cunningham/dangerous-beauty-products_b_4168587.html.

11. L'Oreal Advertisement, *Essence*, February 2019, pp. 1–2.

12. Product description on Buy Better, https://www.buybetter.ng/
    shop/skincare/urbanskin-rx-glow-power-super-clear-and-even
    -kit/; https://urbanskinrx.com/collections/aging-skin/products/
    clear-even-tone-clarifying-glycolic-pads-1.

13. https://biopelle.com/collections/biopelle-stem-cell.

14. Timothy Caulfield, "The Pseudoscience of Beauty Products,"
    The Atlantic, 2015, https://www.theatlantic.com/health/
    archive/2015/05/the-pseudoscience-of-beauty-products/392201/.

15. Federal Trade Commission Complaint against L'Oreal,
    2014, https://www.ftc.gov/system/files/documents/
    cases/140926lorealcmpt.pdf.

16. Federal Trade Commission Complaint against L'Oreal, 2014.

17. Federal Trade Commission, "L'Oréal Settles FTC Charges Alleging
    Deceptive Advertising for Anti-Aging Cosmetics," June 30, 2014,
    https://www.ftc.gov/news-events/press-releases/2014/06/loreal
    -settles-ftc-charges-alleging-deceptive-advertising-anti.

18. Anita Singh, "Helen Mirren admits L'Oreal moisturiser 'prob-
    ably does f--- all,'" *The Telegraph*, August 2, 2017, https://www
    .telegraph.co.uk/news/2017/08/02/helen-mirren-admits-loreal
    -moisturiser-probably-does-f/.

19. https://www.a4m.com/conferences-exhibitors-anti-aging
    -marketplace.html.

20. Sarah Kinonen, "Turmeric Isn't as Magical as We All Thought,

Study Finds," *Allure*, January 18, 2017, https://www.allure.com/story/turmeric-not-beneficial-study-finds.

21. "Allergan Launches New JUVÉDERM® IT Campaign Designed to Reach the Next Generation of Consumers," PR Newswire, October 3, 2018, https://www.prnewswire.com/news-releases/allergan-launches-new-juvederm-it-campaign-designed-to-reach-the-next-generation-of-consumers-300723447.html.

22. Caulfield, "The Pseudoscience of Beauty Products."

23. Matt Novak, "9 Consumer Complaints About Bullshit Memory Drug," *Gizmodo*, April 17, 2017, https://gizmodo.com/9-consumer-complaints-about-prevagen-the-bullshit-memo-1794288389; Maggie Fox, "Jellyfish Memory Supplement Prevagen Is a Hoax, FTC Says," *NBC News*, February 7, 2017, https://www.nbcnews.com/health/health-news/jellyfish-memory-supplement-prevagen-hoax-ftc-says-n704886.

24. Josh Long, "Judge Dismisses FTC Lawsuit Over Quincy Bioscience's Memory Supplement Prevagen," *Natural Products Insider*, October 2, 2017, https://www.naturalproductsinsider.com/blogs/insider-law/2017/10/judge-dismisses-ftc-lawsuit-over-quincy-bioscienc.aspx.

25. "truthinadvertising.org; FTC Complaint Filed Against Maker of Memory Supplement," *NewsRX*, October 10, 2015.

26. Emily Dreyfuss, "Don't Fall for the 'Memory' Pills Targeting Baby Boomers," *Wired*, June 22, 2017, https://www.wired.com/story/dont-fall-for-the-memory-pills-targeting-baby-boomers/.

27. Fayne L. Frey, MD, "6 Claims You'll Find on Skin-Care Products that Are Actually Bogus," *Reader's Digest*, November 18, 2017, https://www.msn.com/en-us/health/healthtrending/6-claims-you%E2%80%99ll-find-on-skin-care-products-that-are-actually-bogus/ar-BBF6HFl?li=BBnbfcL.

28. Hannah Morrill, "Charting: A Brief History of Anti-Aging," *Harper's Bazaar*, April 14, 2016, https://www.harpersbazaar.com/beauty/skin-care/a14980/history-of-anti-aging/.

29. Tina Sugurdson, "Exposing the Cosmetics Cover-Up: True Hor-

ror Stories of Cosmetic Dangers," October 29, 2013, Enviroblog, http://www.ewg.org/research/exposing-cosmetics-cover/true -horror-stories-of-cosmetic-dangers.

30. Trine Tsouderos, "Do anti-aging skin creams work? Mostly no, dermatologists say," *Medicalxpress*, February 4, 2011, https:// medicalxpress.com/news/2011-02-anti-aging-skin-creams -dermatologists.html.

31. "5 Bogus Cosmetic Claims," *Paula's Choice*, https://www .paulaschoice.com/expert-advice/skincare-advice/myths/five -bogus-cosmetic-claims.html.

32. Thomas Cluderay and Tina Sigurdson, "Are Anti-Aging Prod-ucts the Fountain of Youth? Really?" *Enviroblog*, November 22, 2013, https://www.ewg.org/enviroblog/2013/11/are-anti-aging -products-fountain-youth-really.

33. Maggie Fox, "Does your wrinkle cream really work? FDA warns about false claims," *Today*, March 23, 2015, https://www.today .com/health/does-your-wrinkle-cream-really-work-fda-warns -about-bogus-t10391.

34. Fox, "Does your wrinkle cream really work?"

35. *Buhs v. pH Beauty Labs, Inc.*, https://www.truthinadvertising .org/wp-content/uploads/2013/09/Buhs-v.-PH-Beauty-Labs-Inc. -complaint.pdf.

36. https://www.leagle.com/decision/infdco20150528861; file:/// Users/sdoug/Downloads/gov.uscourts.njd.283902.13.0%20(1).pdf.

37. Warning Letter, U.S. Food and Drug Administration to Crescent Health Center, Inc., April 20, 2016.

38. Closeout Letter, from FDA to Crescent Health Center Inc., Decem-ber 15, 2016, https://www.fda.gov/inspections-compliance -enforcement-and-criminal-investigations/warning-letters/crescent -health-center-inc-close-out-letter-12516.

39. Federal Trade Commission, "Marketers Settle FTC Charges That They Used Deceptive Ads in Promoting Products for Mole and Wart Removal, Anti-Aging and Weight Loss," December 23, 2014.

40. Frey, "6 Claims You'll Find on Skin-Care Products that Are Actually Bogus."

41. Frey, "6 Claims You'll Find on Skin-Care Products that Are Actually Bogus."

42. Caulfield, "The Pseudoscience of Beauty Products."

43. Ernst Epstein, MD, "Are We Consultants or Peddlers?" *Archives of Dermatology*, 1998, vol. 134, no. 4, pp. 508–9.

44. Tsouderos, "Do anti-aging skin creams work? Mostly no, dermatologists say."

45. Fayne L. Frey, MD, "Why Buying Eye Cream Is a Waste of Money, According to a Dermatologist," *Reader's Digest*, https://www.rd.com/health/beauty/eye-cream-waste-money/.

46. Michelle Villett, "Does Your Skin Need Hyaluronic Acid?" *Beauty Editor*, March 10, 2014, https://beautyeditor.ca/2014/03/11/hyaluronic-acid-skin-benefits.

47. Danielle Fontana, "18 Beauty 'Facts' You've Heard that Are Totally False," *New Beauty*, June 13, 2016, https://www.newbeauty.com/hottopic/slideshow/2264-beauty-plastic-surgery-myths/.

48. "The Truth about Antioxidants and Your Skin," *Reader's Digest Best Health*, https://www.besthealthmag.ca/best-looks/skin/the-truth-about-antioxidants-and-your-skin/.

49. Jedha Dening, "The 'Proven' Benefits of Antioxidants: Real Science or Sales Pitch?" *Zwivel*, September 19, 2017, https://www.zwivel.com/blog/benefits-of-antioxidants-skin-and-body/.

50. https://intothegloss.com/2016/03/what-is-serum/.

51. Deborah Netburn, "Digitally enhanced Julia Roberts, Christy Turlington ads banned in Britain," *Los Angeles Times*, July 27, 2011, https://latimesblogs.latimes.com/technology/2011/07/julia-roberts-christie-turlington-ads-banned-in-britain-due-to-excessive-airbrushing.html.

52. John Plunkett, "L'Oreal advert featuring Rachel Weisz banned for being 'misleading,'" *The Guardian*, January 31, 2012, https://www.theguardian.com/media/2012/feb/01/loreal-advert-rachel-weisz-banned.

53. Deborah Jermyn, "Introduction—'Get a life, ladies. Your old one is not coming back': ageing, ageism and the lifespan of female celebrity," *Celebrity Studies*, vol. 3, no. 1, March 2012, p. 4.

54. Sara Randazzo, "Lifestyle Lift Shuts Down Most of Its Business, Considers Bankruptcy," *Wall Street Journal*, March 2, 2015, https://www.wsj.com/articles/lifestyle-lift-shuts-down-most-of-its-business-considers-bankruptcy-1425340363; Sara Randazzo, "Protection in Place for Former Lifestyle Lift Patients, Employees," *Wall Street Journal*, April 16, 2015, https://blogs.wsj.com/bankruptcy/2015/04/16/protections-in-place-for-former-lifestyle-lift-patients-employees/; Joan Kron, "Lifestyle Lift Closes for Business," *Allure*, March 3, 2015, https://www.allure.com/story/lifestyle-lift-bankruptcy; Amiya Prasad, MD, "Lifestyle Lift Closes Its Doors Across the US—Patients Seek Continuity of Care," *Dr. Prasad's Blog*, March 31, 2015, https://prasadcosmeticsurgery.com/dr-prasads-blog/lifestyle-lift-closes-its-doors-across-the-us-patients-seek-continuity-of-care/.

55. Jayne O'Donnell, "Cosmetic surgery gets cheaper, faster, scarier," *USA Today*, September 20, 2011, https://usatoday30.usatoday.com/money/perfi/basics/story/2011-09-14/risks-low-cost-cosmetic-surgery/50409740/1.

56. Sara Randazzo, "Protection in Place for Former Lifestyle Lift Patients, Employees," *Wall Street Journal*, April 16, 2015, https://blogs.wsj.com/bankruptcy/2015/04/16/protections-in-place-for-former-lifestyle-lift-patients-employees/.

57. See complaints at Lifestyle Lift Consumer Affairs site, https://www.consumeraffairs.com/doctors/dr_lifestyle_lift.html.

58. See complaints at the Lifestyle Lift Consumer Affairs site.

59. Susan J. Douglas, *The Rise of Enlightened Sexism* (New York: St. Martin's Griffin, 2011), pp. 222–25.

60. Douglas, *The Rise of Enlightened Sexism*, pp. 225–26.

61. Douglas, *The Rise of Enlightened Sexism*, pp. 246–47.

62. Hilde Van den Bulck, "Growing Old in Celebrity Culture," in C. Lee Harrington et al., *Aging, Media, and Culture* (New York: Lexington Books, 2014), p. 67.

63. *Us Weekly* staff, "Plastic Surgery Nightmares," April 2, 2015, https://www.usmagazine.com/stylish/pictures/plastic-surgery -nightmares-2009188/38167/; Brynn Mannino, "10 Worst Celebrity Plastic Surgery Mishaps," *Woman's Day*, May 18, 2013, http://www .womansday.com/life/entertainment/a1310/10-worst-celebrity -plastic-surgery-mishaps-103522/.

64. Van den Bulck, "Growing Old in Celebrity Culture," p. 74.

65. Susan Berridge, "From the Woman Who 'Had It All' to the Tragic, Ageing Spinster: The Shifting Star Persona of Jennifer Aniston," in Deborah Jermyn and Su Holmes, eds., *Women, Celebrity and Cultures of Aging* (Hampshire, UK: Palgrave Macmillan, 2015), p. 116.

66. Jermyn, "Introduction—'Get a life, ladies. Your old one is not com- ing back,'" p. 4.

67. Van den Bulck, "Growing Old in Celebrity Culture," p. 68.

68. Deborah Jermyn and Su Holmes, "Introduction: A Timely Interven- tion," in Jermyn and Holmes, *Women, Celebrity and Cultures of Aging*, p. 4.

69. https://www.theguardian.com/film/2015/may/21/maggie -gyllenhaal-too-old-hollywood.

70. Melanie Williams, "The Best Exotic Graceful Ager: Dame Judi Dench and Older Female Celebrity," in Jermyn and Holmes, *Women, Celebrity and Cultures of Aging*, pp. 147–48.

71. Jermyn and Holmes, "Introduction: A Timely Intervention," p. 3.

72. Pew Research Center, Internet & Technology, "From Plastic Surgery to Vasectomies: Public Opinion on Current Human Enhancement Options," July 22, 2016, https://www.pewinternet .org/2016/07/26/from-plastic-surgery-to-vasectomies-public -opinion-on-current-human-enhancement-options/ps_2016-07 -26_human-enhancement-survey_5-01/.

73. American Society of Plastic Surgeons, "Plastic Surgery Statistics Report, 2016," https://www.plasticsurgery.org/documents/News/ Statistics/2016/plastic-surgery-statistics-full-report-2016.pdf.

74. American Society of Plastic Surgeons, "2017 Plastic Surgery Report," https://www.plasticsurgery.org/documents/News/ Statistics/2017/cosmetic-procedures-ages-55-over-2017.pdf.

75. Duncan Macleod, Ads for Adults, "Dove Pro-Age Women," February 20, 2007, https://advertisingforadults.com/2007/02/dove-pro-age-women/.

76. Karen Grigsby Bates, NPR, "Dove's Pro- (not Anti-) Age Campaign," March 27, 2007, https://www.npr.org/templates/story/story.php?storyId=9155425.

77. Michelle Lee, "The End of Anti-Aging," *Allure*, September 2017.

78. Jermyn, "Introduction—'Get a life, ladies. Your old one is not coming back,'" p. 4.

79. Jermyn, "Introduction—'Get a life, ladies. Your old one is not coming back,'" p. 5.

80. Williams, "The Best Exotic Graceful Ager," p. 155.

81. Williams, "The Best Exotic Graceful Ager," pp. 157–58.

Chapter 5: Visibility Revolts

1. Ron Charles, "Don't be so quick to dismiss 'Book Club'—or fans of 'Fifty Shades of Grey,'" *Washington Post,* May 21, 2018, https://www.washingtonpost.com/entertainment/books/dont-be-so-quick-to-dismiss-book-club--or-fans-of-fifty-shades-of-grey/2018/05/21/8d68d588-5d00-11e8-9ee3-49d6d4814c4c_story.html?utm_term=.a466d34a52b8.

2. C. Lee Harrington et al., "Life course transitions and the future of fandom," *International Journal of Cultural Studies*, vol. 14, no. 6, 2011, pp. 568, 576, 577, 579, 580.

3. Laura Snapes, "Too few films about older women and sex? Thank heavens for Book Club," *The Guardian*, May 31, 2018, https://www.theguardian.com/film/2018/may/31/too-few-films-about-older-women-and-sex-thank-heavens-for-book-club.

4. Deborah Jermyn, "'Get a life, ladies. Your old one is not coming back': ageing, ageism and the lifespan of female celebrity," *Celebrity Studies*, vol. 3, no. 1, March 2012, pp. 4–5.

5. Pepper Baggins, "Psycho-biddy," IMBd, September 29, 2015, https://www.imdb.com/list/ls079191096/; http://www

.tasteofcinema.com/2015/16-creepy-grande-dame-guignol-horror
-films-to-freak-you-out/.

6. Jerry Buck, "TV and Its Audience Growing Older Together," *Aiken Standard*, November 19, 1989, p. 17; Jane Hall, "Sex and the Senior Girls: NBC's *Golden Girls* Are the Toast of TV with Their Mid-Life Miami Spice," *People*, January 6, 1986, https://people.com/archive/sex-and-the-senior-girls-nbcs-golden-girls-are-the-toast-of-tv-with-their-mid-life-miami-spice-vol-25-no-1/.

7. Christyne A. Berzsenyi, "The Golden Girls Share Signature Stories: Narratives of Aging, Identity, and Communal Desire," *Americana: The Journal of American Popular Culture, 1900 to Present*, vol. 9, no. 2, Fall 2010, https://search-proquest-com.proxy.lib.umich.edu/docview/1519978016?pq-origsite=summon.

8. I am grateful to Andre Cavalcante for sharing his thoughts on gay fandom of the show.

9. Brooks Barnes, "Betty White's Sitcom Solution," *Wall Street Journal*, May 4, 2007.

10. Berzsenyi, "The Golden Girls Share Signature Stories."

11. The episode aired November 19, 1986, and was titled "Novel Connection."

12. Jeffrey Scott, "Television Industry Sharpening Their Focus; Networks hope niches are key to ad dollars," *Atlanta Journal and Constitution*, August 1, 1992, p. C1.

13. Lawrence K. Grossman, "Aging Viewers: The Best Is Yet to Be," *Columbia Journalism Review*, January/February 1998, vol. 36, no. 5, p. 68.

14. A. Thorson, "A Gerontologist Reflects on Media Coverage of Older People," in Michael L. Hilt and Jeremy H. Lipshultz, *Mass Media, an Aging Population, and the Baby Boomers* (New York: Routledge, 2005), p. 10.

15. Dominic Patten, "Betty White's Career Is One for the Record Book," *Deadline Hollywood*, September 4, 2013, https://deadline.com/2013/09/betty-white-guinness-world-record-longest-tv-career-578014/.

16. Steve Levitt, "The Most Appealing Celebrity in America is____?"

Q Scores, https://qscores.blogspot.com/2012/05/most-appealing-celebrity-in-america-is.html.

17. Ed Bark, "NBC Canceled 'Harry's Law' for Crime of Skewing 'Old,'" *TV Worth Watching*, May 17, 2012, https://www.tvworthwatching.com/post/Harrys-Law-Kathy-Bates.aspx.

18. "Fall TV: NBC says buy-bye to 'very old' 'Harry's Law' viewers," Show Tracker, *Los Angeles Times*, May 13, 2012, https://latimesblogs.latimes.com/showtracker/2012/05/nbc-bye-harrys-law-viewers.html.

19. Bark, "NBC Canceled 'Harry's Law' for Crime of Skewing 'Old.'"

20. Ed Bark citation, https://www.tvworthwatching.com/post/Harrys-Law-Kathy-Bates.aspx.

21. Bark, "NBC Canceled 'Harry's Law' for Crime of Skewing 'Old.'"

22. "Meryl Streep on Doing Romantic Comedies at 60," *Access Online*, November 20, 2009, https://www.accessonline.com/articles/meryl-streep-on-doing-romantic-comedies-at-60-bette-davis-is-rolling-over-in-her-grave-79305/.

23. Brad Brevet, "'Solo' Slumps in Second Weekend While 'RBG' and 'Overboard' Reach Studio Milestones," *Box Office Mojo*, June 3, 2018, https://www.boxofficemojo.com/news/?id=4404.

24. "Endemol Acquires 'Hot' New Sitcom," *PR Newswire*, June 22, 2010.

25. Alex Strachan, "'Cleveland' has great chemistry," *Leader-Post*, January 24, 2011, p. D7; "TV Land Picks Up Its Sizzling Series 'Hot in Cleveland' for 20 New Episodes," *Right Vision News*, July 8, 2010.

26. "TV Land Picks Up Its Sizzling Series 'Hot in Cleveland' for 20 New Episodes."

27. Rich Heldenfels, "Farewell to 'Hot in Cleveland,'" *Pittsburgh Post Gazette*, June 3, 2015, p. A-9.

28. Finlay Renwick, "Netflix Has Revealed Its Most Popular Shows of 2017," *Esquire*, December 12, 2017, https://www.esquire.com/uk/culture/tv/a14413699/netflix-most-popular-shows-of-2017/.

29. Kate Stanhope, "Marta Kauffman on the Long Road from 'Friends' to 'Grace and Frankie': 'It Wasn't Easy,'" *Hollywood Reporter*, May

7, 2015, https://www.hollywoodreporter.com/live-feed/marta
-kauffman-grace-frankie-friends-793968.

30. Stanhope, "Marta Kauffman on the Long Road From 'Friends'
to 'Grace and Frankie' "; Kate Stanhope, " 'Grace and Frankie'
Offers Fresh Look at Aging, Says Stars Jane Fonda and Lily
Tomlin," *Hollywood Reporter*, April 30, 2015, https://www
.hollywoodreporter.com/live-feed/grace-frankie-offers-fresh
-look-792564.

31. Katie Thomas, "A Polite Silence on Sex Raises Women's Costs,"
New York Times, June 4, 2018, p. B1.

32. Lisa Bonos, "Jane Fonda and Lily Tomlin on 'Grace and Frankie,'
aging in Hollywood and female sexuality," *Chicago Tribune,* March
18, 2017, https://www.chicagotribune.com/entertainment/tv/
ct-grace-and-frankie-friendship-and-womens-sexuality-20170328
-story.html.

33. Anne Jerslev, " 'A real show for mature women' ageing along with
ageing stars: *Grace and Frankie* fandom on Facebook," *Celebrity
Studies*, vol. 9, no. 2, 2018, pp. 189, 191, 194.

34. Barbara L. Marshall, "Sexualizing the Third Age," in C. Lee Harrington et al., *Aging, Media, and Culture* (New York: Lexington
Books, 2014), p. 169.

35. This latter from "Your Sex Life" in *AARP* magazine, April/May
2018, p. 39.

36. Marshall, "Sexualizing the Third Age," p. 171.

37. Herb Scribner, " 'Roseanne' suffers ratings hit. Here's why the
show hit a snag," *Deseret News Entertainment*, May 10, 2018, https://
www.deseretnews.com/article/900018302/roseanne-suffers
-ratings-hit-heres-why-the-show-hit-a-snag.html.

38. Jon Lafayette, " 'Roseanne' Reboot Viewers Came from Republican States," *Broadcasting & Cable*, March 30, 2018, https://www
.broadcastingcable.com/news/roseanne-republican-samba-tv;
Kyle Drennen, "With Roseanne Revival, NBC & ABC See 'Red
States, Ratings Gold,' " https://www.newsbusters.org/blogs/nb/

kyle-drennen/2018/03/29/roseanne-revival-nbc-abc-see-red-states
-ratings-gold.

39. Eileen Reslen, "What Is Roseanne Barr's Net Worth?" *Good House-keeping,* April 3, 2018, https://www.goodhousekeeping.com/life/money/a19662519/roseanne-barr-net-worth/.

40. "Nipped, Tucked and Talking," *People,* September 1, 2003, http://people.com/archive/cover-story-nipped-tucked-talking-vol-60-no-9/.

41. Andi Zeisler, *We Were Feminists Once* (New York: Public Affairs, 2016), p. 124.

42. Ann Hornaday, "'Book Club' celebrates love and sex after 60 with an all-star ensemble and a double-dose of Viagra," *Washington Post,* May 17, 2018, https://www.washingtonpost.com/goingoutguide/movies/book-club-celebrates-love-and-sex-after-60-with-an-all-star-ensemble-and-a-double-dose-of-viagra/2018/05/16/705e9c7a-53f5-11e8-9c91-7dab596e8252_story.html?utm_term=.e9616fe57ca2.

43. G. Oscar Anderson, "The 50+ Moviegoer: An Industry Segment That Should Not Be Ignored,"Washington, DC: AARP Research, March 2017, https://doi.org/10.26419/res.00160.001.

44. Douglas, *Where the Girls Are,* p. 165.

Chapter 6: The War on Older Women

1. Fast Facts and Figures About Social Security 2017, Social Security Administration, https://www.ssa.gov/policy/docs/chartbooks/fast_facts/2017/fast_facts17.pdf.

2. Gerry Hudson, "The Golden Years: One Step Forward or Several Steps Back?" *HuffPost,* February 17, 2012, https://www.huffingtonpost.com/mobileweb/gerry-hudson/the-golden-years-one-step_b_1278869.html.

3. Jessica Bylander, "Meeting the Needs of Aging Native Americans," *Health Affairs,* March 8, 2018, https://www.healthaffairs.org/do/10.1377/hblog20180305.701858/full/.

4. This important point was made by Regan Bailey, litigation director, Justice in Aging, https://www.justiceinaging.org/.

5. Megan Willett, "Here's the hierarchy of luxury brands around the world," *Independent*, October 25, 2017, https://www.independent .co.uk/news/business/heres-the-hierarchy-of-luxury-brands -around-the-world-a8019126.html.

6. https://www.pensionrights.org/publications/statistic/income -received-different-groups.

7. Social Security Administration, "Fact Sheet: Social Security Is Important to African Americans," https://www.ssa.gov/news/ press/factsheets/africanamer-alt.pdf.

8. "Policy Basics: Top Ten Facts About Social Security," Center on Budget and Policy Priorities, August 14, 2017, https://www.cbpp .org/research/social-security/policy-basics-top-ten-facts-about -social-security; Social Security Administration, "Fact Sheet: Social Security Is Important to Women," https://www.ssa.gov/news/ press/factsheets/women-alt.pdf.

9. "Policy Basics: Top Ten Facts About Social Security."

10. Elizabeth O'Brien, "Older women 80% more likely than men to be impoverished," *MarketWatch*, March 2, 2016, https://www .marketwatch.com/story/older-women-80-more-likely-than-men -to-be-impoverished-2016-03-01.

11. "Boomer Expectations for Retirement: Sixth Annual Update on the Retirement Preparedness of the Boomer Generation," https:// www.myirionline.org/docs/default-source/research/boomer -expectations-for-retirement-2016.pdf.

12. Paul Begala, "The Worst Generation," *Esquire*, April 1, 2000, https://www.esquire.com/features/worst-generation -0400?click=main_sr.

13. Alex Kuczynski, "A Caustic Look in the Mirror from Boomers," *New York Times*, Business, August 6, 2001, https:// www.nytimes.com/2001/08/06/business/media/06BOOM .html?scp=104&sq=bABY%20BOOMER&st=cse.

14. Joe Queenan, *Balsamic Dreams: A Short But Self-Important History of the Baby Boom Generation* (New York: Henry Holt, 2001), p. 6.

15. Alex Beam, "No! No! I'm Not a Baby Boomer," *New York Times*, Opinion, December 22, 2005, https://www.nytimes.com/2005/12/21/opinion/21iht-edbeam.html?scp=53&sq=bABY%20BOOMER&st=cse.

16. Nicholas Kristof, "The Greediest Generation," *New York Times*, May 1, 2005.

17. Heather Boushey, *Finding Time: The Economics of Work-Life Conflict* (Cambridge, MA: Harvard University Press, 2016), p. 31.

18. Larry DeWitt, "The Decision to Exclude Agricultural and Domestic Workers from the 1935 Social Security Act," *Social Security Bulletin*, vol. 70, no. 4, 2010, https://www.ssa.gov/policy/docs/ssb/v70n4/v70n4p49.html.

19. Social Security Administration, "Historical Background and Development of Social Security," https://www.ssa.gov/history/briefhistory3.html; Steve Anderson, "A brief history of Medicare in America," Medicare resources.org, February 27, 2018, https://www.medicareresources.org/basic-medicare-information/brief-history-of-medicare/.

20. Dylan Scott, "The 80-Year Conservative War on Social Security," *Talking Points Memo*, January 14, 2015, https://talkingpointsmemo.com/dc/conservative-war-on-social-security-history.

21. Brandon High, "The Recent Historiography of American Neoconservatism," *Historical Journal*, vol. 52, no. 2, June 2009, pp. 475–91.

22. Stuart Butler and Peter Germanis, "Achieving a 'Leninist' Strategy," *Cato Journal*, vol. 3, no. 2, Fall 1983; all quotations from the original document, passim.

23. Bruce Webb, "Social Security Reform: Achieving a Leninist Strategy" (1983)," *Daily Kos*, https://www.dailykos.com/stories/2011/2/15/945309/-.

24. Andrew Prokop, "In 2005, Republicans controlled Washington. Their agenda failed. Here's why," *Vox*, January 9, 2017, https://

www.vox.com/policy-and-politics/2017/1/9/13781088/social
-security-privatization-why-failed.

25. Scott, "The 80-Year Conservative War on Social Security."

26. Link to the original email cited in Ben Adler, "The Real Problem with
    Alan Simpson's Social Security Statements: They're Wrong," *News-
    week*, September 1, 2010, https://www.newsweek.com/real-problem
    -alan-simpsons-social-security-statements-they-are-false-213882.

27. Craig Harrington, "Media Coverage of Social Security Ignores
    Proposals That Assist Beneficiaries," *Media Matters*, https://www
    .mediamatters.org/blog/2013/07/08/media-coverage-of-social
    -security-ignores-propo/194738.

28. Trudy Lieberman, "The Press Plays a Dubious Role," *Colum-
    bia Journalism Review*, April 18, 2012, https://archives.cjr.org/
    campaign_desk/how_the_media_has_shaped_the_s.php.

29. Lieberman, "The Press Plays a Dubious Role."

30. Trudy Lieberman, "CBS Fumbles Again; A lopsided report on
    Social Security," *Columbia Journalism Review*, November 29, 2010,
    https://archives.cjr.org/campaign_desk/cbs_fumbles_again.php.

31. Dean Baker and Mark Weisbrot, *Social Security: The Phony Crisis*
    (Chicago: University of Chicago Press, 1999), p. 5.

32. Lieberman, "The Press Plays a Dubious Role."

33. Stephen Marche, "The War Against Youth," *Esquire*, March 26,
    2012, https://www.esquire.com/news-politics/a13226/young
    -people-in-the-recession-0412/.

34. Lieberman, "The Press Plays a Dubious Role."

35. Lawrence R. Jacobs et al., "Media Coverage and Public Views of
    Social Security," *Public Perspective*, April/May 1995, pp. 9–10, 48–49.

36. Politico's estimate was $2.3 trillion; David Rogers, "POLITICO
    analysis: At $2.3 trillion cost, Trump tax cuts leave big gap," *Politico*,
    February 28, 2018, https://www.politico.com/story/2018/02/28/
    tax-cuts-trump-gop-analysis-430781; the CBO put it at $1.9 tril-
    lion; Kevin Drum, "CBO Projects $1.5 Trillion Trump Tax Cut
    Will Cost $1.9 Trillion," *Mother Jones*, April 9, 2018, https://www

.motherjones.com/kevin-drum/2018/04/cbo-projects-1-5-trillion
-tax-cut-will-cost-1-6-trillion/.

37. Tara Siegel Bernard and Karl Russell, "As the Political Rhetoric
    Heats Up, A Social Security Guide for the Ages," *New York Times*,
    September 29, 2018, p. B2.

38. "U.S. National Debt Passes $22 Trillion," NPR *Weekend Edition*, Feb-
    ruary 16, 2019, https://www.npr.org/programs/weekend-edition
    -saturday/2019/02/16/695420009/weekend-edition-saturday-for
    -february-16-2019?showDate=2019-02-16.

39. Mark Miller, "Social Security and the U.S. deficit: Separating fact
    from fiction," Reuters, November 1, 2018, https://www.reuters
    .com/article/us-column-miller-socialsecurity/social-security-and
    -the-u-s-deficit-separating-fact-from-fiction-idUSKCN1N64GR.

40. Stephen C. Goss, "The Future Financial Status of the Social Secu-
    rity Program," Social Security Administration, https://www.ssa
    .gov/policy/docs/ssb/v70n3/v70n3p111.html.

41. Kathleen Romig and Arloc Sherman, "Social Security Keeps 22
    Million Americans Out of Poverty: A State-By-State Analysis,"
    Center on Budget and Policy Priorities, October 25, 2016, https://
    www.cbpp.org/research/social-security/social-security-keeps-22
    -million-americans-out-of-poverty-a-state-by-state.

42. Bernard and Russell, "As the Political Rhetoric Heats Up, A Social
    Security Guide for the Ages."

43. National Academy of Social Insurance, "Public Opinions on Social
    Security," https://www.nasi.org/learn/social-security/public
    -opinions-social-security.

44. John Gramlich, "Few Americans support cuts to most govern-
    ment programs, including Medicaid," Pew Research Center, May
    26, 2017, https://www.pewresearch.org/fact-tank/2017/05/26/
    few-americans-support-cuts-to-most-government-programs
    -including-medicaid/.

45. "The Generation Gap and the 2012 Election; Section 6: Genera-
    tions and Entitlements," Pew Research Center, November 3, 2011,

https://www.people-press.org/2011/11/03/section-6-generations
-and-entitlements/.

46. Kaiser Family Foundation, "Medicaid's Role for Women," June
22, 2017, https://www.kff.org/womens-health-policy/fact-sheet/
medicaids-role-for-women/.

47. Findings based on a Lexis-Nexis search of articles on proposed cuts
to Medicare and Social Security, or alleged bankruptcy of Social
Security, from 2001–present.

48. Paul Waldman, opinion writer, "Paul Ryan's plan to phase
out Medicare is just what Democrats need," November 15,
2016, https://www.washingtonpost.com/blogs/plum-line/
wp/2016/11/15/paul-ryans-plan-to-phase-out-medicare-is-just
-what-democrats-need/.

49. Michael Hiltzik, "Paul Ryan is determined to kill Medicare.
This time he might succeed," November 23, 2016, https://www
.latimes.com/business/hiltzik/la-fi-hiltzik-medicare-ryan
-20161114-story.html.

50. Waldman, "Paul Ryan's plan to phase out Medicare is just what
Democrats need," https://www.washingtonpost.com/blogs/plum
-line/wp/2016/11/15/paul-ryans-plan-to-phase-out-medicare-is-just
-what-democrats-need/; Danny Vinik, "Can Paul Ryan Actually Privatize Medicare?" November 27, 2016, https://www.politico.com/
agenda/story/2016/11/paul-ryan-trump-privatize-medicare-000241.

51. Jim Tankersley and Michael Tackett, "Trump Proposes $4.75
Trillion Budget," *New York Times*, March 11, 2019, https://www
.nytimes.com/2019/03/11/us/politics/trump-budget.html.

52. Vann R. Newkirk II, "Medicare Is Leaving Elderly Women Behind,"
The Atlantic, March 4, 2016, https://www.theatlantic.com/politics/
archive/2016/03/elderly-women-medicare-issues/472155/.

53. Jonathan D. Ostry et al., "Neoliberalism: Oversold?" *Finance and
Development*, vol. 53, no. 2, June 2016, International Monetary
Fund, http://www.imf.org/external/pubs/ft/fandd/2016/06/
ostry.htm; Christopher Ingraham, "The richest 1 percent now

owns more of the country's wealth than at any time in the past 50 years," *Washington Post*, December 6, 2017, https://www .washingtonpost.com/news/wonk/wp/2017/12/06/the-richest -1-percent-now-owns-more-of-the-countrys-wealth-than-at-any -time-in-the-past-50-years/?utm_term=.72cf18bcef92.

54. Lynne Stuart Parramore, "Bankruptcy is increasingly a rite of passage for America's seniors. It doesn't have to be this way," *NBC Think*, August 8, 2018, https://www.nbcnews.com/think/ opinion/bankruptcy-increasingly-rite-passage-america-s-seniors-it -doesn-t-ncna899206?cid=sm_npd_nn_fb_ma.

55. Deborah Thorne et al., "Graying of U.S. Bankruptcy: Fallout from Life in a Risk Society," SSRN, https://papers.ssrn.com/sol3/papers .cfm?abstract_id=3226574.

56. Judy Molland, "Why the GOP Wants to Gut Social Security," December 10, 2016, https://truthout.org/articles/why-the-gop -wants-to-gut-social-security/.

57. Emily Stewart, "The Republican tax law is becoming less popular, not more," *Vox*, June 22, 2018, https://www.vox.com/policy-and -politics/2018/6/22/17492468/republican-tax-cut-law-poll.

58. Lynne Stuart Parramore, "Bankruptcy is increasingly a rite of passage for America's seniors. It doesn't have to be this way," *NBC Think*, August 8, 2018, https://www.nbcnews.com/think/ opinion/bankruptcy-increasingly-rite-passage-america-s-seniors-it -doesn-t-ncna899206?cid=sm_npd_nn_fb_ma.

Chapter 7: Lifespan Feminism, Bridge Groups, and the Road Ahead

1. I am especially grateful to Andi Zeisler for a conversation that helped inform elements of this chapter.

2. Dr. Nancy Etcoff, "Foreword" in "Beauty Comes of Age: Findings of the 2006 Dove Global Study on aging, beauty and well-being," September 2006, https://static1.squarespace.com/static/55f45174e4 b0fb5d95b07f39/55f45539e4b09d46d4847b60/55f45539e4b09d46d48

47c93/1255277563001/Beauty+Comes+of+Age+2006+Dove+Glo
bal+Study+on+Aging+Beauty+and+Well-being.pdf, p. 4.

3. Barbara L. Marshall, "Sexualizing the Third Age," in C. Lee Harrington et al., *Aging, Media, and Culture* (New York: Lexington
Books, 2014), p. 178.

4. Eric Lindland et al., "Gauging Aging: Mapping the Gaps Between
Expert and Public Understandings of Aging in America," A Frame-
Works Strategic Report, FrameWorksInstitute.org, p. 29.

5. Cited in Robert Love, "The Last Acceptable Prejudice?" *AARP* magazine, October/November 2018, p. 4.

6. Becca R. Levy, "Eradication of Ageism Requires Address the
Enemy Within," *The Gerontologist*, vol. 41, no. 5, 2001, p. 578.

7. Ehud Bodner, "On the origins of ageism among older and younger
adults," *International Psychogeriatrics,* vol. 21, no. 6, p. 1006.

8. Paula Span, "Every Older Patient Has a Story. Medical Students Need to Hear It," *New York Times*, October 12, 2018,
https://www.nytimes.com/2018/10/12/health/elderly-patients
-medical-training.html?action=click&contentCollection=he
alth&contentPlacement=1&module=package&pgtype=secti
onfront&region=rank&rref=collection%2Fsectioncollection-
%2Fhealth&version=highlights.

9. Paula Span, "Ageism Is a 'Prevalent and Insidious' Health Threat,"
New York Times, April 30, 2019, p. D7.

10. Jennifer Smola, "Ohio State age-bias settlement includes back pay
for 2 women, policy changes," *Columbus Dispatch*, May 25, 2018,
https://www.dispatch.com/news/20180525/ohio-state-age-bias
-settlement-includes-back-pay-for-2-women-policy-changes.

11. "California jury awards $31M in age discrimination lawsuit," Asso-
ciated Press, June 26, 2018, https://www.apnews.com/2823071eda
8e4aa69a3be4b58e421978.

12. Joan A. Greve, "This Is the Age Americans Feel Best About Their
Appearance," *Time*, July 10, 2014, https://time.com/2972944/
gallup-appearance-senior-citizens.

13. Sandra Pepera, "Why Women in Politics?" Women Deliver, February 28, 2018, https://womendeliver.org/2018/why-women-in-politics/.

14. "The Status of Women in the U.S. Media 2017," Women's Media Center, March 21, 2017, https://www.womensmediacenter.com/reports/the-status-of-women-in-u.s.-media-2017, p. 105.

15. Joe Berkowitz, "Twenty-nine women directors the Golden Globes could have nominated this year, and didn't," Fast Company, https://www.fastcompany.com/90277567/for-absolutely-no-reason-here-are-29-women-directors-who-made-outstanding-films-in-2018.

16. "The Status of Women in the U.S. Media 2017," p. 32.

17. A. J. Katz, "Here's the Median Age of the Typical Cable News Viewer," TVNewser, January 19, 2018, Adweek, https://www.adweek.com/tvnewser/heres-the-median-age-of-the-typical-cable-news-viewer/355379.

18. Michael M. Grynbaum, "'Edged out,' 5 Anchorwomen at NY1 File a Discrimination Lawsuit," New York Times, June 20, 2019, p. A24.

19. JC Lupis, "The State of Traditional TV: Updated with Q2 2017 Data," Marketing Charts, December 13, 2017, citing Nielsen data, https://www.marketingcharts.com/featured-24817

20. https://tvseriesfinale.com/tv-show/murphy-brown-season-11-ratings/; https://tvseriesfinale.com/tv-show/the-cool-kids-season-one-ratings/.

21. Ken Hughes, "Richard Nixon: Domestic Affairs," The Miller Center, University of Virginia, https://millercenter.org/president/nixon/domestic-affairs.

22. I draw here from Stuart Hall's important essay "Gramsci and Us" in his very important book The Hard Road to Renewal: Thatcherism and the Crisis of the Left (London: Verso, 1988), pp. 161–73.

23. Jared Keller, "The IMF Confirms That 'Trickle-Down' Economics Is, Indeed, a Joke," Pacific Standard, June 18, 2015, https://psmag.com/economics/trickle-down-economics-is-indeed-a-joke.

24. Joseph E. Stiglitz, People, Power, and Profits: Progressive Capitalism for an Age of Discontent (New York: Norton, 2019), p. xii.

25. Era Dabla-Norri et al., "Causes and Consequences of Income

Inequality: A Global Perspective," International Monetary Fund,
June 2015, p. 7.

26. Elizabeth Anderson, *Value in Ethics and Economics* (Cambridge, MA:
Harvard University Press, 1993), p. 182 and passim.

27. Stiglitz, *People, Power, and Profits*, p. 239.

28. Helen K. Black et al., "The Lived Experience of Depression in
Elderly African American Women," *Journal of Gerontology*, vol. 62B,
no. 6, 2007, S392–S398.

29. Megan Brenan and Lydia Saad, "Global Warming Concern Steady
Despite Some Partisan Shifts," Gallup, March 28, 2018, https://
news.gallup.com/poll/231530/global-warming-concern-steady
-despite-partisan-shifts.aspx.

30. American Economic Association, "AEA Professional Climate Survey: Main Findings," May 18, 2019, https://www.aeaweb.org/
resources/member-docs/climate-survey-results-mar-18-2019.

31. "Survey of European economists finds sizable gender gaps in
opinions," *International Labour Organization*, February 5, 2018,
https://www.ilo.org/global/about-the-ilo/newsroom/news/
WCMS_616815/lang--de/index.htm; Ann Mari May et al., "Are
Disagreements Among Male and Female Economists Marginal at
Best?: A Survey of AEA Members and Their Views on Economics
and Economic Policy," *Contemporary Economic Policy*, vol. 32, no. 1,
February 25, 2013.

32. Transcript of Lawrence Summers's remarks at the NBER conference, posted by the Women in Science and Leadership Institute,
University of Wisconsin–Madison, https://wiseli.engr.wisc.edu/
archives/summers.php#conference-info.

33. WISLI response posted by the Women in Science and Leadership
Institute, University of Wisconsin–Madison, https://wiseli.engr
.wisc.edu/archives/summers.php#conference-info.

34. "US, China and Saudi Arabia top list of military spending,"
Al Jazeera online, May 2, 2018, https://www.aljazeera.com/
news/2018/05/china-saudi-arabia-top-list-military-spending
-180502060524362.html.

35. Keerty Nakray, "Gender Budgeting and Its Implications for Feminist Research," Conference Proceedings – Thinking Gender – the NEXT Generation, UK Postgraduate Conference in Gender Studies, June 21–22, 2006, University of Leeds, UK, e-paper no.11, http://gender-studies.leeds.ac.uk/files/2013/02/epaper11-keerty-nakray.pdf.

36. Christine Lagarde, "Every Woman Counts: Gender Budgeting in G7 Countries," *IMFBlog*, May 13, 2017, https://blogs.imf.org/2017/05/13/every-woman-counts-gender-budgeting-in-g7-countries/.

37. "Why national budgets need to take gender into account," *The Economist*, February 23, 2017, https://www.economist.com/finance-and-economics/2017/02/23/why-national-budgets-need-to-take-gender-into-account.

38. Bradley Sawyer and Selena Gonzales, "How does infant mortality in the U.S. compare to other countries?" Kaiser Family Foundation, July 7, 2017, https://www.healthsystemtracker.org/chart-collection/infant-mortality-u-s-compare-countries/#item-start; The World: Infant Mortality Rate, 2017, geoba.se, https://www.geoba.se/population.php?pc=world&type=019&year=2017&st=crworld&asde=d&page=1.

39. Austin Clemens and Heather Boushey, "Disaggregating Growth: Measuring who prospers when the economy grows," Washington Center for Equitable Growth, March 28, 2018, https://equitablegrowth.org/research-paper/disaggregating-growth/?longform=true.

40. Jessica Deahl, "Countries Around the World Beat the U.S. on Paid Parental Leave," NPR, *All Things Considered*, October 6, 2016, https://www.npr.org/2016/10/06/495839588/countries-around-the-world-beat-the-u-s-on-paid-parental-leave; Emily Carter and Lucille Sherman, "U.S. is only developed nation without mandated paid maternity leave," September 28, 2017, Politifact Missouri, https://www.politifact.com/missouri/statements/2017/sep/28/claire-mccaskill/us-only-developed-nation-without-mandated-paid-mat/.

41. Ronnie Downes, Lisa von Trapp, and Scherie Nicol, "Gender bud-
    geting in OECD countries," *OECD Journal on Budgeting*, vol. 2016,
    no. 3, https://www.oecd.org/gender/Gender-Budgeting-in-OECD
    -countries.pdf.

42. Sheila Tobias, "Toward a Feminist Analysis of Defense Spending,"
    Frontiers: A Journal of Women Studies, vol. 8, no. 2, 1985, p. 65.

43. Jared Keller, "The Navy Basically Just Admitted That the Littoral
    Combat Ship Is Floating Garbage Pile," *Task & Purpose*, August
    12, 2018, https://taskandpurpose.com/navy-littoral-combat-ship
    -problems/; Martin Matishak, "The 10 Most Expensive Weapons
    in the Pentagon's Arsenal," *Fiscal Times*, March 22, 2016, https://
    www.thefiscaltimes.com/Media/Slideshow/2016/03/22/10-Most
    -Expensive-Weapons-Pentagon-s-Arsenal?page=1.

44. John M. Donnelly, "Zombie Zumwalt: The Ship Program That
    Never Dies," *Roll Call*, May 21, 2018, https://www.rollcall.com/
    news/policy/zombie-zumwalt-the-ship-program-that-never-dies.

45. Matishak, "The 10 Most Expensive Weapons in the Pentagon's
    Arsenal."

46. Planned Parenthood, *2016–17 Annual Report*, p. 34, https://www
    .plannedparenthood.org/uploads/filer_public/d4/50/d450c016
    -a6a9-4455-bf7f-711067db5ff7/20171229_ar16-17_p01_lowres.pdf.

47. "Older Americans Policy Paper," National Committee to Preserve
    Social Security and Medicare, October 3, 2018, https://www
    .ncpssm.org/documents/older-americans-policy-papers/older
    -americans-act/.

48. Philip Bump, "Assessing a Clinton argument that the media helped
    to elect Trump," *Washington Post*, September 12, 2017, https://
    www.washingtonpost.com/news/politics/wp/2017/09/12/
    assessing-a-clinton-argument-that-the-media-helped-to-elect
    -trump/?utm_term=.643feb5706b9.

49. "Lowey Introduces Legislation to Provide Social Security Earn-
    ings Credit to Caregivers," press release, August 27, 2015, https://
    lowey.house.gov/media-center/press-releases/lowey-introduces
    -legislation-provide-social-security-earnings-credit.

50. Robert B. Biancato and Meredith Ponder, "The Public Policies We Need to Redress Ageism," *American Society on Aging*, Fall 2015, https://www.asaging.org/blog/public-policies-we-need-redress -ageism.

51. Paula Span, "The Gray Gender Gap: Women on Their Own," *New York Times*, October 11, 2016, p. D7.

52. Dean Baker and Mark Weisbrot, *Social Security: The Phony Crisis* (Chicago: University of Chicago Press, 1999), p. 119.

53. Jenny McCarthy, "The new feminist war: young women vs. old women," *The Spectator*, January 27, 2018, https://www.spectator .co.uk/2018/01/the-metoo-fury-has-spilled-over-into-a-feminist -war/; Penny Nance, "Young Women Are So Over Hillary's Old-School Feminism," *The Federalist*, February 15, 2016; Christina Cauterucci, "Feminism's Generation Gap," *Slate*, February 8, 2016, https://slate.com/human-interest/2016/02/gloria-steinems-gaffe -exposed-feminisms-generation-gap.html.

54. Josephine Livingstone, "Time Is a Feminist Issue," *New Republic*, February 20, 2018, https://newrepublic.com/article/147124/myth -metoo-generational-divide.

55. Tarana Burke, biography, https://www.biography.com/people/ tarana-burke.

56. Anna North, "The #MeToo generation gap is a myth," *Vox*, March 20, 2018, https://www.vox.com/2018/3/20/17115620/me-too -sexual-harassment-sex-abuse-poll.

57. Zeeya Merali, "Pulsar Discoverer Jocelyn Bell Burnell Wins $3-million Breakthrough Prize," *Nature*, https://www.nature.com/ articles/d41586-018-06210-w.

INDEX